"Conditioning To Win"

©
1974
Equine Research
PUBLICATIONS
15048 Beltway Drive
Dallas, Texas 75240

DEDICATION

To the brave and innovative research scientists and professors throughout the world who recognize the horse as an animal worthy of serious scientific study.

Don M. Wagoner
Editor/Publisher

TABLE
OF CONTENTS

Introduction

The popularity of competitive events for the horse has increased at tracks and arenas throughout the world at a phenomenal rate within recent years. As a result of this increased popularity, the rewards to be gained from excelling in these events have grown at comparable rates. The natural response to increased rewards has been an increased intensity of competition.

The highly competitive environment within which the horseman of today is forced to function offers a very small margin of error. He must either keep his animals conditioned to their physical peak or he must be willing to accept something less than frequent success. The days of competing successfully with equine atheletes of marginal athletic ability are gone forever.

Equine conditioning covers a broad spectrum. Nutrition, exercise physiology, equine psychology, and husbandry are all important elements. In many instances, proper training techniques are vital to the success of a conditioning program. It is well to remember however, this text is not a "training manual."

Training techniques, in general, vary from horseman to horseman depending on what "works best" for each individual. Training techniques, in particular, often vary from horse to horse depending upon the nature of each individual animal. Many useful training suggestions are to be found in CONDITIONING TO WIN. However, these are offered simply as practical means by which certain conditioning goals may be achieved. It is not our intent to suggest that any of the techniques presented in this book are the *only* ones to use. In fact, it is our suggestion that all horsemen be extremely flexible in their approach to any training methods and be extremely objective in the evaluation of anyone's "training tips."

This book is offered as a text on equine conditioning. In that regard, every practical area of the subject has been presented. The text portion of this book covers the conditioning needs of all ages and types of horses in great depth. The final chapter (The Art and Science of Conditioning) is a practical approach to the text material. This final chapter consists of interviews of persons well known and respected throughout the horse industry. The reader can greatly benefit from the scientific and applied knowledge contributed by these recognized experts in their various fields.

CONDITIONING TO WIN is a complete and current reference on the subjects of equine conditioning and exercise, but it is more than that. It is a companion volume to FEEDING TO WIN. Our goal with these two volumes is to offer the horseman the most comprehensive, the most current, and the most scientifically sound information available. It is hoped that these two volumes in combination will supply the horseman with the ultimate "guide" to the achievement of equine health, soundness, beauty, and performance excellence. We sincerely hope the reader will feel we have accomplished these goals.

Don M. Wagoner
Editor/Publisher

1

Basic Conditioning Theory

Equine conditioning can be better understood and appreciated when compared to the process of conditioning the human body. Although exercise is basic to any conditioning program, exercise alone cannot build peak condition. Firm, agile muscles are part of a well toned, highly conditioned body, but true winning condition is built on an even broader foundation. The utmost peak of physical and mental health, for the individual animal, constitutes real winning condition. Aside from muscle tone, physical health includes many other qualities such as resistance to disease, endurance, stamina and coordination.

Top class athletes, whether man or animal, need to have an excellent mental attitude. The drive to compete and win is a part of mental well-being. The athlete has confidence in himself and, therefore, exhibits a high desire to really try in any competitive situation.

Scientific knowledge, even common sense alone, dictates that a good diet is basic to proper conditioning. High quality nutrition helps maintain the strong, trim athletic body. A well balanced diet is necessary for the human athlete and the equine athlete. Discussion of equine nutrition will not be offered in great detail in this text since it is fully presented in the companion publication, **Feeding To Win.**

The mammalian body, human or animal, displays an amazing complex of muscles and bones. The bony and muscular skeletons complement each other to perfection. The design, or the way the body is put together, allows an almost limitless number of motions provided by an organized and efficient system of movement. (1) Different physical activities call upon different groups of muscles in varying proportions. For this reason, in addition to general toning up programs, specific physical activities require unique exercise for those regions of the body used most strenuously.

The professional football player doesn't play four full quarters on his first day at training camp, and the same principle should apply to the horse going into training. Exercise must be increased gradually at regular intervals. Without proper conditioning, the chances of strain and injury to the poorly prepared muscles, tendons and ligaments would be terrific. Everyone is familiar with that uncomfortable "day after" soreness following overuse of unconditioned muscles, tendons and ligaments. Regular, periodically increasing exercise is the way to begin every intensive conditioning program. Once endurance and strength are developed they can be maintained easily by regular exercise.

The American Medical Association strongly recommends that strenuous activity be begun gradually until endurance is established. (2) Logically, the horse must be treated in the same manner. Exercise must always be within the limits of the animal's current state of physical fitness.

Again, conditioning exercises can be either general or specific. Hiking or long distance walking is an excellent general conditioner for humans, according to the American Medical Association. (3) Walking helps to develop the heart and lungs and also exercises the back and legs. Walking is a good conditioner for the horse, too. The same exercise basics apply to the horse; for this reason, plenty of walking and trotting are included in equine conditioning programs.

Ideally, a horse is walked before and after strenuous exercise. Obviously, walking helps to "warm" the horse up before vigorous exercise and helps to prevent too rapid cooling after the exercise. It should also be noted that the hoof of the horse is a specialized structure designed to pump blood by the pressure exerted on the foot when walking. Before exercise, walking increases the circulation throughout the body of the horse and prepares him for the exercise. After exercise, walking helps to slowly decrease the body circulation and therefore aids the animal's recovery from the stress of exercise. (4)

The tennis player requires specific conditioning exercises for his arms, shoulders and legs such as push ups and knee bends. These regions and their associated muscle groups are used most vigorously while playing tennis. From this standpoint it is easy to see that horses intended for specific performance areas will need a certain amount of unique exercises for muscles used most strenuously in addition to the general conditioning needs common to almost all types of horses. For example, the race horse requires special attention for the legs while the jumper requires an extremely strong back and hindquarters. Another example is developing the strength and balance for the quick stops and starts required of a roping horse.

The Lucien Laurin conditioned entry of Secretariat and Riva Ridge come in 1st and 2nd in the 1973 Marlboro Cup.

Specific exercise in a conditioning program has a second purpose. Recognized weak areas are carefully exercised and developed to potential by individualized care. This includes injuries that require special attention and conformational defects which increase tendencies to particular injuries. The football player recuperating from knee surgery has an individual exercise regime slanted toward bringing that knee back to its original potential. The same goes for a running horse with bucked shins or a jumper with pulled back muscles.

Regarding competitive sport injuries the American Medical Association states, "The doctor's authority on medical matters should be absolute and unquestioned." (5) The same rule applies to veterinary advice; the future ability of the athlete, human or horse, should be protected at all times. This may mean withdrawing from an important race or horse show—but, the opportunity to have another chance in competition is preserved.

Slow, steady progression of exercise levels in a conditioning program is also fundamental in building mental well-being in an athlete. Carefully planned and well executed conditioning regimes are essential in establishing confidence in an athlete. This confidence, in turn, helps to form the basis for the kind of drive and desire we often recognize in human and equine athletes as "heart." The promising young swimmer should not be expected to compete against Mark Spitz, and the same principle should be followed with horses new to a competitive situation. A young race prospect should not be expected to compete with seasoned horses, and the novice cutting horse shouldn't be asked to hold a really tough calf. Confidence is a fragile quality and must be protected in the new competitor.

Security is another important factor in molding good mental attitudes. Young boys need the attention of their coach; they need to know someone cares about their athletic performance. Along this same line, horses must have individual attention and pleasing surroundings to build security. The horse needs to have that secure feeling that "someone cares" before he willingly gives his most in athletic performance.

A properly conditioned athlete has a general appearance of superior health, both mentally and physically. Whether the athlete is a man or horse, the muscles will be toned and smooth—ready to respond. The heart and lungs will be developed to capacity to insure performance with maximum efficiency. Every athlete in winning condition possesses the qualities of strength, endurance, stamina, flexibility and the will to win. The athlete is content with himself and confident that his body is prepared to face any physical challenge.

Before training for physical activity begins, the prospective human athlete is normally subjected to a thorough physical examination. This sensible practice is no less valuable in the case of the equine athlete. A physical exam by a qualified medical person will make certain that the athlete's body is able to withstand the rigors of training. Another purpose of the exam is to uncover any weak areas so that provisions can be made in the conditioning program and possible injuries avoided.

A veterinarian should perform the initial complete physical examination, plus subsequent periodic checks to accurately determine the horse's state of physical health. Blood tests and fecal examinations are examples of procedures the veterinarian may use to look for signs of disease or heavy parasite infestation. The exams are normally scheduled at least once a year and frequently more often, depending upon what the horse is required to do.

Winning condition is built and maintained only on a foundation of good general health. Throughout any conditioning program the serious horseman carefully watches the state of health of his horse. A healthy horse has good expression—bright, alert eyes and a proud, erect carriage of the whole body. Aside from general appearance, there are three good indexes of physical condition that every horseman can and should check periodically. In fact, many well known trainers record these indicators daily during a conditioning regime.

Temperature, pulse and respiration, or breathing rate, can be determined by simple tests. The normal temperature for a horse falls between 99 and 100.6 degrees F. (6) A clean rectal thermometer, lightly greased with vaseline or a similar jelly, is used to take a horse's temperature. It is placed full length into the rectum and left for two or three minutes. Then the thermometer is removed, cleaned, and read.

The pulse rate is a measure of the heart activity—or at what rate the heart is pumping blood. The normal range of pulse rates in horses is 32 to 44 beats per minute. (7) Easy locations to take a horse's pulse are the arteries that run around the inside of the jaw, at the back of the fetlock and at the inside of the elbow.

The respiration, or breathing, rate is how often a horse inhales and exhales. The normal respiration rate is 8 to 16 per minute. (8) To take the respiration rate, the in and out motion of the ribs or the rise and fall of the flank is observed. Each combination of in and out (or rise and fall) is counted as one.

Each of these measurements should be taken while the horse is calm and at rest; for example, between feeding and the daily exercise. Pulse and respiration rates increase greatly with exercise and excitement. Temperature will also show a slight increase when the horse is excited.

The horseman who really knows his horses and observes them daily

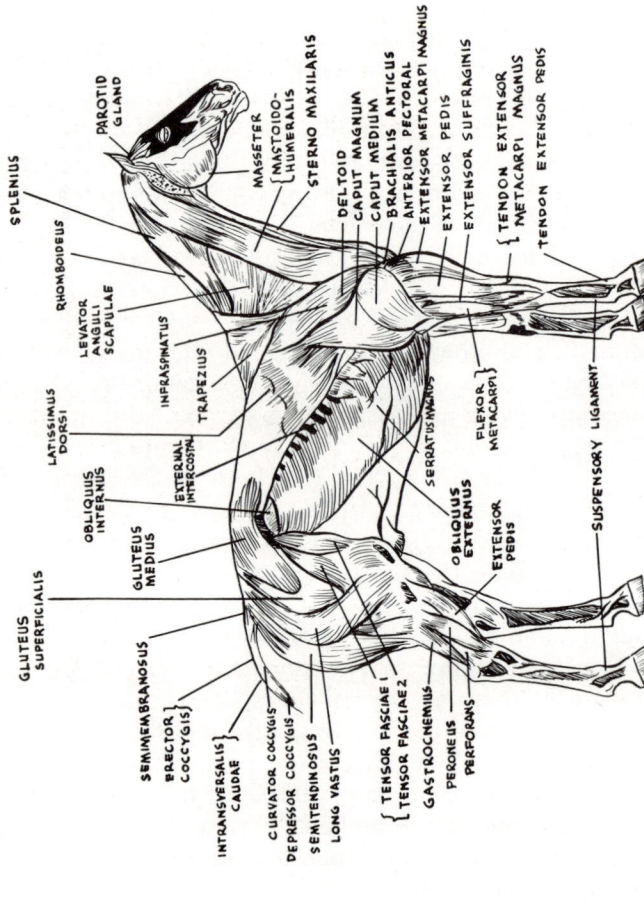

taken from Horseman's Veterinary Guide, The Western Horseman, Inc., 1963

The power of muscular contraction, combined with the skeletal system, provides the force for movement in the horse.

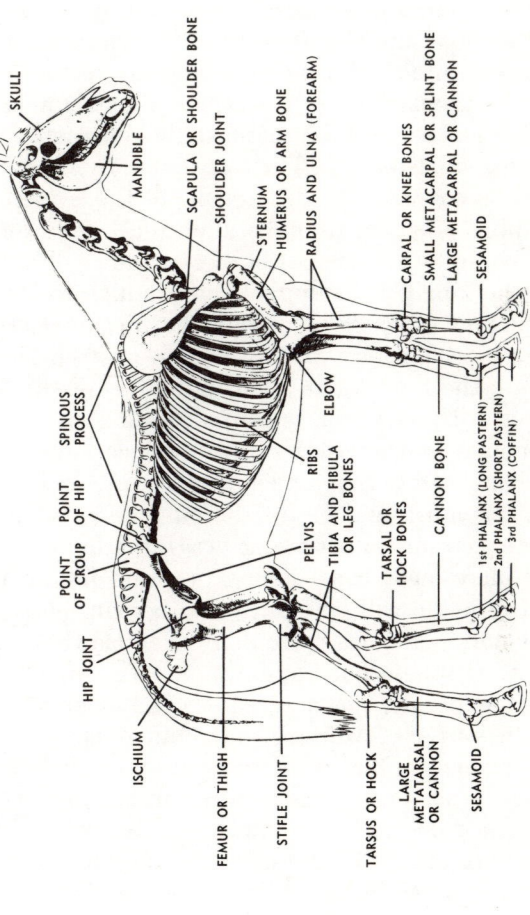

taken from Horseman's Veterinary Guide, The Western Horseman, Inc., 1963

The skeleton of the horse, as illustrated above, dictates form and relative athletic ability.

for any changes will be able to determine fairly accurately when one is not healthy. To develop and maintain condition fit enough to compete and win, the horse *must* be healthy. Athletic performance makes great demands on the horse's body and, naturally, a healthy body is more able to withstand the rigors of physical activity.

As previously stated, horses are similar in many respects to people; the limitless variation among the equine population, like the human population, makes generalizations notoriously unreliable. Each horse is an individual and this individual is constantly changing both physically and mentally. Appearance and disposition of the horse are influenced by the day to day variations in external stimuli to which he is exposed. Nearly every day potentially represents a new situation, requiring special attention. The horseman, by knowing his horse, should be able to recognize the daily results of these factors and best adapt a conditioning program to make allowances for them.

Each horse, when compared to another, will exhibit unique characteristics making this horse truly different from any other. The horse is not a machine from which to grind performance. To obtain full benefit from the horse's potential, the trainer must be able to understand and appreciate the limitations and capabilities of the horse in the various situations with which he is confronted.

The unique characteristics of a horse can greatly influence the way in which he will accept and react to any conditioning program. Obviously, this must be aken into account and evaluated when formulating and executing conditioning programs for horses.

When planning a conditioning program for an individual horse the age of the horse will be a factor to be considered. As a general rule, younger horses require more daily exercise than older horses in order to stay fit. On the other hand, the physical capabilities of the younger horse are generally not as great as the older horse and caution must be used not to over-exercise the younger horse.

The temperament of a horse is another unique characteristic that will require individual consideration in the conditioning program. For example, a rank horse might do better with additional and more strenuous exercise. On the other hand, when a horse isn't trying, a period of rest might bring back the confident, competitive temperament.

Special provisions also have to be made for the soundness of the horse. If the horse has any inherent conformational weaknesses or unsoundnesses already present, the conditioning program will certainly have to be planned to avoid extra stress on weak areas in an effort to protect them from further injury.

The physical characteristics of the horse, such as weight, size and

Lump It Luke, a Thoroughbred from Hollywood Park, tries out swimming as an exercise to help maintain condition at the Inglewood track pool.

height must be individually considered. For example, a mare with the pedigree and performance record to be an outstanding broodmare prospect might be extremely small and fine-boned. In other words, she possesses several highly desired characteristics breeding wise, but may not be capable of carrying and producing outstanding offspring without special care and assistance.

A horse with the "cow sense" and stability demanded of a superior cutting horse might be hampered by weight or extreme physical size limiting the agility of the animal. There are countless examples of physical characteristics which, by their nature, will require special provisions in a conditioning regime.

Just like people, horses have different degrees of intelligence. Some are mentally alert and quickly advance in conditioning programs. Others may be deficient in intelligence. This type of horse may be easily upset by anything new and may require especially gentle handling to benefit from any type of conditioning program.

There is a mysterious quality found in some horses, commonly called "heart," which makes a great difference in the manner a horse develops and performs. The horse with a lot of heart possesses an abundance of tenacity, courage and a keen desire to excel. Although "heart" is normally not recognized until a horse has excelled in some dramatic "chips are down" situation, the astute horseman can often detect it earlier. Horses with this quality are inherently able to take more intensive conditioning than an average horse and, all the while, maintain a strong drive to compete and win.

The unique characteristics of the horse require that each be conditioned in a slightly different way to derive a willing, 100 per cent performance. There is no substitute for knowing one's horse and realizing that he is a unique, living animal with his own capabilities, limitations and requirements. A person who thinks he knows any two horses that are *exactly* alike is not yet ready to join the ranks of true horsemen.

Swaps, the 1955 Kentucky Derby winner and voted horse of the year as a four-year-old, has sired a select group of offspring with earnings totaling nearly six million dollars.

REFERENCES CITED

1. Walls, Katharine F., Ph.D., **Kinesiology; The Scientific Basis of Human Motion,** Philadelphia, Pennsylvania, W. B. Saunders Company, 1966.
2. Bauer, W.W., M.D., Editor, **Today's Health Guide,** Chicago, Illinois, Department of
Health Education of the American Medical Association, 1970.
3. Bauer, W.W., M.D., Op. Cit.
4. Williams, Waynon, "Walk Your Horse," The Quarter Horse Journal, Volume 24: 4, 1971,
pp. 76-77.
5. Bauer, W.W., M.D., Op. Cit.
6. Swenson, Melvin J., D.V.M., M.S., Ph.D., Editor, **Dukes' Physiology of Domestic Animals,**
Ithaca, New York, Cornell University Press, 1970.
7. Ensminger, M.E., B.S., M.A., Ph.D., **Horses and Horsemanship,** Danville, Illinois, The
Interstate Printers and Publishers, Inc., 1969.
8. Straiton, E.C., **The Horse Owner's Vet Book,** Philadelphia, Pennsylvania, Farming Press
Ltd., 1973.

Jogging to promote sound, strong development is a fundamental step in every conditioning program.

2

Psychology As It Relates To Conditioning

A horse can be in peak physical condition and still be a poor competitor. The will to win and drive to compete are entirely dependent upon the mental well-being of the animal. Therefore, "horse psychology" is an extremely important part of any conditioning program. The trainer who makes an attempt to understand his horses, the one who really thinks of a horse as a living, breathing animal—not a machine to grind out performance, is invariably the man who gets the most from his horses.

The horse of today has strong mental characteristics directly related to the way of life in the days before domestication. Because of this, it benefits any horseman to have a functional knowledge of the natural history of the horse.

Fossil remains have furnished scientists with fairly complete records of the evolutionary history and changes of the horse. First records of ancient ancestors of the horse date as far back as 50 million years ago. (1) This tiny, primitive horse is called Eohippus, literally "dawn horse," by students of natural history. From skeletal remains, scientists know that Eohippus was about 12 inches tall and had four toes on each foot. The teeth of this small ancestor were much different than those of our horse of today.

Eohippus lived in the forests of Europe and North America. Because he ate leaves and possibly a few small fruits in the forest, Eohippus had a front set of teeth for nipping and a back set of teeth for crushing and grinding. (2) This little creature's teeth prove him incapable of

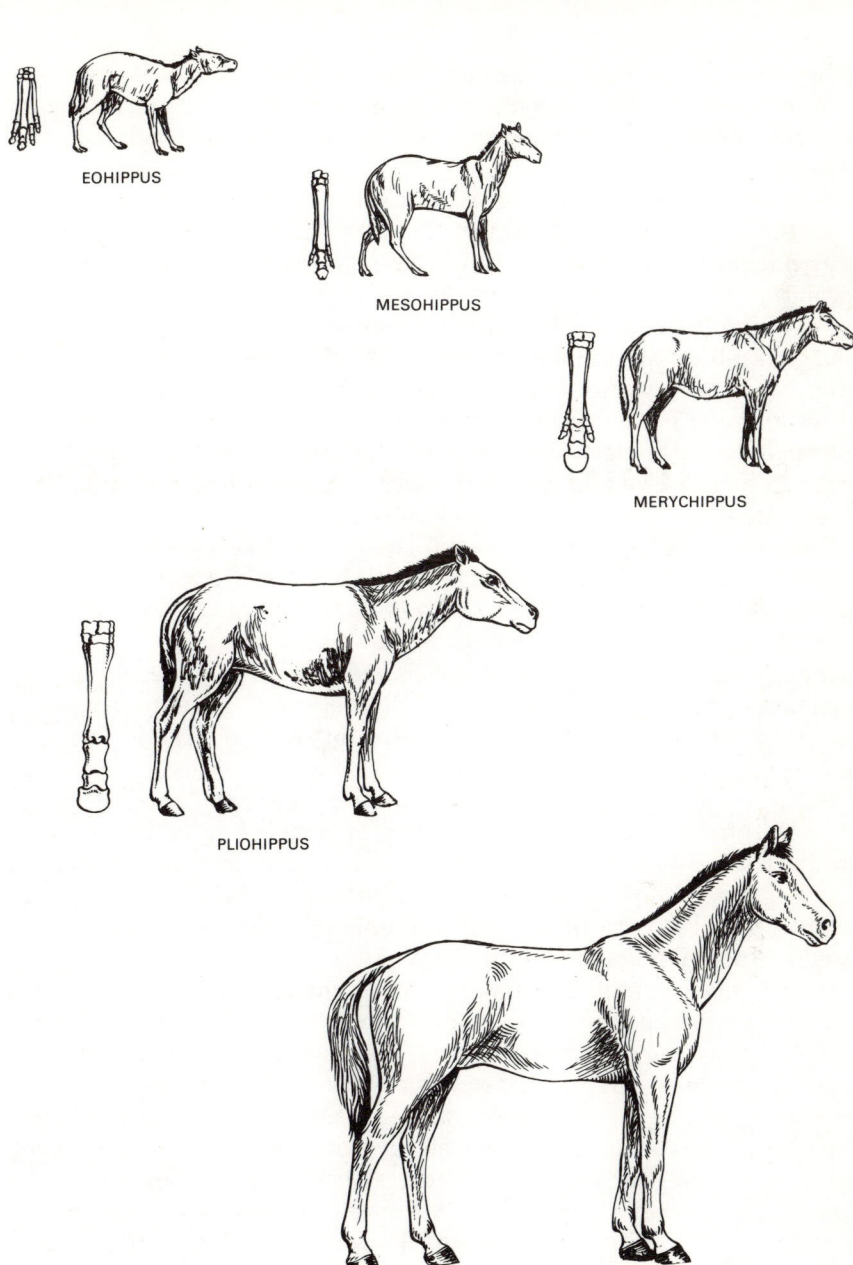

EOHIPPUS

MESOHIPPUS

MERYCHIPPUS

PLIOHIPPUS

EQUUS

The evolutionary progress of the horse.

living on a diet of rough grass like today's horses. Scientists have been able to determine from fossils and other segments of natural history that the dawn horse lived a simple life of browsing for food in forested regions.

Over the millions of years, evolutionary changes appeared in the ancestors of the horse. Following history, at ten to twenty million year intervals, progressive changes furnish scientists with enough information to identify a new ancestor of the horse.

Following Eohippus, the larger, three-toed Mesohippus developed. This was about 36 million years ago. (3) Mesohippus was still small, probably about two feet tall, but the head looked more like the horse as we know it. The face was more slender, although the eyes were still set far back in the head. The teeth of Mesohippus were not adapted to grazing, so it is thought that this ancestor lived in forests and along river banks. (4)

Eventually, open grazing became the way of life for the horse and Merychippus developed. This horse was about the size of a small pony, but he still had three toes. The center toe was much larger, with the smaller side-toes looking similar to dew claws. Changes had taken place in the whole skeleton of the horse. The legs were longer and slimmer—more adapted to running. The leg was becoming a specialized structure to carry weight and move forward efficiently. The skull of Merychippus appeared more long and slender than his forerunners.

Because open grazing was becoming the primary life pattern for the horse, dental changes evolved to suit this new lifestyle. The teeth of earlier horses would have been rapidly worn away by rough grass. The teeth of Merychippus were longer and stronger than those of his ancestors. The long crowned teeth had enamel ridges with cement between, much like the horse of today. (5)

Over a span of millions of years, more changes took place and the one-toed Pliohippus developed about 13 million years ago. (6) The teeth of Pliohippus provide evidence that it was a successful grazer. The teeth were even more elongated than Merychippus and more suitable to stand up under the constant wear of sand and dirt in the grass. Pliohippus was about four feet tall, growing in size over the generations. Its skull was longer and more slender with the eyes set very similar to our horses of today. Advanced species of Pliohippus are thought to have looked very much like the horse of this era.

No one knows exactly how evolution progressed, yet we do know that Equus, or the living horse as we know it, appeared about a million years ago. (7) Twenty-five thousand years ago man was still hunting the horse for food. (8) Domestication of the horse didn't take place until five or six thousand years ago. (9)

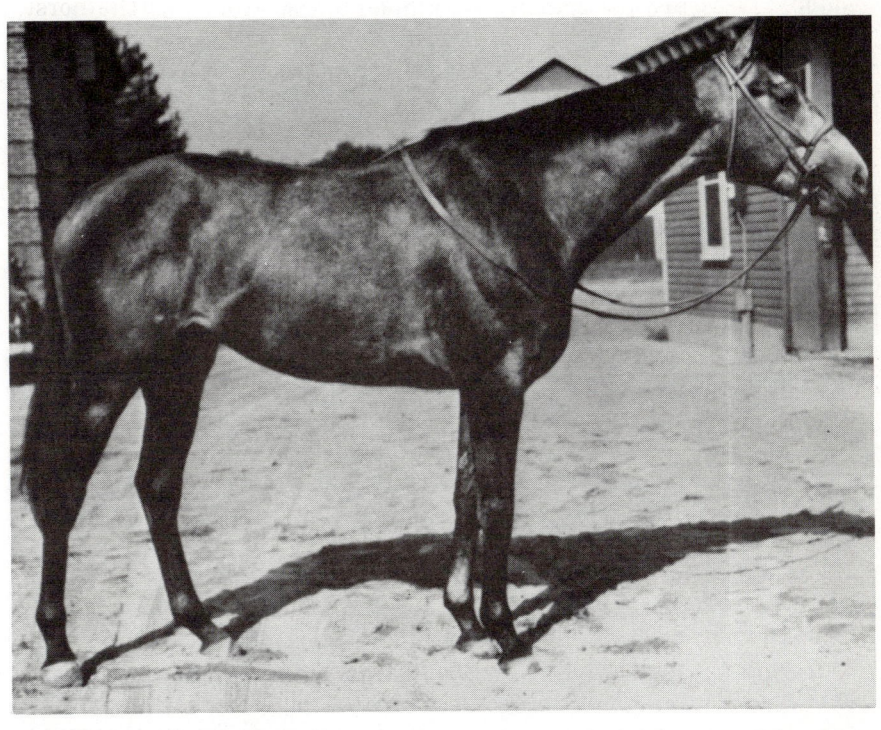

courtesy of The Blood-Horse

Winning condition, both mentally and physically, are largely responsible for Native Dancer's famous winning form.

The development of the modern horse took place over a period of more than fifty million years. By selective breeding to facilitate survival, the horse made many functional changes to better adapt to its changing environment.

The small forest dwelling animal developed into an animal adapted to living on prairies and plains. The horse became progressively larger and stronger. The four-toed foot which provided good footing on the moist forest floor gradually evolved into the one-toed foot, or hoof, as we know it today. For running on the hard surfaces of open grazing areas, the hoof is much more suitable than four toes. The horse adapted to escape his enemies by a quick burst of speed. It became a grazing animal equipped to eat and derive nutrients from harsh grasses. The brain of the horse had become more complex, as more cunning was needed for survival in open areas.

Understanding equine psychology in order to develop performance potential is a valuable tool for the horseman. Strong mental characteristics of the horse can be directly related to primitive instincts.

The horse was originally a herd animal because survival often depended upon being part of a herd. As a part of a group, the horse is used to looking toward a leader. In today's horse, the herd instinct is still strong and the need for security is related to this herd instinct.

Security, for the horse, centers around where the animal lives and the surrounding company. Whether kept in a stable or pasture, the horse is a naturally gregarious animal and, as a rule, likes company.

Routine also promotes security for the horse and encourages calm and well being. A regular pattern of life, but not to the point of boredom, is thought to contribute much to the mental well-being of the horse. (10)

Before domestication, the horse was conditioned to run rather than fight when frightened or alarmed. This is believed to contribute to 1) the relatively high degree of nervousness or excitability in today's horse, and 2) the relatively low pain threshold that makes a horse so sensitive to touch. This sensitivity, predominant along the neck and shoulders, is a characteristic often taken advantage of by the trainer.

.With the onset of domestication, the horse was taken from his natural habitat, roaming and grazing free and wild, and placed in an artificial environment. Apart from the herd, where he acts instinctively, the horse is dependent entirely on the will of man. (13) Some of the natural nervousness and uncertainty of the horse is the consequence of this total dependence on man. Even though the horse is superior to man in size and strength, it is forced to place trust in man and obey him. (14)

This is quite a responsibility for the horseman. He needs to gain the

courtesy of the Blood-Horse

Little Current adding the Belmont to his list of accomplishments.

respect and confidence of the horse to help the horse accept strange and frequently fearful situations. The horse must learn what to do under certain circumstances so that it can face similar situations without fear and uncertainty. The process of learning is largely a change in behavior. (15)

Scientists really don't know exactly what happens as an animal learns, but they can carefully observe the animal's behavior and see the effects of learning. In this sense, the horse must learn, or change his behavior, to accept man as a partner—and a dominant partner at that. As previously mentioned, the horse is accustomed to looking toward a leader and this characteristic is an aid to man (or the trainer).

The seasoned trainer, therefore, realizes that top performance on the part of the horse requires that it have confidence in him. In other words, the horse recognizes that the trainer is instrumental in banishing its fears—the horse learns to trust the trainer.

Learning is a major part of conditioning a horse to compete and win. However, everyone recognizes that there are differences in animals and you can't teach all things to all animals. Animals, even within the same species, have different learning potentials.

The learning potential of an animal is closely related to its environment and experiences. (16) The animal's experience is a factor in establishing behavioral patterns and these behavioral patterns can sometimes interfere with learning. The really great trainer is the one who is aware of the previously established patterns of an animal and tries to avoid interference by fitting his training techniques into these behavioral patterns.

For example, the horse, as one in a herd, is accustomed to being guided by the behavior of a leader. The average horse doesn't have much individual initiative compared to many other animals, and is often uncertain how to behave when alone. (17) When the trainer or rider is confident, consistent and quietly forceful, the horse is relatively at ease. It knows what behavior is expected and is guided by the personality of the person. If the rider loses confidence and becomes uncertain, the horse dhes too.

As in any learning situation, it is mandantory that the lesson be completely understood and within the capabilities of the animal. Also, the horse is like people in that it learns best when not fatigued—physically or mentally.

Numerous experiments with school children have proven that those getting rest from physical and mental activities exhibit the best performance. Other studies show that youngsters in good physical condition perform better than others not so physically fit. It is not unreasonable to assume that the same would hold true for the horse.

courtesy of Don Sugart Photography

Noted barrel racer and trainer Martha Josey riding Scorpion Gill, owned by Darrell Kissee of Miami, Oklahoma.

Therefore, conscientious exercise and learning regimes are closely related and should both be incorporated in any good conditioning program.

One way animals learn is by cause and result. This basic form of learning consists of making the connection between an act and a reward. (18) The cause and result, or response and reward (or punishment) *must* be closely related in time.

A stimulus is anything that elicits a response. An unconditioned stimulus is one that naturally causes a response, with no previous practice. A conditioned stimulus is the type that results in the desired response only after repeated trials.

I. P. Pavlov, the Russian physiologist, did much work with classical conditioning. He found that he could cause dogs to salivate, or drool, at the blinking of a light if this stimulus (the blinking light) appeared often enough just prior to the serving of food. (19) This type of stimulus, resulting in a desired response only after repeated practice, is the kind used most often in training horses. The stimuli, use of leg pressure, rein pressure, etc., are frequently referred to as cues.

The sensitivity of the horse to touch is a great aid to the horse trainer. For example, in the early stages of training, the horse responds readily to cues such as heavy reins and leg pressure by "getting away from" any possible discomfort. This is even more true of discomfort caused by the bit because the mouth is a very sensitive area.

At the beginning of training the trainer presents a stimulus that almost naturally causes the desired response. One example is direct rein pressure—the horse is being "pulled" in the direction it is supposed to go and learns this quickly. Later, the trainer introduces a new cue by rein pressure on the neck as well as pulling the horse with the opposite rein. Eventually the horse learns to respond to only the light pressure on the neck, which would have meant nothing to the horse at first.

With a young horse, the horseman should always start with the simplest and most obvious maneuvers. No training session should begin with something new—rather, it should begin with a familiar lesson and gradually work up to the new. (20)

Reinforcement is a learning aid; punishment and reward are two types of reinforcement. Reward tends to strengthen or reinforce an act and obviously punishment has just the opposite effect. (21) An example of reward reinforcement is luring a horse into a trailer or pen with feed. More complicated is the example of a horse learning that the sooner he performs the desired response, the quicker the training session is over.

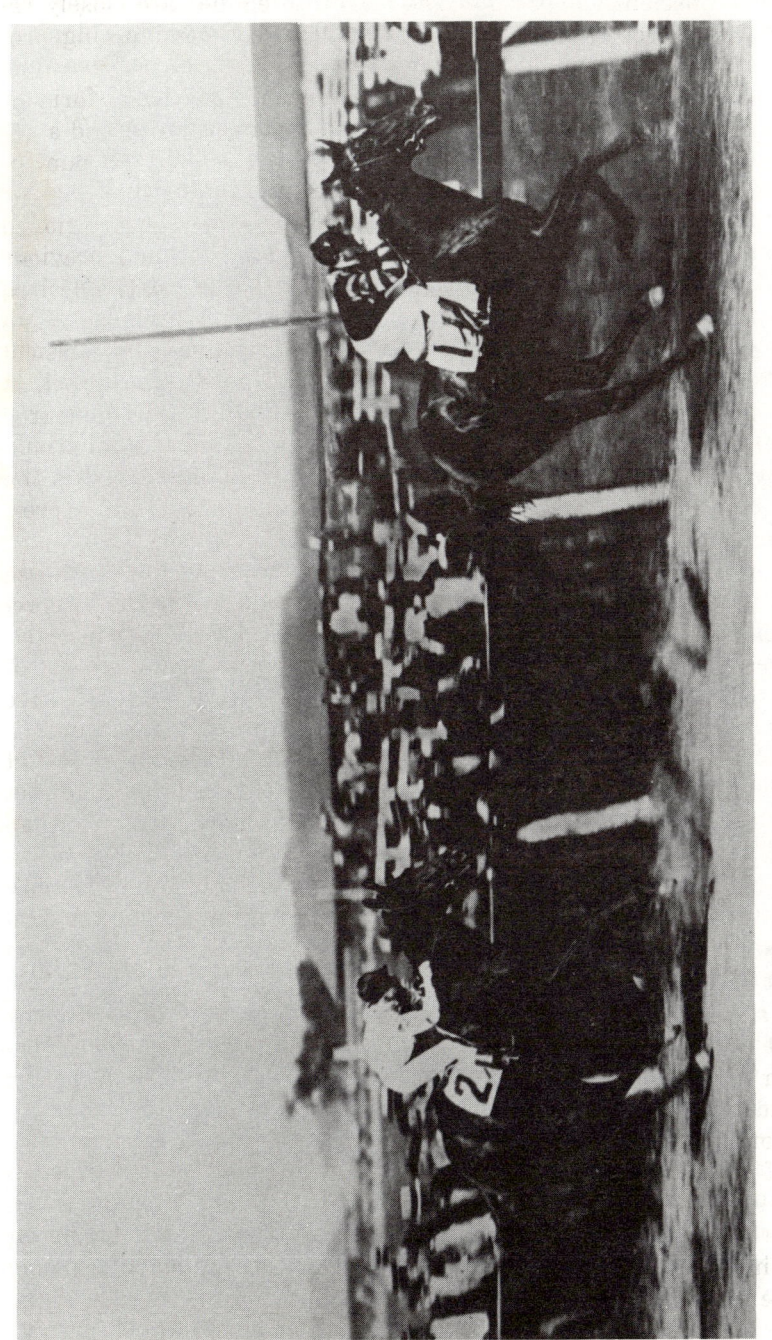

Man O' War, pictured here in typical form, had a game cock as a stall companion.

In some cases, the horse may enjoy running, jumping obstacles, chasing cattle, etc. and the training regime itself may be a kind of reward. Just the sight of the trainer could be a form of positive reinforcement.

On the other hand, punishment tends to suppress an act. The intensity of the punishment is extremely important. The trainer must know the horse and be able to select the type and intensity of punishment required for that particular horse.

For punishment to be an effective training tool, it must be given almost *simultaneously with the mistake* so the horse can easily link the act and the punishment together. Also, corrective measures, or punishment, must be given *each time* the horse makes the mistake. And equally important, *the severity of the punishment should be comparable to the seriousness of the infraction.* All of this demands patience and consistency on the part of the trainer. Training a horse is frequently tedious and has dead levels, but it is mandatory that the trainer not become lax or exasperated.

The horseman should be certain that the horse has thoroughly learned one thing before going on to another. Sometimes it seems like this will never happen. In this case, many trainers follow the practice of taking the horse out of training for a rest period. The rest period gives the horse a chance to "digest" what has been presented and is frequently followed by rewarding results.

The reinforcement, or tuning up, schedule is very important. The frequency of reinforcement depends on the level of training and how often the horse is used. Naturally, the young horse not yet ready for competition will need reinforcement, or practice, more often than the finished horse.

It is also important to remember that the horse should not be made to continue to execute a maneuver just because it has learned to do it right. Many horses are "burned out" in this way before they ever get to the arena, race track or show ring. The opposite extreme, or too little exercise is detrimental also. A horse must be kept in good physical condition by routine exercise. Stamina and endurance come only when the horse is properly conditioned and conditioning is a special relationship between the physical and mental states of the horse.

Another important point is that the rider (trainer, exercise boy, jockey, etc.) needs to be an accomplished horseman. If the rider is continually bouncing and floundering all over the horse, using his legs to regain balance, the horse will be easily confused. The horse interprets this leg pressure and rein pressure as cues or signals and doesn't know how to react.

When teaching or training a horse the trainer must be certain to go slowly making sure that every lesson is thoroughly understood by the horse. This gradual, consistent learning is a major factor in helping a horse develop confidence and overcome his natural fears.

Vices

The horse is a sensitive animal and usually expresses emotions in a way that most humans can recognize. (22) For example, the nostrils can dilate, quiver, expand and contract. The ears can prick sharply forward or be plastered flat against the neck. A horse's tail can be either buried between the legs or hanging free and loose. When familiar with an individual animal, the eyes can be very expressive. Every astute horseman recognizes these equine indicators of emotion.

The sensitive nature and inherent nervousness of the horse make it susceptible to vices or bad habits. This kind of behavior is both troublesome and unwanted. Most horsemen are quite willing to talk about vices and their possible remedies. In fact, the subject is included in almost every publication concerning the horse. Some of the recommended remedies are ridiculous, while others could be classified as cruel or inhumane. Before trying to remedy a vice, it is most important to try to determine the cause. For example, a horse often develops the habit of tail wringing if it is constantly badgered by a rider who is forever picking or tapping at the horse with bat or spurs. This problem, if it hasn't gone on too long, is easily solved by stopping the continual annoyment of the horse. Most vices, however, are much more difficult to understand and often no apparent reason can be determined.

Anxiety is a major problem in human learning behavior—apprehensions, especially related to reward and punishment, are very powerful. (23) It is reasonable to assume that the same would apply to a naturally sensitive and intelligent animal like the horse.

As humans, we handle our natural fear of the unknown by evaluating a situation, drawing conclusions, making decisions and acting accordingly. The horse is forced to rely on his instincts for survival and trust his handler to guide him through the paces demanded.

When a horse lacks the security provided by a consistent, thoughtfully planned conditioning program, this insecurity or excessive nervousness can easily manifest itself in the form of a vice. Cribbing, kicking, balking, hard-to-catch, halter-pulling, etc. are only a few of the many ways a horse may express his lack of trust and respect for the horseman.

Boredom is a major factor in causing vices in horses—especially those horses kept in stalls most of the time. A horse can very easily become bored when he is not turned out of the stall or subjected to forced exercise at regular intervals. Contrary to the practice of some "weekend horsemen," exercise on the weekends only is not enough to keep the average, mature horse from becoming bored.

Without the opportunity for regular free or forced exercise a stall-kept horse will frequently develop vices. Limited access to a paddock or a more intensive conditioning program may help the bored horse who has acquired bad habits such as cribbing or weaving.

Numerous trainers also follow the practice of putting something in the stall with a nervous horse to help the horse combat boredom. A gentle goat, in many cases, makes an excellent companion for the bored or nervous horse. In other instances, a tether ball hanging in the stall can give a horse "something to do" when he must be stalled for long intervals.

Often, horses will "sour" simply because they are excessively bored with their particular area of performance. This is a highly individualized situation and is many times caused by the novice horseman who continually insists that a horse repeat a maneuver simply because he has learned to do it correctly. The experienced horseman tends to allow the horse to quit when he has properly executed a maneuver—this helps to keep the horse fresh and eager to perform.

When the horse is bored with the routine of the performance demanded of him, he often purposely develops bad habits in an effort to "get out of doing it." The horse is simply trying to tell his handler that he's tired of this. The barrel horse who "ducks off the barrels" could be a bored horse rather than a problem horse. The reining horse is another prime example of a type easily soured by excessive repetition. For this reason, many top trainers in the western performance area seldom ask a finished reining horse to run through a complete reining pattern when not at a show.

Vices are usually the result of incompetent or thoughtless handling of horses. A trainer should plan his conditioning program carefully, making a conscientious attempt to take into consideration the psychological conditioning of the horse. He should take note of the indicators of emotion in the horse and try to take advantage of them, while making allowances for individual characteristics of the horse.

A true cribber. This habit is commonly the result of boredom.

REFERENCES CITED

1. Jones, William E., D.V.M., Ph.D., and Bogart, Ralph, Ph.D., **Genetics of the Horse**, East Lansing, Michigan, Callabus Publishers, 1971.
2. Simpson, George G., **Horses**, New York, New York, Oxford University Press, 1970.
3. Moore, Ruth, **Evolution**, New York, New York, Time-Life Books, Inc., 1968.
4. Simpson, George G., Op. Cit.
5. Simpson, George G., Op. Cit.
6. Moore, Ruth, Op. Cit.
7. Edwards, E. H. and Geddes, C., Editors, **The Complete Book of the Horse**, New York, New York, Arco Publishing Company, Inc., 1973.
8. Ensminger, M. E., B.S., M.A., Ph.D., **Horses and Horsemanship**, Danville, Illinois, The Interstate Printers and Publishers, Inc., 1969.
9. Simpson, George G., Op. Cit.
10. Edwards, E. H. and Geddes, C., Op. Cit.
11. Edwards, E. H. and Geddes, C., Op. Cit.
12. Smythe, R. H., **The Mind of the Horse**, Brattleboro, Vermont, The Stephen Greene Press, 1965.
13. Williams, Dorian, **The Book of Horses**, Philadelphia, Pennsylvania, J. B. Lippincott and Company, 1971.
14. Williams, Dorian, Op. Cit.
15. Allen, Thomas B., Editor, **The Marvels of Animal Behavior**, Washington, D.C., The National Geographic Society, 1972.
16. Allen, Thomas, B., Op. Cit.
17. Smythe, R. H., Op. Cit.
18. Allen, Thomas B., Op. Cit.
19. Allen, Thomas B., Op. Cit.
20. Williams, Moyra, **Horse Psychology**, South Brunswick, New York, A. S. Barnes and Company, 1969.
21. Allen, Thomas B., Op. Cit.
22. Smythe, R. H., Op. Cit.
23. Stein, M. R., Vidich, A. J., and White, D. M., **Identity and Anxiety**, The Free Press of Glencoe, 1963.

3

Conformation and Athletic Ability

The conformation of a horse, or "the way he is put together," is a major factor in determining what the animal can do. Within reason, the area of performance is normally not the critical element. Athletic ability is largely dependent upon basic conformational factors. Consequently, conformation is a primary consideration in any conditioning program.

By knowing what factors constitute good conformation and what injuries are most likely to occur with specific conformational weaknesses, the horseman can better plan a conditioning program for his individual horse. Also, he can more easily select animals with the capabilities of producing winning offspring.

Before domestication, horses best physically equipped to survive in their surroundings were the animals that reproduced. Today, the horseman selects breeding animals often simply by his own idea of how they should look, with insufficient consideration given to sound conformation. This is possibly a good reason why so many horses, both race and performance, are rendered lame through competition.

Unfortunately, when no longer capable of performing due to an injury, many horses are put into breeding programs. If the injury was due to a weakness in conformation, this certainly can play a big part in producing defective animals with lowered athletic potentials.

Conformation is a highly heritable trait. In other words, much of it is directly inherited from the conformation of the sire and dam. Total athletic ability is made up of conformation, age, health, overall condition, training and breeding. The horseman has considerable control over health, condition and training, but breeding and conformation are different matters. The best he can do is select horses with good conformation and devise personalized conditioning programs to work around any weaknesses which may be present.

There are differences in the conformational traits of various breeds, and within breeds as well. These differences are generally the result of selection methods to develop horses to perform specific tasks. In many ways, these differences are not very great. A superb Quarter Horse and a superb Standardbred will often have different overall dimensions, yet they will possess many common conformational traits. Examples are the overall balance, symmetry, adequacy without excess of muscle, slope of shoulder and pasterns, straightness of leg, alert eyes that are set wide apart, and large nostrils. These will be similar and are usually necessary for the horse to be an acceptable athlete.

Large nostrils, for instance, allow a generous intake of oxygen which is especially important for any equine athlete. Another specific example is the good throatlatch, free of excess fat and muscling. This is a desirable conformational trait for a good reason. All of the things that keep a horse going—air, food, blood, the total nerve supply—pass through the throatlatch. When a horse with a heavy throatlatch tucks his head, these supplies are cut off. (1)

Conformation is one of the major factors in determining the potential soundness of limbs. Most unsoundness is directly caused by stress, strain and concussion. Defective conformation causes extra stress on the faulty areas of the animal. Even though conformational defects can be due to a variety of causes, environmental as well as hereditary, there is a distinct relationship between conformation and lameness.

The horseman should make an effort to determine whether a conformational defect is inherited or acquired. If it is inherited, he will certainly want to eliminate the problem from his breeding program. Pedigree, breeding records and close relatives of the faulty horse are indicators of whether or not a specific defect is inherited. Most inherited conformational defects are not characteristic of any one breed, but spread throughout the entire horse population.

If one divides a horse in half, between the head and tail, over half of the animal's weight is on the front legs. Since the front legs support more weight, they are forced to absorb more concussion than the hind limbs. For this reason, lamenesses of the front legs are generally more common than those of the back limbs.

The angles of the shoulder and the fetlock both serve as built in shock absorbers. Straight legs between both of these structures results in evenly distributed concussion through the leg. Ideally, the angle of the hoof and the pastern are exactly the same. Deviations

Crown Prince is generally considered to represent the most desirable features of conformation for the Thoroughbred horse.

cause extra stress on the fetlock joint, ligaments and tendons.

Specific defects in conformation are predisposing to specific types of lamenesses. For example, base narrow conformation of the front legs places a greater amount of strain on the outside of the legs. Because of this, base narrow horses are especially prone to windpuffs, ringbone and sidebone on the outside of the leg. (2) In the same respect, base wide conformation places excess stress on the inside of the leg. Horses with this conformational fault are especially susceptible to similar injuries on the inside of the leg.

Bowed tendons, sesamoiditis and suspensory ligament injuries are very common with the long, sloping pastern. In this case, the pastern is simply too long for the rest of the leg and causes excessive stress.

An upright, or straight, pastern lacks the shock absorbing effect of a normal, sloping pastern. Therefore, concussion on the fetlock joint, pastern joint and navicular bone is especially severe with this type of conformation. Horses with this fault in conformation have tendencies to develop osselets, ringbone and navicular disease. Even worse is a straight pastern *and* a straight shoulder. All of the shock is absorbed right through the middle of the foot where the navicular bone is located. (3)

The back legs drive extremely hard to push a horse forward so the column of bones in the hind leg is a system to spread pressure evenly throughout the structure. Any conformational defects in the hind limb cause excess stress on the hocks due to the uneven distribution of pressure.

Sickle hocks, cow hocks and thin hocks are types of poor conformation that place excessive strain on the hocks. These conformational defects frequently cause curb, bone spavin and bog spavin. Back legs that are too straight are predisposed to lamenesses such as bog spavin and upward fixation of the patella (knee cap).

There are many examples of poor conformation due to improper alignment of the bones of the knee. Calf knees, bucked knees, knock knees, bow legs and bench knees are a few examples. In each of these situations, because of the abnormal bone position, weight is not correctly distributed over the leg. Consequently, these horses are particularly prone to injuries of the foreleg. Splints and popped knee are two of the most commonly occurring types of lamenesses due to improperly aligned bones.

Abnormal conformation of the feet can also cause certain kinds of lamenesses. Flat feet, where the sole of the foot is not concave, are easily bruised because the sole is in constant contact with the ground. Other forms of faulty foot conformation, such as narrow feet, frequently result in contracted heels and navicular disease.

courtesy of The United States Trotting Association

The Standardbred stallion, Adios, is thought to demonstrate superior conformation for his breed.

Muscling is a major part of conformation and athletic ability. Muscular contraction causes movement, and muscles in good tone and condition respond quickly to messages from the nervous system. A poorly conditioned horse is injured easily because the muscles are unable to respond quickly enough to prevent joint damage and strain. (4) Add to this the extra strain caused by faulty conformation and the result can be crippling.

Following is a discussion of particular kinds of lamenesses that can be caused by poor conformation. It is very important to remember that poor conformation is not the *only* cause of the following kinds of lamenesses. By understanding the conformational aspects of these lamenesses however, the horseman can design conditioning programs to keep stress on the weakest areas of the animal to a minimum.

Inflammation is a big part of nearly all lamenesses. Body tissue reacts to injury by way of the process called inflammation. Swelling, heat, pain and redness are characteristics of inflammation. As a rule, treatment of lamenesses is designed to either speed up the inflammation or reduce the inflammation—two entirely different approaches.

Treatment to reduce inflammation includes ice packs and pressure bandages to reduce pain and swelling. X-ray treatments and anti-inflammatory injections (such as corticosteroids) are also used for this purpose. These techniques are aimed at cutting down the inflammation because of undesirable side effects.

On the other hand, treatments to speed up or increase the inflammation include firing, blistering, hot packs and liniments. These kinds of treatments are used most frequently with chronic conditions to reinforce the healing process. (In other words, turn a chronic condition into an acute one, in hope of a better chance of healing.) These treatments should be used only with veterinary assistance and advice because they can drive bacterial infections deeper.

Again, it is very important to remember that the following types of lamenesses are often the result of causes other than poor conformation. They are presented in detail to help devise conditioning programs with minimal stress on the weaker areas of the individual horse.

Bowed Tendons (Tendinitis)

Predisposing influences are long, weak pasterns and horses too heavy for their tendon structures—anything that increases concussion. The flexor tendons in the foreleg not only bend the joint, but serve as the chief supporters. These tendons are the weight-bearing or shock-absorbing mechanism in the gallop and must absorb massive

This famous Orren Mixer painting exemplifies ideal Quarter Horse conformation.

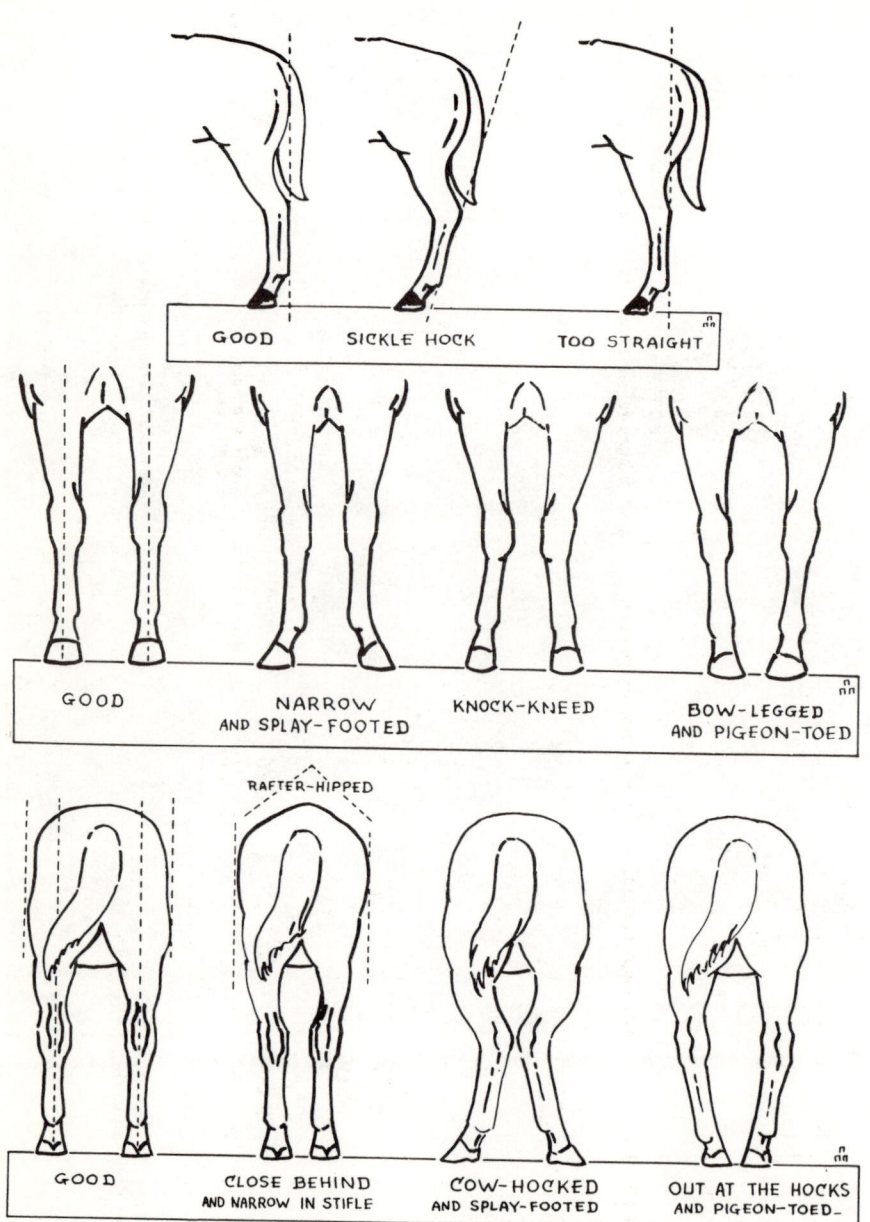

GOOD SICKLE HOCK TOO STRAIGHT

GOOD NARROW AND SPLAY-FOOTED KNOCK-KNEED BOW-LEGGED AND PIGEON-TOED

RAFTER-HIPPED

GOOD CLOSE BEHIND AND NARROW IN STIFLE COW-HOCKED AND SPLAY-FOOTED OUT AT THE HOCKS AND PIGEON-TOED

taken from **Horseman's Veterinary Guide,** *The Western Horseman, Inc., 1963*

General examples of good conformation and commonly occurring faults are pictured above.

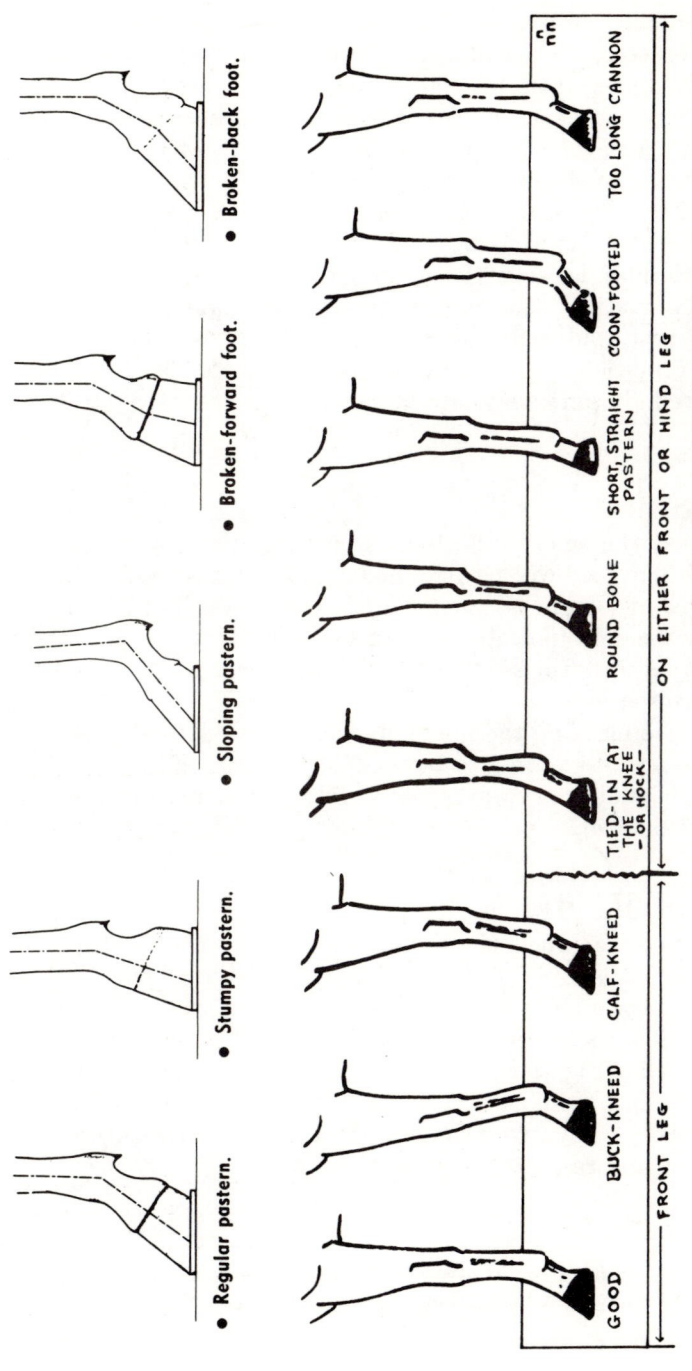

taken from Horseman's Veterinary Guide, The Western Horseman, Inc., 1963

The diagrams above illustrate some of the many variations of knee and pastern conformation in the horse.

forces. For example, an average horse with jockey over three-eighths of a mile generates a thrust of nearly two million foot-pounds. (5)

This is hard enough on normal tendons, but poor conformation makes the concussion even greater. Add to this an unconditioned tendon and sheath and you can imagine the results. Bowed tendon is a strain and tearing of a tendon, most commonly the superficial flexor tendon. The affected leg will be hot and swollen, with this bulky swelling being referred to as a "bow."

Tenosynovitis may occur with, or as a result of, bowed tendon. In this case, inflammation also involves the synovial sheath of the tendon. Complete rest, cold packs, blistering and firing are common treatments. If the condition is extremely severe, surgery to split the tendon may be required. Surgery may also be used as an alternative to firing and blistering.

Bruised Sole

With flat feet, the sole of the foot is easily bruised by stones and rough ground. The foot will be inflamed and lameness readily apparent. The degree of lameness depends upon the severity of the bruise. Red stains in the sole indicate the bruised area. If a sole abscess if present, the area may appear bluish. The horse will usually favor the heel of the bruised foot.

In cases of sole bruising the horse should be rested. Cold packs and anti-inflammatory drugs can also be used. If the bruised area becomes an abscess it should be cut away, treated with iodine and covered until the surface heals over.

Contracted Heels

Contracted heel (or foot) does not necessarily involve only the heel—the whole foot can be included. In this condition the foot becomes narrower than normal. The front feet are most commonly affected. Contracted heels result from a lack of frog pressure which usually causes the frog to shrink and recess in the foot. Lameness may not be obvious until the problem becomes severe. Methods of treatment (usually corrective trimming and shoeing) are designed to expand the foot and re-establish frog pressure.

Curb

Curb is an enlargement at the back of the hock due to inflammation and thickening of the plantar ligament. Any kind of poor conformation of the hock which places excessive strain on the ligament is

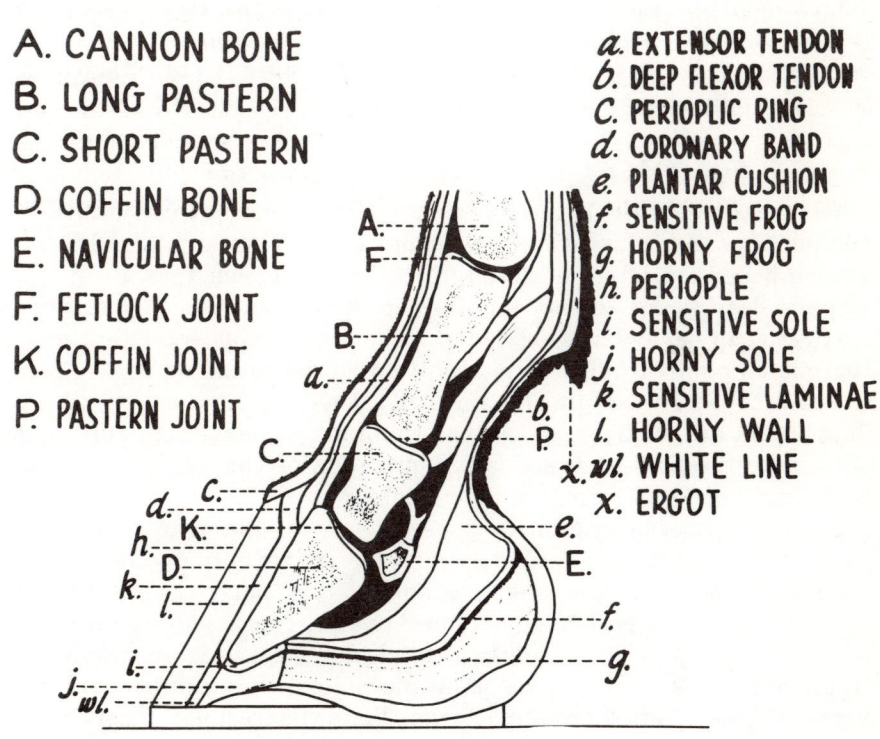

A. CANNON BONE
B. LONG PASTERN
C. SHORT PASTERN
D. COFFIN BONE
E. NAVICULAR BONE
F. FETLOCK JOINT
K. COFFIN JOINT
P. PASTERN JOINT

a. EXTENSOR TENDON
b. DEEP FLEXOR TENDON
c. PERIOPLIC RING
d. CORONARY BAND
e. PLANTAR CUSHION
f. SENSITIVE FROG
g. HORNY FROG
h. PERIOPLE
i. SENSITIVE SOLE
j. HORNY SOLE
k. SENSITIVE LAMINAE
l. HORNY WALL
wl. WHITE LINE
x. ERGOT

- Median section of pastern and foot.

*taken from **Horseman's Veterinary Guide**, The Western Horseman, Inc., 1963*

This diagram of the foot and pastern is provided for reference purposes. Particular note should be taken of the enclosed position of the navicular bone.

especially predisposing to curb. When observing the animal from the side, a swelling below the point of the hock can easily be seen.

If the condition is acute there will be heat, swelling and lameness. Exercise usually increases the lameness. The horse will stand with the leg elevated and the heel at rest. In chronic cases, although the blemish is readily apparent, the animal may not be lame.

Treatment for acute curb includes rest, cold packs and corticoid injections into the swelling. In chronic cases, firing and blistering may be necessary. When poor conformation is the cause of curb, the condition is usually chronic because the cause is continual.

Navicular Disease (Podotrochleosis)

Navicular disease is a term that describes numerous conditions involving the navicular (distal sesamoid) bone. This is a small boat-shaped bone completely enclosed in the hoof between the joint and the deep flexor tendon. Conformation that increases concussion may result in navicular disease. Since the bone is completely enclosed, there is no room "to give" and vibration from concussion causes friction, wear and tear on the navicular bone. This results in inflammation and damage to the bone and surrounding structures. As the disease progresses there is inflammation of the navicular bursa, cartilage degeneration and bone erosion.

Navicular disease ordinarily appears only in the front feet. The horse will stumble, take shorter strides and eventually develop a shuffling gait. When standing, the animal may point the toe of one foot or stand with both feet extended. Later, the horse will also appear to be sore in the shoulders. Navicular disease is incurable, so treatment is designed to ease pain and extend the usefulness of the horse. This is often done by posterior digital neurectomy ("nerving"), and corrective shoeing.

Osselets

Osselets is an arthritic condition of the fetlock joint. When the joint capsule is inflamed, with no new abnormal growth, the condition is referred to as "green osselets." The fetlock joint will be hot, swollen and very painful for the horse. Complete rest, antiphlogistic packs, ice packs and corticoid injections are common methods of treatment.

Green osselets can progress to "true osselets." New bone growth characterizes this condition. The bony growths most commonly appear at the site where the joint capsule was torn from its attachment. Hot, extremely painful swellings show up around the fetlock joint. The horse moves with a short, choppy gait, refusing to completely extend

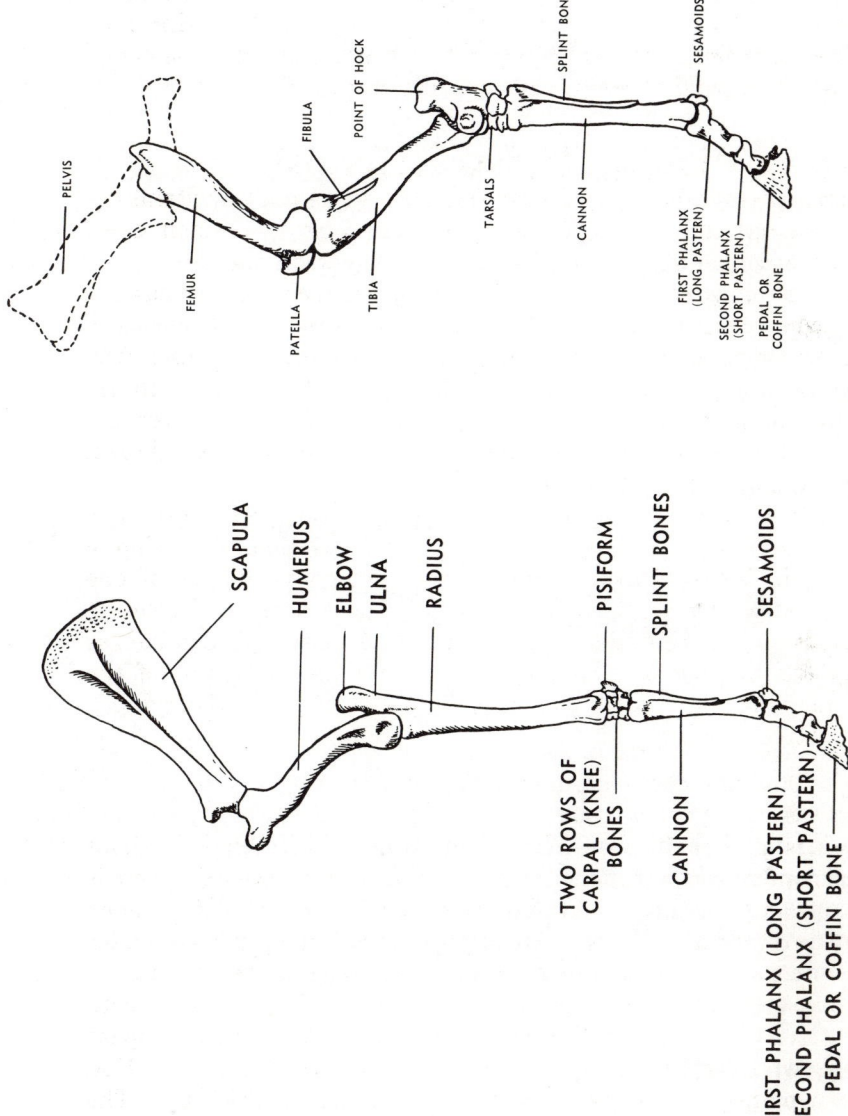

taken from Horseman's Veterinary Guide, The Western Horseman, Inc., 1963

It is important to note the bone structures of the fore and hind legs of the horse as these are involved in most conformationally caused lamenesses.

the limb. Exercise increases the lameness. Treatment for true osselets, usually a chronic condition, involves rest with limited exercise. Blistering, firing, radiation therapy and/or surgical removal may also be employed.

Increased concussion to the fetlocks, resulting from upright pasterns, is the major conformational cause.

Popped Knee (Carpitis)

This is an inflammation of the joint capsule of the carpus (knee). The joint capsule may be torn, the ligament may be torn and/or small bits of bones chipped off. The knee is usually swollen and tender. Lameness is a "swinging leg" type—the horse generally will move with a shortened stride and swing the affected leg around instead of flexing the knee. In older, or chronic cases bony growth may develop in the knee and associated structures. Also the horse may not appear to be lame until exercised.

Rest is the best treatment. Excess fluid may need to be removed from the joint to relieve pain. Corticosteroid injections, blisters, firing or surgery may be required in severe cases. Improper bone alignment of the foreleg is the major conformational influence on popped knee.

Ringbone

The term "ringbone" refers to any bony enlargement below the fetlock. True ringbone is classified as either high or low. High ringbone involves the pastern joint and low ringbone involves the coffin joint. Any kind of poor conformation that increases stress on the pasterns or tendon and ligament attachments may cause ringbone. (For example, base wide and base narrow conformation, upright pasterns.)

True ringbone is really osteoarthritis and may affect all four limbs, but it usually appears only in the front limbs. Osteoarthritis simply means that the cartilage in the joint wears away and the respective bone structures degenerate. Eventually, new, abnormal bone growth appears in the joint area. These new bony structures are the primary characteristics of ringbone.

Lameness may either develop rapidly or very slowly. The only treatment is aimed at relief of pain as there is no cure for ringbone. Some treatments (counter-irritants) may even lead to further destruction of the joint.

Sesamoiditis

Sesamoiditis is an inflammation of the proximal sesamoid bones and/or ligaments. Calcification and new bone growth may occur on the

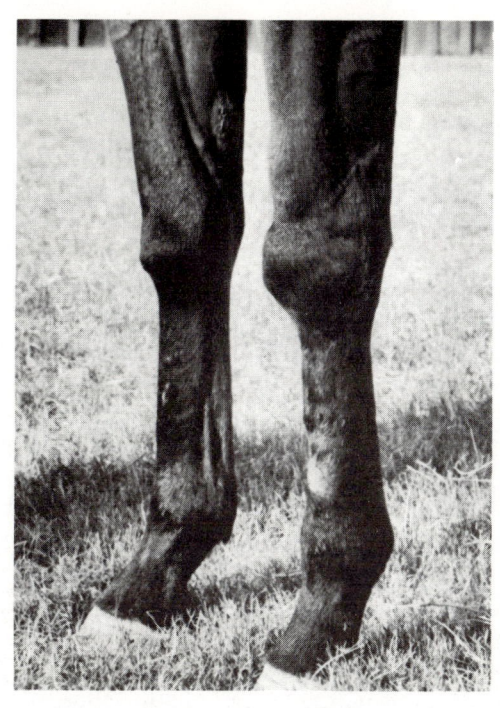

Equine Research Publications Staff Photo

A classic case of carpitis (popped knee) which probably resulted from faulty conformations.

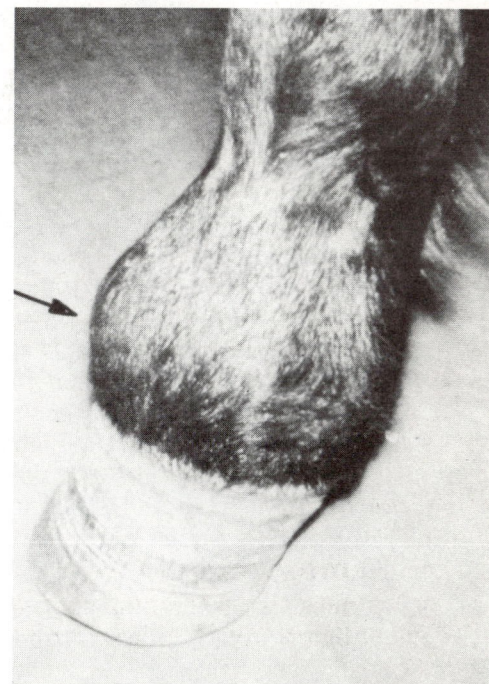

reproduced with permission of the publishers of Equine Medicine and Surgery, 2nd Edition

An example of severe ringbone in the horse.

surfaces of both the bone and associated ligaments. The proximal sesamoids are small, curved bones located in pairs behind the fetlock joint. They are shaped somewhat like half-moons; concave on the surface toward the joint and convex on the outer surface.

Pain and swelling of the fetlock joint are signs of sesamoiditis. When the horse is in motion, pain is most evident when weight is placed on the affected limb. A very effective treatment is to immobilize the limb with a cast. Inflammation can usually be reduced by alternating hot and cold packs. Although long, sloping pasterns decrease concussion on the fetlock joint, they increase stress on the surrounding ligaments. Therefore this type of conformation predisposes straining and inflammation of the associated structures of the fetlock joint, i.e., sesamoiditis.

Sidebones

This condition is an ossification, or change into bone, of the lateral cartilages. These cartilages slope up and backward along the sides of the foot and extend up to above the coronary band. Poor conformation that increases concussion often produces sidebones.

Lameness and pain may or may not be present. Rarely is a horse lame from sidebones. If the horse is lame, it will be most evident when he turns. No treatment is needed when neither lameness nor pain are present. Sidebones can be removed surgically, usually only for cosmetic reasons. Advanced cases of sidebone may produce contracted feet, in which case corrective shoeing is indicated. The quarters of the hoof can be grooved to allow expansion of the foot and relief of pain if necessary.

Spavin

Spavin is a general term that applies to lameness originating in the hock. Poor conformation that places extra stress on the hocks is a very common cause of spavin.

Bog spavin is a chronic enlargement of the hock due to distension of the joint capsule with synovial fluid. The swelling rarely causes an animal to be lame, but does result in an ugly blemish. Treatment to remove excess fluid from the joint is generally all that is required. Blisters, liniments, sweats and pressure bandages as attempts to remove the blemish are not often successful. Research in recent years indicates that injection of a steroid hormone, with properties very similar to adrenocorticoids, into the affected joint may be successful in reducing the distension of the hock. (6)

Bone spavin (or jack spavin) is a gradual bone destruction on the

This horse is an illustration of the common conformational defect, cow hocks. This condition predisposes the hock to bog spavin which this horse has also. (Notice enlargement of left hock.)

inside of the hock usually followed by new bone growth that greatly enlarges the hock. Bone spavin is a "cold" lameness at first that slowly progresses to a constant lameness. The stride of the horse with bone spavin is shortened and there is a tendency to jerk the leg forward when the hip is raised instead of flexing the hock. When standing, the horse almost always rests the toe on the ground with the heel slightly raised. Rest and corrective shoeing often make a horse sound; however, surgery may be required in severe cases.

Splints

Each horse has eight splint bones. These are small bones that taper to a point on the lower end. They run down the back and near the edge of the cannon bone and are attached at the knee (or hock). The bottom end of the splint bone is atached to the cannon bone by a strong ligament. As a horse grows older, this ligament is replaced by bone. The splint bones bear some of the weight coming down the knee (or hock) and since there isn't an opposing force on the other end of the bone, a considerable amount of strain is placed on the ligament.

This movement causes irritation and damage to the bone surfaces and ligament. Constant irritation results in subsequent new bone growth which appears as small swellings along the cannon bone. These enlargements can occur anywhere along the cannon bone, but most frequently show up about three inches below the knee. If it occurs, lameness is most evident when the horse trots.

Rest is a very important part of treatment for splints. Cold bandages, antiphlogistic packs, blistering, firing and surgical removal are all techniques for treating splints, depending upon the severity. Bench knees commonly cause splints because there is more concussion to the bones.

Upward Fixation of the Patella (Knee Cap)

Horses with long, straight hind legs are most susceptible to upward fixation of the patella. The patella becomes fixed (or "stuck") when the leg is extended and the limb is locked in extension as the horse tries to pull it forward. This condition can be very painful for the horse. In some cases, there is only a momentary "catching" of the patella when the horse walks—the leg never really locks. If the horse is forced to move, he will drag the front of the hoof on the ground.

The first time upward fixation of the patella occurs the horse can be given a tranquilizer and an attempt made to return the patella to its normal position. Using a sideline to pull the leg forward, the patella should be pushed upward and sideward. Occasionally, forcing the horse

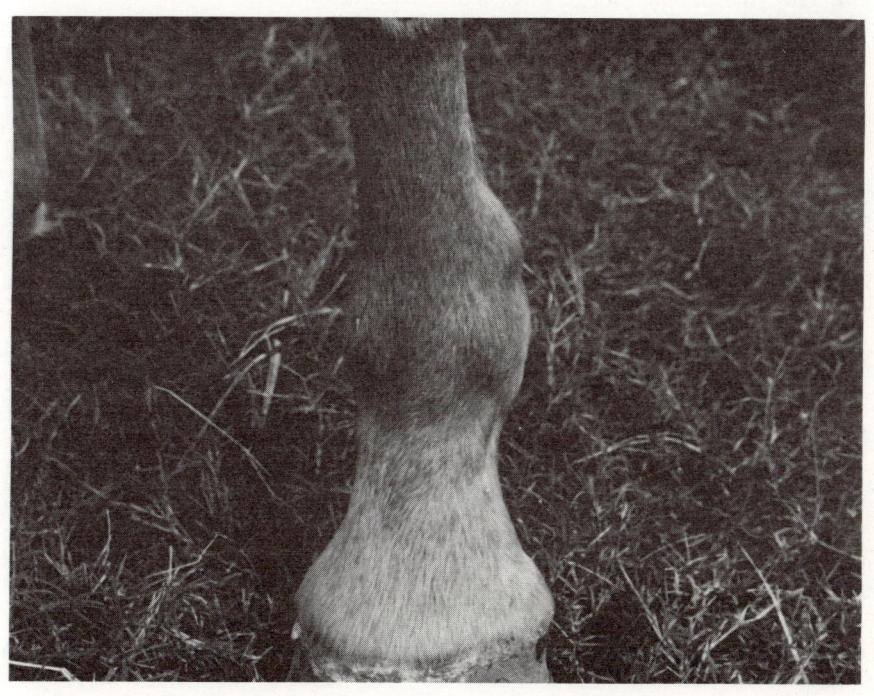

The swollen appearance characteristic of windpuffs.

to make a sudden move will cause the patella to slip back into place. If this condition keeps recurring surgery may be needed.

Windpuffs

Windpuffs rarely cause lameness. They are swellings of the joint capsule caused by excess synovial fluid, usually involving the fetlock or hock joint. No heat, pain or lameness accompanies windpuffs. Rest will generally reduce the size of the swelling, but no other treatment is necessary. Windpuffs rarely go away, they are usually present throughout the life of the horse affected with them.

The horse's ability to perform an athletic task for any length of time is directly dependent upon his conformation. There have been some outstanding individuals with glaring conformational defects, but we'll never know how much better they might have been, were it not for the defect.

The "perfect" horse has never been born and probably never will be, so the horseman must strive to get the best performance from the animals he has. To condition a horse properly, and get the most from him, allowances must be made for any weaknesses in form.

REFERENCES CITED

1. Beeman, Marvin, D.V.M., "Conformation ... The Relationship of Form to Function," The Quarter Horse Journal, Volume 25: 3, 1972, pp. 82.
2. Adams, O.R., D.V.M., M.S., **Lameness in Horses**, Philadelphia, Pennsylvania, Lea and Febiger, 1966.
3. Beeman, Marvin, D.V.M., Op. Cit.
4. Strong, Charles L., M.V.O., M.C.S.P., **Horses' Injuries**, London, England, Faber and Faber, Limited, 1967.
5. Reed. W. O., "Bowed Tendons Heal Slowly in Horses," Journal of the American Veterinary Medical Association, Volume 148: 4, 1966, pp. 390.
6. Van Pelt, R.W., D.V.M., Ph.D., "Intra-Articular Injection of 6 α-Methyl, 17 α-Hydroxyprogesterone Acetate in Tarsal Hydrarthrosis (Bog Spavin) in the Horse," Journal of the American Veterinary Medical Association, Volume 151: 9, 1967, pp. 1159-1171.

GENERAL REFERENCES

Catcott, E. J., D.V.M., Ph.D., and Smithcors, J. F., D.V.M., Ph.D., Editors, **Equine Medicine and Surgery**, Wheaton, Illinois, American Veterinary Publications, Inc., 1972.
Lamkin, William G., D.V.M., "Control of Orthopedic Inflammation," Quarter Racing World, Volume 5: 5, 1972, pp. 64-67.
McKibbin, Lloyd D., D.V.M., "A Review of Splints," The Backstretch, Volume 12: 1, 1973, pp. 12.
Putnam, Harold D., D.V.M., "Lamenesses," Quarter Racing Record, Volume 13: 4, 1973, pp. 16
Siegmund, O. H., Editor, **The Merck Veterinary Manual**, Rahway, New Jersey, Merck and Company, Inc., 1967.

courtesy of the International Arabian Association

Excellent Arabian Conformation

* BASK+, AHR25460
(Witraz x Balalajka)

Legion of Merit Champion

U.S. National Champion Arabian Stallion 1964
U.S. National Champion Arabian Park Horse 1965
U.S. National Reserve Champion Arabian Formal Driving Horse 1967
U.S. National Reserve Champion Arabian Combination Horse 1967

Imported in 1963 from Poland by Lasma Arabians, Scottsdale, Arizona

4

Evaluating Performance Potential Scientifically

Peak condition largely contributes to ultimate performance capability. The proper combination of nutrition and exercise is instrumental in developing peak condition. In other words, the individual performs only as well as his body will allow.

A businessman, working daily in an office, couldn't possibly run a four minute mile. His body just isn't up to it. In the same sense, the family pleasure horse certainly isn't able to turn in a winning performance in a steeplechase. In both cases the results would be disasterous!Therefore, in situations not so exaggerated, we need to have some way to measure states of condition. What are signs of good condition and how can they be recognized?

With the human athlete this doesn't present too much of a problem. Reams of research and clinical studies provide physicians with plenty of techniques, equipment and standards to accurately determine the physical condition of a man. The horse, however, hasn't had the benefit of nearly as many refined, detailed studies as the human.

In the last 15 years there has been an increase in this area of equine research and valid testing procedures have been developed by several studies. Even so, the results of these studies have not always been absolutely conclusive. There are two general approaches when determining the relative condition of a horse.

First, the general state of health is a good indicator of condition.

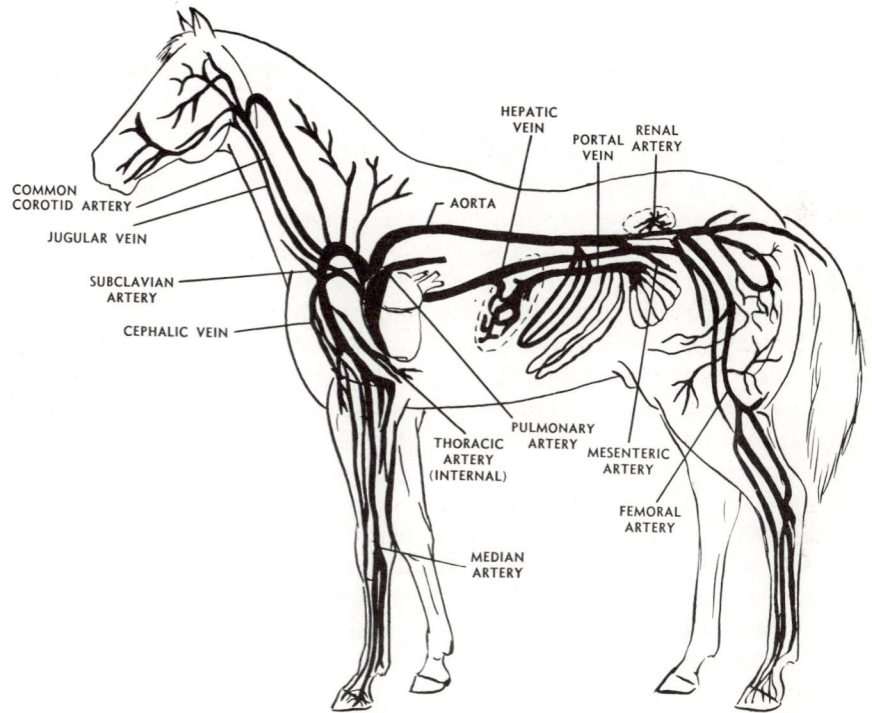

*taken from **Horseman's Veterinary Guide**, The Western Horseman, Inc., 1963*

The circulatory system pictured above is the basis for many of the performance evaluations of the horse.

Since health is such a major part of condition, it certainly follows that a horse cannot possibly be in good condition without being in good health.

The second approach is to determine how the horse's body reacts to work, or physical stress. When a horse is properly conditioned for the goal he is expected to achieve he should be able to perform the required work without detrimental physical side effects.

A horseman, like an athletic coach, needs to know the relative state of condition of the athlete with which he is working. This knowledge should indicate to the horseman the type and level of conditioning program required. Continued scrutiny will allow the trainer to determine what progress the horse is making and how to "step up" the conditioning regime to develop the horse to his full physical potential.

Determining the level of condition and the athletic potential of an animal is a horseman's tool for formulating individualized conditioning programs for specific horses. Regular checks of the state of condition will uncover weak areas where additional work is needed. The full potential of the horse, as an athlete, can then be more readily developed.

Many measurements related to condition concern the circulatory system. This system is made up of a pump (the heart) and a network of vessels for carrying blood throughout the body. The following discussion is intended to explain only the fundamentals of the circulatory system so that the basic concepts of measurements of condition can be more fully understood. The reader who desires more than a simply functional knowledge should refer to texts on equine anatomy and physiology.

The heart is a hollow, muscular organ that forces blood circulation through the body by regular contractions. The blood is in constant motion, so this is quite a task for the heart as the principle force for propelling the blood. Blood circulation, continual movement of a fluid, is extremely complex, involving intricate pressure relationships, nervous impulses, chemical as well as engineering principles, etc. Each heartbeat of the horse forces about 1/15th of the total blood volume into the arteries. (1)

The vessels of the circulatory system include arteries, veins and capillaries. The networks of the arteriole and venous portions of the system can be compared to a tree with many branches, each getting successviely smaller. Oxygenated blood is carried away from the heart and distributed to the body by the system of arteries. These vessels have thick, muscular walls which can control the amount of blood that flows at one time, thus aiding in maintaining blood pressure.

As the branches become smaller the oxygenated blood goes through

Citation, 1948 Triple Crown winner, is shown in peak racing condition. This top-flight runner was later retired to the King Ranch.

a system of tiny vessels called the capillary network. Capillaries are extremely small vessels, but it is here that the vital exchanges take place that nourish every cell in the body. The walls of the capillaries are very thin, semi-permeable membranes. A semi-permeable membrane allows selective passage of materials. In this case, the water, oxygen and nutrients carried by the blood are allowed to go out through the walls of the capillaries and the waste products from the cells pass into the vessels to be carried away.

The blood then goes through the veins, or venous return portion of the circulatory system. Veins carry deoxygenated blood to the heart. Veins have thin walls, with very few muscles, but there are valves in the veins. These valves prevent the blood from returning to the capillaries and make it possible for the muscle contractions from normal body movements to help push blood back to the heart. Blood pressure is much lower in the veins than it is in the arteries.

Through the pulmonary artery, the heart pumps this deoxygenated blood to the lungs to be supplied with oxygen. The capillary beds at the end of the air passages in the lungs are the site of the actual gaseous exchanges. The oxygen in the air is exchanged for the waste product, carbon dioxide, which is carried back by the deoxygenated blood. This newly oxygenated blood is returned to the heart through the pulmonary veins and is then pumped by the heart through the arteries for continuing circulation throughout the body.

This system of oxygen transport supplies the muscles of an animal's body with the energy needed to meet the requirements of the animal's body during athletic competition. Blood is the body fluid that carries oxygen, nourishes all cells, removes waste products, fights disease and many other functions—but, what is it?

Blood consists of a straw-colored fluid called plasma in which all the cellular components of the blood are suspended. Red blood cells (erythrocytes), white blood cells (leukocytes) and platelets (thrombocytes) are the cellular portions of blood.

Erythrocytes are specialized cells designed to carry oxygen. Present in erythrocytes is the iron-containing compound, hemoglobin, which gives the erythrocytes their unique ability to carry oxygen. Leukocytes serve primarily to fight infection and maintain resistance to disease. The major function of thrombocytes is to aid in the clotting of blood.

Blood analysis, which should be performed only by a qualified veterinarian, can be used to give an indication of the general state of health of a horse and also the stamina, or performance capability, of the animal. Under sanitary conditions, a blood sample is taken from a horse and sent to a laboratory to be analyzed.

courtesy of The Complete Book of the Quarter Horse, Arco Publishing Company, Inc. of New York, Nelson C. Nye

The immortal Peter McCue, one of the greatest early sires of short-running horses in history, with his owner-jockey Milo Burlingame.

Laboratory analyses valuable to the horseman include hematocrit value (packed cell volume or PCV), hemoglobin concentration, red blood cell count and white blood cell count. The counting procedure is simply a microscopic count of the number and types of cells circulating in the blood of the animal at a specific time. (2) The hematocrit value is the percentage of whole blood that is red blood cells. It is obtained by centrifuging a sample of blood for a specific time until the blood separates into its component parts. The hematocrit value, or PCV, is an indication of *both* the number and size of erythrocytes present. The normal range of hematocrit values in horses is 31 to 55 per cent. (3)

There is a wide range in normal values because PCV is easily influenced by many factors. Even small amounts of physical exertion or excitement can be reflected in an increased PCV. One study reported that a 4% increase was observed in a horse when the blood sample was collected by a veterinarian rather than the usual groom, and in other horses at least a 2% increase was reported. (4) Another study reported that exercise, pain, fever and excitement can result in a 30% or more increase in this value. (5)

Differences among individual breeds are also responsible for such a wide variation of normal hematocrit values. Light horse breeds, the Thoroughbred especially, have higher normal hematocrit values than breeds of heavy horses. (6) Sex and age can also be influencing factors on this value. Stallions normally have a higher value, with geldings exhibiting the lowest normal values, and two-year-olds were found to have lower mean values. (7) However, 35% is considered to be about the average PCV for horses. (8)

The red blood cell count should normally fall between 9 to 12 million cells per cubic millimeter of blood for light or hot-blooded horses and 7 to 10 million cells per cubic millimeter of blood for draft or cold-blooded horses. (9) A blood count lower than this is termed anemia, which has many causes including nutritional deficiencies and disease. A higher than average red blood cell count is called polycythemia and often occurs at higher altitudes before the horse has had a chance to physically adjust to the altitude. Serious diseases can cause the red blood cell count to be greatly elevated permanently; examples are emphysema and heart disease. Temporary increases in the red blood cell count often occur when the horse is nervous or excited and also with a reduced fluid intake which results in a lowered plasma volume (or "more concentrated" blood).

For the horse, a white blood cell count between 8,000 and 11,000 cells per cubic millimeter of blood is considered to be normal (10), while a higher count usually indicates some type of bacterial infection. The normal range of thrombocytes is 150,000 to 450,000 cells per cubic

La Prevoyante, a 1970 bay filly out of Arctic Dancer by Buckpasser, came in first in all twelve of her two-year-old starts to earn $417,109.

courtesy of The Blood-Horse

millimeter of blood for draft horses, with light horses averaging approximately half as many. (11)

Hemoglobin concentration is measured in grams per 100 milliliters of blood and most horses have normal concentrations of hemoglobin between 13 and 15 grams per 100 milliliters of blood. However, the cold-blooded horses will have a lower normal value; usually 12 to 13 grams per 100 milliliters. (12) Because hemoglobin is contained in the red blood cells, the wide range in normal concentrations is due to the same factors causing variation in hematocrit values.

The blood is an excellent indicator of an animal's state of health. Usually, signs of illness can be detected much earlier by changes in the blood rather than changes in the physical appearance of the animal which generally occur at a later time. Also, blood analysis can be used as a tool to estimate the ability of an animal's body to react to physical exertion.

From the standpoint of the equine athlete, measurements regarding the erythrocytes are most frequently considered when attempting to determine the state of condition or performance potential of the horse. Obviously, this is because of the oxygen carrying ability of the red blood cells. Without an adequate oxygen supply to meet the requirements of working muscles, the equine athlete could not successfully cope with the physical demands of athletic competition. The hematocrit value or PCV, hemoglobin concentration and red blood cell count are measurements generally used in this respect.

In the animal body, oxygen consumption increases with work. During physical exertion the higher heart rate and hematocrit value in the horse demonstrate methods the animal's body uses to meet these increased oxygen requirements. The protein compound hemoglobin in the red blood cells absorbs oxygen from the air and releases it to the cells in the body.

Each gram of hemoglobin can combine with only a specific amount of oxygen, 1.36 milliliters. (13) For this reason, measurements taking into account the presence and amount of hemoglobin are an indication of the oxygen carrying capacity of the blood and are thought to be an index of performance potential. This applies especially to athletic competition demanding superior endurance, such as racing.

In fact, one study (14) concluded that hemoglobin concentration and total blood volume can be used to predict racing performance and also the physical "readiness" of the animal to race. This same study found that endurance training increases these values and that they are significantly higher in well conditioned horses. Horses subjected to endurance training exhibited a 34% higher total hemoglobin and 19% higher total blood volume.

An example of potential developed to winning peak is the Thoroughbred, Carry Back, the Champion Three-Year-Old Colt of 1961.

Another study in Australia (15) found that PCV, hemoglobin concentration and the red blood cell count in the horse increases with training. While attempting to establish the range for normal blood values in Thoroughbreds in Australia, from the standpoint of racing performance, these researchers concluded that optimal and suboptimal levels need to be established. This is because, while studying Thoroughbred winners, they found that the majority of winners had blood values above the average for the breed—thus suggesting that optimum values are an index of superior racing performance and physical fitness. These same researchers also concluded that the need for high blood values (PCV and hemoglobin concentration) increased as the distance of the race increased because of the higher demands made on the body.

In horses, the PCV is considered to be a better evaluation of the blood's oxygen carrying capacity than is the red blood cell count or hemoglobin concentration. (16) This certainly suggests that the PCV would be the most valuable blood analysis in attempting to assess performance potential and physical fitness of a horse. With regular exercise and good nutrition this value normally increases.

However, a word of caution is warranted when considering PCV (or hematocrit values)—there are many factors that can influence the number of erythrocytes circulating in the bloodstream of the horse at a given time. The spleen of the horse is a storage area for erythrocytes and the animal has a terrific capacity for releasing large numbers of erythrocytes into circulation when it is exercised or excited. As previously stated, the number of circulating erythrocytes also varies with other factors such as age, sex and breed of the specific horse. For this reason, much caution should be exercised to assure that blood samples are taken under similar conditions when the animal is relatively calm.

Because of this extreme variability in the number of circulating red blood cells in the horse, most scientists consider a single analysis to have a questionable value. To really benefit from the results of a blood test, or to consider the results valid, one needs to know what the "normal" value is for that individual horse. Blood analysis, as part of regular physical examinations, can help to set up normal ranges of values for individual horses.

Since the oxygen requirement for any animal does increase with exercise, the total blood volume of a horse is also used as a method for evaluating performance potential and physical fitness. Obviously, since all the blood can't be drained from a horse to measure it without killing the horse, there is an indirect technique for obtaining this value. A specific amount of dye is injected into the bloodstream of the animal and allowed adequate time to circulate and thoroughly mix in the bloodstream. A blood sample is then taken and the dilution of the dye calculated to indirectly determine the total amount of blood.

As with other blood values, the light horses have significantly higher total blood volumes, as a percentage of body weight, than heavy horses. (17) Since studies indicate that performance is closely related to the oxygen carrying capacity of the blood, total blood volume can be used as a valid means of estimating performance potential. For example, one study found that total blood volumes increased 19% in trained horses and concluded that this can be used to predict racing performance and to determine the level of fitness. (18) In general, a larger total blood volume (in relation to the size of the animal) indicates a larger oxygen capacity for that particular animal and the total blood volume increases when the horse is subjected to physical training.

The erythrocyte sedimentation rate (ERS) is occasionally used in assessing the level of fitness. The ERS is measured in standard tubes by the distance in millimeters the erythrocytes settle in a certain time interval. Compared to other species of domestic animals, the erythrocytes of the horse settle rapidly. For example, the normal range of ERS values for the horse is 2 to 12 millimeters in 10 minutes, while the average value for cattle is 2.4 millimeters in 7 hours. (19) Because so many variables can affect the ERS in horses, this value is considered to be of limited use in veterinary practice. (20) However, it is suggested that the ERS becomes slower as the peak of physical fitness is reached.

The heart rate of a horse has also been used as a means of scientifically evaluating performance potential. The heart rate of a horse increases when physical exertion increases. If the maximum heart rate for an individual animal has been determined by previous monitoring, then the heart rate during exercise can be used as an indication of "how hard" the horse is working on a specific exercise level.

As it is difficult to count the heart rate when a horse is exercising, several methods have been developed to handle the electrical monitoring equipment needed. These include a treadmill set-up, a wagon or sulky to carry the equipment, wireless transmission of electrical signals (telemetry), and recordings on magnetic tape.

One study using heart rates as a method of evaluating physical fitness and predicting racing performance concluded that horses with relatively low resting and recovery heart rates after exercise have the greatest endurance. (21) This same study found that horses with lower heart rates during exercise had faster winning times in races. Compared to horses less physically fit, these horses had smaller increases in heart rates during exercise.

Since no special equipment is needed to determine the heart rate of a horse before and after exercise, horsemen can fairly easily use this as an index of physical fitness. However, it must be remembered that heart rates can vary quite a bit among individual animals, so the horseman must make a conscientious effort to determine the resting rate for each animal.

To compare the fitness of different horses, it is mandatory that they receive the *same* amount of exercise and have the heart rate taken at the *same* intervals after exercise. To make a valid comparison of how quickly these animals recover from exercise, the heart rates must be counted at specified intervals after the exercise session has ended. For example; one minute, two minutes, five minutes, etc. after the conclusion of the physical exertion.

Research has also been carried out attempting to relate the horse's heart size with performance potential. This is done using interpretations from an electrocardiogram (ECG, EKG). Like other muscles, heart muscle exhibits electrical activity upon contraction which spreads through the surrounding tissues and can be recorded by an electrocardiograph.

Assuming that a larger mass of heart muscle requires a longer time interval to be activated, a specific portion of the ECG (the QRS interval) is thought to indicate heart size of the animal. This time interval is measured in milliseconds and the concept is termed "heart score." The theory behind the heart score concept is that a larger heart, in relation to the size of the animal, is better able to meet the oxygen requirements of the animal's muscles during exercise. There are many variables that can influence the ECG including specific placement of the electrocardiograph leads, posture of the animal, heart rate, disease—plus the age and sex of the horse.

One study (22) determined that, under racing conditions in Australia, the best race horses have higher than average heart scores. Also, those horses with high heart scores averaged larger money earnings per race. In this study a heart score of 120 milliseconds or more was considered indicative of superior racing performance potential. In addition, these researchers commented that heart score should not be used as an absolute index of racing performance since performance is under the influence of many other variables, also.

Electrocardiography in the horse is a relatively new area of study and the basic theories are not positively concrete. Obviously, more study is needed in this area. Heart score is considered to be only an indicator of superior athletic ability—definitely not a hard and fast guide.

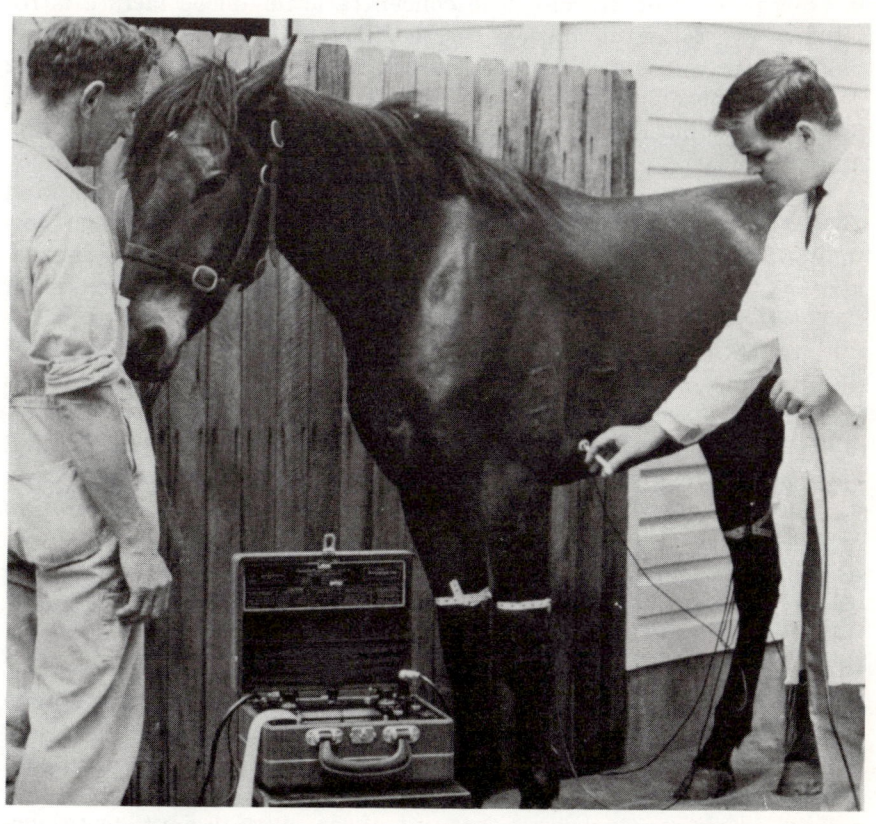

reproduced with permission of the publishers of **Equine Medicine and Surgery,** *2nd Edition*

The procedure and equipment used to record an electrocardiogram (used in the heart score concept) are shown above on a Standardbred gelding.

Study has also been conducted regarding the use of the blood lactate level of a horse to determine working capacity. (23) As in the human body, working muscles produce lactic acid that is dispelled into the bloodstream. After exercise, the concentration of blood lactate is related to the degree of muscle fatigue. By comparing the amount of blood lactate present when the horse is at rest and after exercise, a determination of the strenuousness of the exercise can be made. In other words, blood lactate level is thought to reflect how hard the animal worked.

Further study into the relationship of blood lactate levels and muscle utilization involved investigation of the three major types of muscle fibre. (24) These are classified on the basis of contractile characteristics and oxidative capacity: slow twitch (ST), fast twitch, high oxidative (FTH) and fast twitch, low oxidative (FT).

Since it was found that older horses had a higher percentage of FTH fibres than young horses, it seemed probable that endurance conditioning developed greater oxidative capacity in the muscles of horses.

The extent of use of all three types of muscle fibre was monitored according to temperature, glycogen levels and glucose levels. All evidence pointed to the conclusion that ST and FTH fibres are always engaged at the start of a horse's exercise but that FT fibres are not used until the horse attains near maximal speed. In other words, this possibly means that the extent of use of ST and FTH fibres is in direct relation to fatigue since they sustain prolonged use. It also means that the fibre which constitutes 43% of the cross-sectional area of horse muscle, the FT fibre, remains inactivated except at high speeds for extended periods of time, i.e., under racing conditions.

It would seem, therefore, that to condition the FT fibres one would have to exercise a horse at racing capacity. This is not considered normal procedure for the very reason the research scientists experimented with "very willing horses"—it leads to exhaustion. No conditioning program can achieve its purpose if the horse is constantly having to take rest breaks or is physically broken down from overwork.

It can only be assumed that the normal racing schedule of a horse adequately exercises the FT fibres or that, until a safer method is devised, the solution would probably be to maintain a horse in peak condition and rely on this good condition to naturally provoke the needed response from the FT fibres.

During exercise, the body of a horse is forced to make adjustments to meet the increased oxygen and energy needs of working muscles. The effectiveness with which the animal makes these adjustments is a determiner of the athletic ability of the horse. The heart, the blood

Peppy Otoe, 1973 A.Q.H.A. Honor Roll Champion Trail Horse owned by Sue Ann Smith, exhibits winning condition.

and its components are extremely important factors influencing the endurance and stamina of the horse—or the athletic potential.

REFERENCES CITED

1. Edwards, E. H. and Geddes, C., Editors, **The Complete Book of the Horse**, New York, New York, Arco Publishing Company, Inc., 1973.
2. Frandson, R. D., B.S., D.V.M., M.S., **Anatomy and Physiology of Farm Animals**, Philadelphia, Pennsylvania, Lea and Febiger, 1965.
3. Ensminger, M. E., B.S., M.A., Ph.D., **Horses and Horsemanship**, Danville, Illinois, The Interstate Printers and Publishers, Inc., 1969.
4. Archer, R. K. and Clabby, J., "Effect of Excitation and Exertion on the Blood."*
5. Persson, Sune, "Normal Variations in Hematocrit."*
6. Marcilese, N. A., "Blood Values in Light and Heavy Horses."*
7. Stewart G. A. and Steel, J. D., "Hematology and Racing Performance," in **Equine Medicine and Surgery**, Wheaton, Illinois, American Veterinary Publications, Inc., 1972, (Catcot and Smithcors, Editors).
8. Schalm, Oscar W., D.V.M., Ph.D., **Veterinary Hematology**, Philadelphia, Pennsylvania, Lea and Febiger, 1965.
9. Swenson, Melvin J., D.V.M., M.S., Ph.D., Editor, **Dukes' Physiology of Domestic Animals**, Ithaca, New York, Cornell University Press, 1970.
10. Swenson, Melvin J., D.V.M., M.S., Ph.D., Op. Cit.
11. Swenson, Melvin J., D.V.M., M.S., Ph.D., Op. Cit.
12. Swenson, Melvin J., D.V.M., M.S., Ph.D., Op. Cit.
13. Frandson, R. D., B.S., D.V.M., M.S., Op. Cit.
14. Persson, Sune, "Blood Volume and Working Capacity."*
15. Stewart, G. A. and Steel, J. D., Op. Cit.
16. Schalm, Oscar W., D.V.M., Ph.D., Op. Cit.
17. Marcilese, N. A., Op. Cit.
18. Persson, Sune, "Blood Volume and Working Capacity," Op. Cit.
19. Swenson, Melvin J., D.V.M., M.S., Ph.D., Op. Cit.
20. Morgan, H. C., D.V.M., M.S., "Value of the Erythrocyte Sedimentation Rate."*
21. Marsland, W. P., "Heart Rate Response to Exercise in Standardbreds."*
22. Steel, J. D. and Stewart, G. A., "Electrocardiography and Racing Performance," in **Equine Medicine and Surgery**, Wheaton, Illinois, American Veterinary Publications, Inc., 1972, (Catcott and Smithcors, Editors).
23. Asheim, A., V.D.M., Ph.D.; Knudsen, O., V.D.M., Ph.D.; Lindholm, A., V.D.M.; Rulcker, V.D.M., Ph.D.; and Saltin, B., Ph.D., "Heart Rates and Blood Lactate Concentrates of Standardbred Horses During Training and Racing," Journal of the American Veterinary Medical Association, Volume 157: 3, 1970, pp. 304-312.
24. Lindholm, Arne, D.V.M., Ph.D., **Muscle Morphology and Metabolism in Standardbred Horses at Rest and During Exercise**, Stockholm, Sweden, 1974. (From the Department of Biochemistry, Royal Veterinary College and the Department of Physiology, Gymnastik-och idrottshögskolan.)

* Contained in:
  Catcott, E. J., D.V.M., Ph.D. and Smithcors, J. F., D.V.M., Ph.D., Editors, **Progress in Equine Practice**, Volume II, Wheaton, Illinois, American Veterinary Publications, Inc., 1969.

5

Care and Conditioning
of Young Horses

(Birth to Breaking)

The time from birth to weaning is an especially important segment in the life of a horse requiring the very best care that can be provided. The process of being born, in itself, is a great stress and many of the events occurring at this time can have a lasting influence on the ability of the horse.

Although birth is a very natural process, sometimes things do go wrong which may jeopardize the future performance potential of the horse. Consequently, it is important that the horseman be familiar with the signs of foaling problems in the mare and with the other processes and events surrounding time of foaling. Then, if something does go wrong, the horseman can recognize it and immediately provide for assistance.

To give the foal every possible chance of becoming a winner, proper care for the broodmare is essential. Most horsemen allow their mares to foal outside, under normal circumstances. In the case of bad weather, or if the mare is expected to need assistance, it is usually more practical to move the mare into a stall. The foaling stall should be larger than an average stall to allow plenty of room for the mare and foal, and attendants if needed. Sixteen feet by sixteen feet is usually considered adequate. During inclement weather a larger stall will provide the opportunity for more self exercise for both foal and mare.

It is important that the stall be well ventilated and bedded with soft, clean material. For the protection of the mare and foal, the interior of the stall should be as smooth as possible. The health and safety of both mare and foal should always be the prime consideration regarding any preparations or actions taken at the time of foaling. The stall should also be well lighted and near equipment that might be needed such as water facilities and veterinary supplies. Adequate preparation at foaling time can insure against lost time if any assistance is required.

Regarding the time of foaling, mares are especially individualized and may exhibit very few indicators of the coming event. The signs vary so widely that knowing the mare and being familiar with her usual pattern is one of the very best indicators of foaling time. Although there aren't any sure signs leading up to foaling, one can look for general indicators. Individual mares may present several, none, or all of the following characteristics. Initially the mare begins to "make a bag," or the udder begins to develop. This development starts anywhere from two to six weeks before the mare actually foals. (1) Usually one to two days prior to foaling, milk will ooze down and the teats "wax" over. Generally, the wax falls away and milk begins to drip from the teats within 12 to 24 hours of foaling. (2)

As a rule, when the mare is getting ready to foal she will be restless, nervous and possibly unfriendly. She may frequently lie down and get back up, exhibiting signs of slight discomfort. Again, the signs are extremely variable and many mares foal when it is least expected. For this reason the conscientious horseman should be adequately prepared several weeks before he expects the mare to foal. Some foals arrive virtually unannounced.

Once uterine contractions begin, producing labor pains, the "water bag" will rupture. This is the only sure sign of imminent foaling. Normally the foal is born within 15 to 30 minutes of this time. (3) In an ideal situation the attendants are hidden from the mare's view so they can observe without interfering with the natural process of birth.

Most veterinarians agree that the umbilical cord should never be cut after the foal is born. Generally, the cord breaks spontaneously when most of the placental blood has drained into the foal. If the cord is severed by the attendants immediately after birth the foal may be robbed of as much as a third of its total blood supply. (4) After the cord has broken, the stump should be quickly disinfected with tincture of iodine, merthiolate or metaphen. Within one to $1^1/2$ hours after birth the normal foal will be standing and nursing. (5) Delays longer than this should be regarded as a sign of danger. Again, the stall should be free from protruding objects so that the foal will not injure

himself when trying to stand and take those first few wobbly steps.

Since birth is a very natural process, one should never try to "help" the mare unless it is obvious that something is wrong. Prolonged labor or abnormal presentation of the foal are conditions that usually require immediate veterinary assistance.

Normally a foal is born completely surrounded by the amnion (encased in a membrane sac) and will kick the sac open when emerging from the birth canal—this initiates the start of breathing. Occasionally a foal doesn't manage to break this membrane and swift assistance is needed to prevent suffocation of the foal. The attendant should quickly rupture the sac and make certain that the foal's mouth and nostrils are clear of membrane and fluid.

To help insure the best possible health of the foal from the very first, injections of tetanus antitoxin and antibiotics are routinely administered after birth. These are measures to protect the foal from general infections and are ideally given within the first 48 hours of life. (6)

Another common practice is that of "balling out" or giving an enema to the foal. Some veterinarians recommend this treatment for every foal, while others say only those foals indicating the need for an enema should receive one. General signs of constipation include abdominal pain, as in colic, straining and sweating. An enema of warm, soapy water or glycerin will normally give the foal quick relief. However, if this treatment doesn't work, a veterinarian's assistance is recommended.

These practices are commonly carried out at foaling time to insure the foal will have every chance to develop to his full potential. Since the colostrum, or first milk of the mare, is very effective in warding off disease, a normal foal needs no other treatment.

The horseman should be able to recognize the abnormal or sick foal so that it can receive the special care it will need to prevent permanent injury. General indications of illness in a foal are weak or labored breathing and fever. The normal rectal temperature of a foal falls between 100° and 101°F. (7) One should also look for signs of diarrhea, constipation, swellings, nasal discharges, etc. Notice, too, if the foal moves around and nurses easily. With careful observation it is easy for the horseman to determine when something is wrong with the foal. If a problem is present, there should be no hesitation in calling a veterinarian quickly. A sick foal may not make it until morning.

In some cases a foal may be orphaned. Possible reasons include death of the mare, injury to her udder, twins, or any factor that will prevent the foal from nursing. An orphan foal will need special attention, especially within the first three hours of foaling.

The primary concern is to find something to replace the colostrum which the foal would have normally received from his dam. The colostrum is a very important sourse of vitamins, nutrients and immunity against disease. If another mare is present that has foaled about the same time it is possible to get colostrum from her. In many cases this mare can serve as a foster dam.

If a foster dam is not available, an artificial milk replacer must be used. There are commercial preparations available for this purpose. In addition to food sources, an orphaned foal needs adequate levels of vitamins and antibiotics. It is a common practice to maintain the orphaned foal on antibiotic injections for five days after birth. (8) The veterinarian can help the horseman formulate a diet for the orphaned foal to be sure to provide all of the needed nutrients. It is also important to use dry feed, too, and wean the foal onto a totally dry ration as soon as possible. Milk replacers in the pelleted form are a good choice; label directions should be followed carefully.

When a foal is about two weeks old, whether orphaned or on the mare, it should be allowed to eat what it wants. A foal usually will begin to nibble a little grain and hay on its own at this time. The mare may have to be tied up for short periods to allow the foal to eat. It is beneficial to encourage any foal to eat supplemental feed as soon as possible. Feeding the foal helps promote early development and an easier weaning. Also, the mare can get back into breeding condition more rapidly if the foal eats supplemental feed instead of relying solely on her milk.

In a special situation where mare and foal must be stall kept, the foal should be provided with its own grain box. This is because it is generally unsatisfactory for the foal to eat with the mare. If she does allow the foal to eat with her, the mare usually eats much faster than the foal and he may not get all the feed he wants. Also, if a foal is put on creep feed later in life, this early feeding can help condition the foal against accidentally overeating. (9)

When mares are kept in pasture or large paddocks, it is a good practice to creep feed foals. Normal pasture or hay usually doesn't furnish an adequate source or proper balance of nutrients for a growing foal. Also, the digestive tract of the foal is not sufficiently developed to handle the form and concentration of nutrients found in roughage. One alternative is to wean foals early, at three to four months of age, and feed them a dry feed especially formulated for foals. This method requires exceptionally good management and health programs. However, some foals simply should not be weaned this early. Borderline cases should be discussed with a veterinarian.

A creep feed is a specially designed enclosure to allow the foals to eat a specific diet while keeping the dam out. This is usually accomplished by fencing off a small area with the entrance large enough for the foals, but small enough to keep the dams from following. A board can be placed horizontally across the entrance for this purpose and adjusted as the foals grow. The creep feed should be placed in an area where the mares come regularly, such as by a water trough.

Foals are naturally curious and will generally investigate the facility when they are very young. Once inside, when the foal has found the feed, he will usually make it a regular habit to come back and eat all that he wants. The feeder should be kept clean, and all of the foals observed to make sure that the timid ones are getting their fair share. Foals on creep feed are accustomed to eating independently and usually suffer far fewer weaning setbacks.

Supplemental feeding of foals is designed to make up for any naturally occurring nutritional deficiencies in pasture or hay. Ideally, supplemental feed furnishes only those nutrients that are lacking and doesn't increase those already present in adequate amounts. A foal can easily be overfed. Overfeeding a foal can have extremely undesirable effects on physical health and athletic ability. For example, too generous supplementation of diets with iodide sources has been shown to cause goiter in significant numbers of foals. An iodide-excess goiter may cause developmental and functional defects that seriously limit athletic performance. Weakness, poor muscle development and contracted tendons are defects commonly reported. (10)

Exercise and the amount and quality of feed given are primary factors involved in conditioning. The exercise must be regular and graduated—always within the limits of the foal's strength. Mares and foals may begin an exercise program when the foal is three to four days old (11) with the exercise in a small area at first so the foal will not tire. One obvious method is to ride the mare and allow the foal to follow. Careful observation should then be made for any signs of tiredness in the foal since it cannot take very much physical exertion at this age.

On pasture a healthy foal will get plenty of exercise on its own. In fact, the ideal situation is to raise foals on good, clean, healthy pasture with other mares and foals. (12) Playing with other foals will insure that the young horse gets adequate amounts of exercise to promote sound growth. Depending upon the climate, the pasture should certainly provide shade and/or shelter.

However, if special conditions require that a mare and foal be kept up, a forced exercise program will need to be implemented. Foals are individuals and will require different amounts of exercise. The fundamental rule is to allow adequate exercise without over-exertion. Phys-

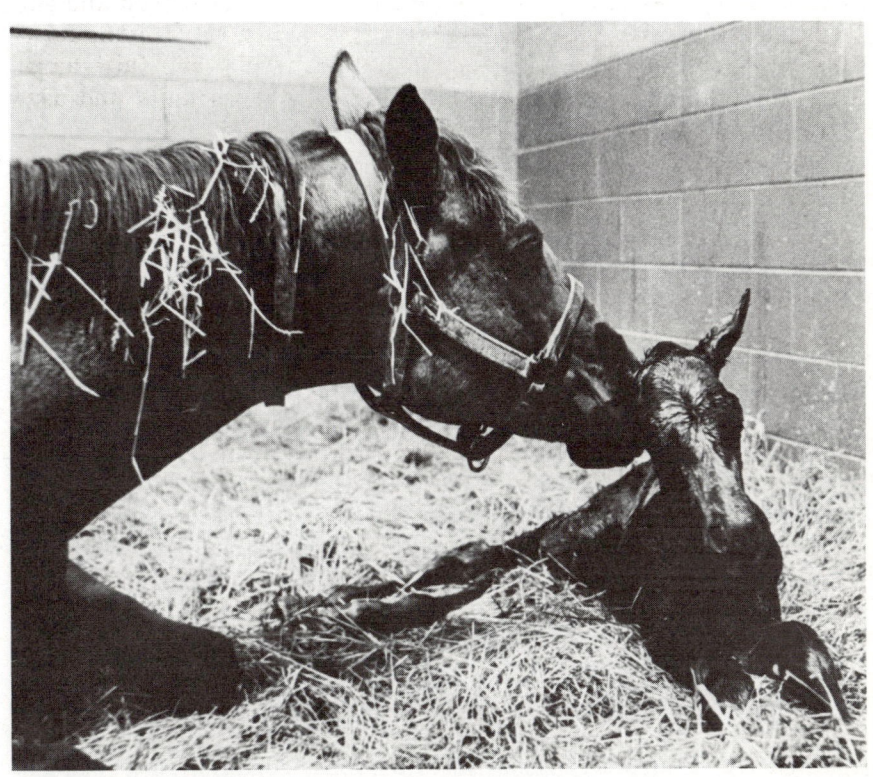

This mare will give her newborn foal the best care she can. The rest is up to the horseman to insure fulfillment of the foal's athletic potential.

ically and mentally, the foal is very immature and exercise should always be kept well within the current level of the foals's abilities. Even when foals are playing together, racing around a pasture, a steady pace is rarely kept up for any length of time. The healthiest of foals will tire rapidly; their muscles and bones are just not ready for any continuous work.

No matter what type of facilities you have, the first few days following foaling, when the mare and foal are kept inside, provide an excellent opportunity for gentling the foal. The primary rule is to handle the foal gently and carefully. Generally it is advisable to tie the mare up in the stall so that she can see her foal, but won't be in the way. Calmly catch the foal by putting one arm around the front of the chest and the other arm around the foal's rump. Handling up to and including halter breaking may be done at this time. A helper can put a clean, well-fitting halter on the foal. A foal should never be lifted with one hand underneath the chest as this can easily break the soft ribs. During the next few days the foal can be taught to lead. With a light lead, both the mare and foal can be led around the stall. Initially, the foal may struggle, but he will naturally follow the dam and this method usually arouses the least resistance on the part of the foal.

Continuing these lessons daily, with sessions *never* longer than 15 minutes, the foal will eventually progress to the stage where he can be led by himself, beside the mare instead of following, or even alone. During these early lessons it is also important to use verbal commands. The foal will begin to learn what they mean and have a good, basic foundation in obedience for later lessons.

In a stall kept situation the mare and foal should be regularly led to a pen to provide for adequate amounts of self exercise. Physically and mentally, a foal is not ready for regimented exercise, as with the longeing or round pen methods, until he is five or six months old, at least.

Because the period from birth to weaning is particularly vital in insuring the development of a sound and healthy mature horse, health management is also very important for proper condition of a foal. The feet of foals should be periodically checked to get them gradually accustomed to the procedures for later shoeing. Necessary trimming should be done when the individual foal needs it; this will vary widely depending upon the climate, ground surface, etc. Since young bones are so soft and pliable, corrective trimming at this time can help to alter some conformational defects. However, corrective trimming must be done properly and only when needed. An experienced farrier, by observing the foal when he is standing and in motion, can determine what will be needed.

Weaning is a shocking experience, but it's much easier for a foal already on supplemental feed and accustomed to playing with others. The sudden separation is a panic-stricken time for both the mare and foal, so the horseman must know exactly what he is going to do and do it *calmly*. He should draw up a safe, sensible plan and stick to it.

The majority of foals are weaned by the time they are five to six months old. Basically, the procedure is to separate the mare and foal swiftly and completely so they can neither see nor hear each other. This is the major factor in helping both to settle down once they have gotten over the initial shock of separation. Every effort should be made to avoid injury to both the mare and foal during the procedure.

This requires that there be safe fencing; no barbed wire, low gates, or split, rotten or loose rails. A deeply bedded stall with few projections is ideal. Aside from physical facilities, the persons handling the horses must exhibit quick, secure and calm actions. Things will go smoother and the horses will be less nervous if the handlers stay calm.

At first the foal will need to be kept securely in a stall or other safe enclosure, with plenty of fresh feed and clean water. The weanling gradually begins to eat well, relax and look around at his new surroundings with curiosity. After one or two days the average foal will be calm enough to be turned out into a large paddock for self exercise. The time the weaned foal is in the stall, small pen, etc., can be used to accustom it to humans and handling if this has not been previously done.

If the foal has been eating supplemental feed well and has been handled and taught to lead before weaning, it can usually be turned out on pasture with other weanlings within a few days of the actual weaning. The horseman who appreciates the importance of early care and takes foal conditioning seriously will have healthier, better looking and easire to handle weanlings.

At the time of weaning the young horse starts his life on his own. The way the young horse is handled at this time and for the next several months can greatly affect the animal for the rest of his life. Physically and mentally, the horseman wants to build the type of young horse who is able to calmly accept breaking as the next progressive step in learning. Plenty of time and patience are required to properly develop a young horse physically and mentally to this point. Many people begin working with young horses at the time they are weaned, while others delay the initial work for several months. However, no actual regimented, forced lessons should begin before the horse is at least six months old. He won't be equipped, physically or mentally, to handle it.

Self exercise is very important for the young horse. Just like a child, running is a favorite form of play for the young horse. Fresh air and sunshine are extremely instrumental in building a strong, healthy weanling. Running and playing on natural footing, as in a pasture, are ideal for proper bone and muscle growth and development. (13) Of course, it is mandatory that the pasture be safe and well fenced. Extreme care should be taken to remove any objects on which the young horse might injure himself. Old wells, cisterns, abandoned barns—any hazards—must be fenced off to make a safe pasture for young horses.

Depending upon the development of the individual horse and the practices of the horseman, there is much variation as to when forced exercise begins. The most important point to remember is that the horse is still a baby. He can't be expected to react and learn as an adult horse would. *Slowly* and *gently* are the key words describing the proper handling of young horses.

If the weanling hasn't previously been taught to lead, this generally should be done before anything else. It is a common practice of many horsemen to break a young horse to lead while he is still on the mare. The accepted belief is that this makes weaning and following events a little easier—for both the weanling and the horseman. In any case, the weanling should be taught only one lesson at a time and the horseman should make certain that each lesson is completely understood and learned before attempting to introduce something new.

It is important to remember that this is a *young* horse who is just developing the ability to concentrate. Therefore, even the simplest lesson may be hard for him to understand. Patience on the part of the horseman is a vital factor in building a good mental attitude in the young horse.

Halter breaking and teaching the weanling to lead does not need to turn into a fight between the horse and the man. The weanling should be allowed a couple of days to settle down and get used to the new stall. When the young horse is first handled, extreme care must be taken not to frighten him—he must learn to trust the handler and not be afraid.

The handler should concentrate on making smooth, calm movements in the stall, gradually getting nearer the weanling, talking to him and scratching him, until the halter can be gently slipped over his head. Because the young horse could easily injure himself by struggling, he should not be tied up until he has thoroughly learned to lead and respect the lead rope. Halter breaking is far safer and easier if the young horse has been handled from an early age.

Encouraging the weanling to move forward often presents the first problem when teaching one to lead because, at this age, the young

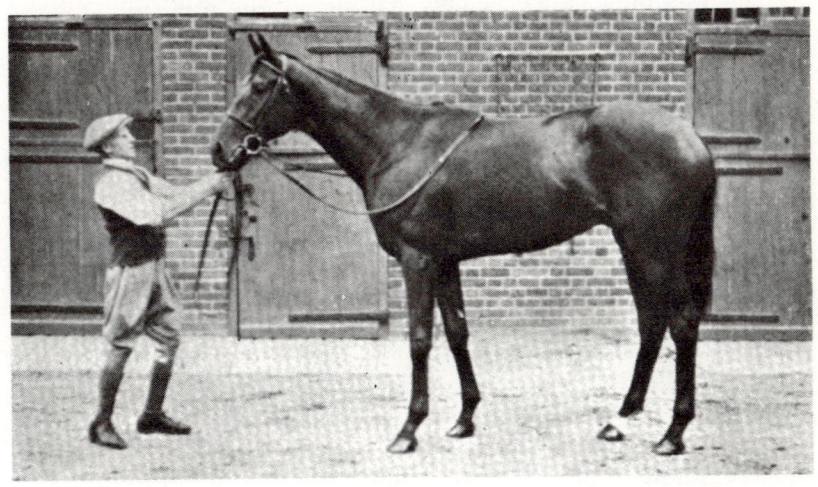

Nasrullah, the English bred Thoroughbred stallion brought to the United States by the late A. B. Hancock, Jr., led the American Sire List five times.

horse may be stronger than the handler. Instead of simply trying to drag the horse it's a good idea to also use other measures to encourage the horse forward.

For example, a lariat can be looped around the hindquarters of the weanling and be used with the lead rope. By holding the lead rope in one hand and the lariat in the other, the horseman can easily coax the weanling with the lariat when he fails to respond to the lead rope. If the young horse still balks and pulls back, additional help may be needed. A helper can stand behind the young horse and gently "shoo" him forward while the other person urges with the two types of ropes. If the shooing doesn't work, the degree of encouragement from the helper can be gradually increased. Again, if the weanling has not been previously handled, halter breaking will certainly be a much more difficult task.

When the weanling can be easily led out of the stall and walked around, always under control, he can be tied up for daily grooming. This should be gently, yet thoroughly, done with the handler watching for any sudden movements on the part of the horse. The weanling may be fidgety during grooming and should be patiently accustomed to human handling.

After about a week of being led out of the stall, walked around, tied and groomed, the weanling will probably be ready for more advanced lessons such as longeing, round pen work, etc. However, this depends upon the individual horse—some may not learn as rapidly as others and won't be ready to concentrate on something more difficult.

It is also a good idea to avoid starting something that can't be finished. In other words, ideally, the lesson should not be stopped before the young horse actually learns it. If the horse learns that he can "get away" with something, it will only be harder for the horseman to get him to do it the next time. Both the handler and the horse should be ready for a new lesson before attempting it.

If not sufficiently prepared, the lesson can turn into a frustrating experience for the horse and the trainer. In an extremely short time the handler can destroy all the confidence and trust the young horse has in him. It can take a long time for the weanling to regain confidence in the handler after a short session of severe punishment brought on by simple misunderstanding and unpreparedness.

When the horse is handled can also make a big difference. Ideally, the weanling should be relaxed and quiet. In this state of mind the young horse will seldom get carried away to the point of being uncontrollable. If the weanling is in the proper mood, firmness and patience on the part of the handler are generally the most that will be required.

In most cases the handler is simply asking for trouble when he tries to work with the young horse that is overly rambunctious, energetic, nervous or irritable. Logically, the young horse is not going to be receptive to learning under these circumstances. If the young horse is like this from standing in a stall all day, it often helps to let him run off the excess energy and nervousness in a paddock before starting the lessons. Developing a good mental attitude is extremely important in conditioning the young horse.

The actual amount of forced exercise will vary greatly with the individual horse. The only basic rule is to never overwork the young horse. He is still growing, his bones are soft and one doesn't want to create any hysical problems to deal with later. The amount of forced exercise must increase gradually as the young horse develops the strength and mental ability to "take a little more."

Among trainers, the methods and duration of forced exercise for young horses are widely diversified. Longeing, leading and ponying are by far the most common methods of exercise. Many trainers recommend exercising the young horse in sand to equally develop the muscles of his body. A round pen, about 50 feet in diameter with a few inches of sand, is a great conditioning aid. A horse may be conveniently exercised with or without a longe line in such a pen. Using a longe line is preferable with the young horse because of the control it gives the handler and the basic training incorporated in the exercise.

Many horsemen follow the practice of longeing weanlings for five to six minutes and yearlings for ten to fifteen minutes in light to medium depth sand. Of course, this must depend upon the stage of condition of the individual young horse and the footing provided by the surface where he is being exercised. Exercise in very soft footing is extremely tiring and can be easily overdone.

Other commonly used methods include starting the horse with ten to fifteen minute sessions of easy jogging and loping on regular footing. Longe line, round pen and leading from another horse are ways this initial exercise is enforced. With one of these methods the young horse can be gradually worked up to 20 to 25 minute, maximum, exercise sessions.

Every trainer strives to always keep the horse under control, especially when exercising at faster speeds, such as a lope. If the young horse ever learns that he can "get away" from the horseman, completely out of control, an extremely bad habit can be developed. The trainer must be certain that the young horse has acquired the necessary obedience for a new lesson before attempting it.

The amount of exercise is not as important as the reaction of the horse to it. The horseman needs to know each individual horse well enough to recognize when it has had enough exercise and is beginning to tire. Fundamentally, one is developing muscles, coordination and balance in the young horse and there isn't any one rule that can possibly apply to every young horse.

Mentally, during this conditioning period prior to breaking, one is instilling in the young horse the ability to concentrate and obey. If the yearling already responds willingly to verbal commands from the handler, breaking will generally be a calmer and easier process for both the horse and the handler.

Throughout the period between weaning and breaking, the young horse is also becoming accustomed to situations with and without other horses around. In other words, he is learning to adapt to a variety of different situations and developing his ability to concentrate when faced with different surroundings. The trainer is simply broadening the experiences of the young horse so he will be better able to learn and perform in the various situations with which he may be faced in later life.

Many trainers make it a practice to turn yearlings in large pens or paddocks several hours per day before and after the forced exercise sessions. This opportunity to run and stretch is very beneficial to the development of the young horse.

Forced exercise should be on a regular basis and thoughtfully planned, with much attention given to each individual horse. Mentally, the handler strives to keep the horse interested in the lessons by not overdoing it. This is to help develop a positive attitude in the young horse regarding his relations with humans.

During the winter it can be very impractical to exercise the young horse daily. Cold rain, sleet, frozen ground and snow can certainly hamper a forced exercise program. If facilities allow, walking young horses inside to avoid keeping them stalled for long periods of time is recommended. If possible, turning the yearlings into large pens with adequate shelter is a good practice. Any opportunity for self exercise during a period of little or no forced exercise should be taken advantage of during the winter conditioning program.

The practices vary, but the object is the same. Young horses need exercise to promote the best physical and mental development. They simply will not "do well" when cooped up in a stall for extended periods of time.

Exercise is not the only consideration of the conditioning program for a young horse during the weanling to breaking period. Well planned health management is important. Also grooming, including trimming and shoeing, when needed, is a major segment of conditioning the young horse. The horse, ideally, is accustomed gently and

courtesy of The Upjohn Company

Good health management is an integral part of every conditioning program; this includes periodic worming. The stomach tube method is illustrated above.

slowly to all the practices with which he will be faced in later life. This includes picking up feet, as the farrier will do, brushing all over, clipping and so on. If the young horse is gently and conscientiously introduced to these practices, they will present no problem later on. Again, extreme care must be taken not to frighten the young horse or force him to accept things he is not ready to accept. The trainer is building the basis for his behavior as an older horse. Sometimes even the most insignificant things can have a lasting effect on the horse.

A well planned conditioning program for the young horse, during this period from weaning to breaking, greatly enhances his prospects for later competition. He has had experience concerning close associations with humans and knows how to act and what to expect. His capability to learn things easily and willingly has been increased. He has developed self control and respect for human authority.

REFERENCES CITED

1. Catcott, E. J., D.V.M., Ph.D., and Smithcors, J. F., D.V.M., Ph.D., Editors, **Equine Medicine and Surgery**, Wheaton, Illinois, American Veterinary Publications, Inc., 1972.
2. Catcott, E. J., D.V.M., Ph.D. and Smithcors, J. F., D.V.M., Ph.D., Editors, Op. Cit.
3. Ensminger, M. E., B.S., M.A., Ph.D., **Horses and Horsemanship**, Danville, Illinois, The Interstate Printers and Publishers, Inc., 1969.
4. Toms, T., B.V.Sc., "Care and Management of Thoroughbred Foals," in **Progress in Equine Practice**, Volume One, Wheaton, Illinois, American Veterinary Publications, Inc., 1966.
5. Ensminger, M. E., B.S., M.A., Ph.D., Op. Cit.
6. Catcott, E. J., D.V.M., Ph.D. and Smithcors, J. F., D.V.M., Ph.D., Editors, Op. Cit.
7. Rossdale, Peter D., M.A.F.R.C.V.S., **The Horse**, Arcadia, California, The California Thoroughbred Breeders Association, 1972.
8. Catcott, E. J., D.V.M., Ph.D., and Smithcors, J. F., D.V.M., Ph.D., Editors, Op. Cit.
9. Knappenberger, R. E., D.V.M., "The Foal from Birth to Growing Yearling," in **Progress in Equine Practice**, Volume One, Wheaton, Illinois, American Veterinary Publications, Inc., 1966.
10. Baker, H. J., D.V.M. and Lindsey, J. R., D.V.M., "Equine Goiter Due to Excess Dietary Iodide," Journal of the American Veterinary Medical Association, Volume 153: 12, 1968, pp. 1618-1630.
11. Knappenberger, R. E., D.V.M., Op. Cit.
12. Rossdale, Peter D., M.A.F.R.C.V.S., Op. Cit.
13. Ensminger, M.E., B.S., M.A., Ph.D., Op. Cit.

Conditioning for Specific Events

As an athlete, the horse competes in quite a variety of events. Competitive events differ among age groups, breeds and, of course, purpose. These range all the way from racing to jumping, to polo, to western events such as calf roping and cutting, etc. In fact, the variety of competitive events for the horse is almost limitless.

When considering conditioning of horses aimed toward winning in competition, one must take into account that on the one hand many conditioning procedures are identical no matter what the task. On the other hand specific tasks will require specific conditioning in many instances.

The track star who is a champion pole vaulter normally wouldn't be expected to win an 880 meter race. He hasn't been conditioned and trained for this event. The same principle holds true for the horse. What the individual animal does, or in which events he is expected to compete, will usually determine what type of specific conditioning the individual horse needs.

Certainly, the basic fundamentals of a conditioning program apply to all horses, no matter what their area of performance. But, different tasks do require slightly different types of conditioning in some instances, and widely differing types of conditioning in others.

Also, it is well to remember that training techniques vary widely among horsemen. Two good trainers may use methods, in a particular situation, that appear to be completely opposite and yet their efforts may result in equal successes. On the other hand, these same two trainers may be in complete agreement as to the proper method to be used in some other situation.

It is obvious that very few, if any, training techniques can be considered to be the only "right one." Therefore it should be understood that this text is concerned primarily with conditioning. Training techniques are presented simply as guides to achieve proper condition. The techniques themselves are good ones and have proven successful for many trainers. However, they are neither offered nor should they be considered "sacred."

courtesy of The Blood-Horse

Dahlia—the first Thoroughbred mare to earn over one million dollars.

6

Conditioning Thoroughbred Race Horses

The Thoroughbred race horse is a unique animal. By way of selective breeding, a horse specialized to run relatively long distances with superior speed has been developed. This type of animal—bred exclusively for racing—requires specialized conditioning to develop speed and distance and maintain soundness.

The initial breaking and training of the horse as a yearling is very important as it can have a life-long effect on its performance ability. Thoroughbred yearlings are generally broken to bridle and saddle in the late summer or early fall of the year. Most colts have been allowed to run out at night and exercise riderless during the day so that the initial muscle development has begun. There are several common methods for exercising the Thoroughbred yearling. Simply turning the young horse out into a large, safe paddock for self exercise is one example. Longeing, leading and ponying are other examples of exercise methods frequently used.

Only competent, calm and experienced persons should be used for the breaking of yearlings. In the stall the yearling is efficiently bridled in a *calm* manner. All movements should be made in a smooth and deliberate manner so that the young horse is not frightened.

After the yearling becomes thoroughly used to the bridle, the saddle is put on the horse. Some yearlings may require several sessions to become accustomed to the bridle while others may accept both bridle

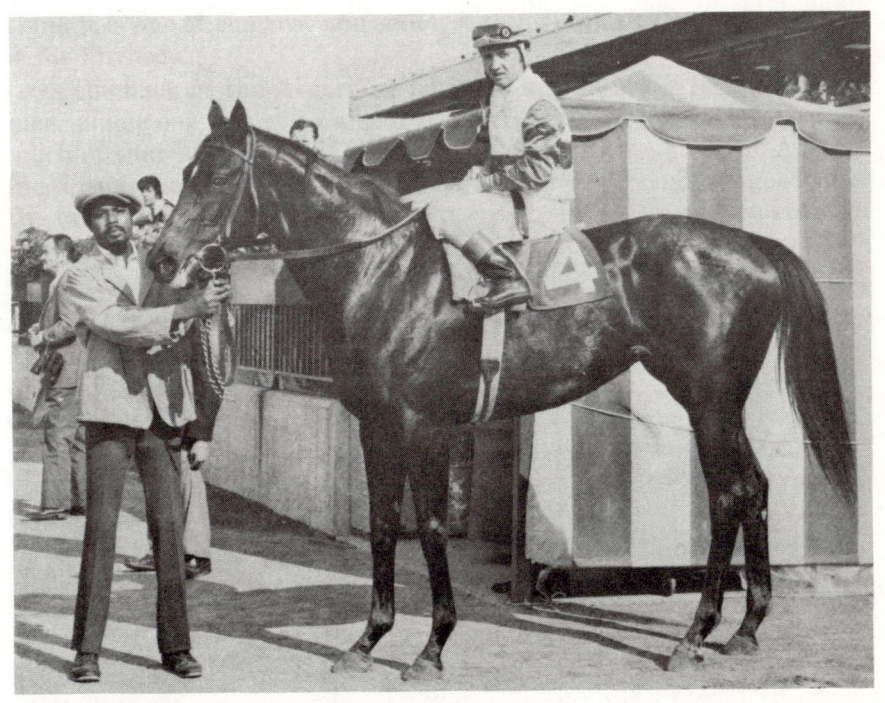

Already touted by many to be perhaps the finest Thoroughbred filly of all time, Ruffian displays highly desirable conformational characteristics.

and saddle on the same day. The trainer should slowly and gently place the pad and saddle (with the stirrups taken up so they won't dangle) on the horse. He will then pull the girth up only enough so that the saddle won't fall off. When the yearling stands calmly with the saddle, the girth can be gently taken up more.

The next step is to walk the yearling around in the stall until he doesn't seem to mind the saddle. Then is the time for the yearling to get used to a little weight in the saddle. Most trainers have a boy hang over the saddle so the horse can feel a little weight on his back. Slowly and smoothly the boy gets into the saddle. The young horse should be allowed to stand quietly for a few minutes before he is led around in the stall. If he isn't too unruly, he can be led outside, with the boy on his back. The first session should not be longer than 20 to 30 minutes because the horse has not yet developed muscles to carry more weight than his own. If the yearling gets tired, the session should be stopped.

Gradually the yearling proceeds to being ridden without being led. In small areas, the young horse learns to walk and turn in all directions. The majority of Thoroughbred establishments handle young horses in groups so that they become accustomed to other horses being handled around them.

The exercise sessions are gradually increased as the horses become more fit and manageable. Short periods of jogging and eventually cantering are incorporated into the program as the yearlings become stronger. A lead pony is often helpful with yearlings as they are usually willing to "follow the leader."

It is *very* important that yearlings be taught to stand quietly. If they don't stand quietly at home, how can they be expected to stand quietly in the saddling paddock or starting gate at the track? Numerous trainers also insist that all horses be taught to back since situations often arise when they are required to back up in a starting gate.

When yearlings can be handled easily enough, they are exercised on the track. It is recommended that exercise sessions begin with the young horses standing quietly in a line across the track. No fast work is done until the horse is sufficiently developed to handle it. For example, when yearlings can stand two to three total miles a day of walking, jogging and galloping *without* any signs of strain or excessive tiredness, small amounts of fast work can be initiated. Yearlings should be galloped head-to-head some of the time to get used to being bumped and jostled by other horses on the track.

An eighth of a mile is the usual distance for the slow, early breezes. As the horse grows and develops, the speed and distance are increased to fit the individual needs of the yearling. As a rule, yearlings are

Early lessons for racing prospects often include exercise in groups.

usually galloped every day to insure maximum muscle development, with breezes coming every three days, or about twice a week.

It is important to remember that the yearling is growing during this entire period and that it is fundamental to keep him sound. Extra-special attention should be paid to the legs, watching for any signs of soreness or injury. The horse should be rested if he shows any indication of soreness. A trainer should never hesitate to call for veterinary assistance. The early stages of conditioning are aimed at developing the yearling so he can later realize his full racing potential.

After two to three months of this beginning conditioning, the good race prospect should be able to easily gallop two miles without being winded and, on an average track, surface breeze a quarter mile in 23 to 24 seconds. Three-eighths in a time of :36 to :39 is indicative of excellent speed in a yearling.

At this time, the yearlings are nearly two-year-olds and many are sent home for a winter rest or a short rest and winter training. Others are taken south for the winter racing season.

Two-Year-Olds

The winter is usually a comparative rest period for two-year-olds. From late fall until early February the general routine calls for easy gallops, weather permitting, and much of the remaining time spent in a paddock or stall.

In northern areas, many young horses get much of their winter exercise in closed sheds. Therefore many have a tendency to put on too much weight. On days when young horses cannot be exercised outside, they should be walked for an hour or more inside so they won't be difficult to get back into condition later in the year.

Whatever the case, the early conditioning of the two-year-old should be slow and gradual, as with yearlings. Most trainers begin with a month of long, slow gallops—generally working up to at least two miles daily. Periods of walking and jogging are also included.

After this initial "hardening up," the two-year-old should be in shape for easy breezes. However, this is the *average* horse. Some horses may require additional slow work, especially if they are recuperating from an injury or were allowed to get overly fat during the winter rest. Slow quarter-mile breezes, such as 26 to 27 seconds, are a common starting point. The speed is built at a gradual rate so the individual horse can make safe and sound progress. Breezes are slowly increased to three furlongs, usually in 41 to 42 seconds, and a few half-miles in 55 to 56 seconds. With proper conditioning, the average two-

Young Thoroughbreds becoming accustomed to the starting gate.

year-old should eventually be able to go a half-mile in 50 seconds easily.

During this period of slowly building speed it is very important that young horses be taught to stand quietly in the starting gate. Before the young horse can successfully break from the starting gate, he must be thoroughly used to it and see that there is nothing to fear. Some two-year-olds take to such gate training quickly, others frequently take up to a month. The young horse should be taught to walk into the gate, through the gate, and stand quietly in the gate with the doors open and shut.

Many trainers have two-year-olds stand in the gate 15 minutes or so, every day for weeks, before they ever learn to break away from the gate. This, naturally, develops the kind of horse that is calm and well-mannered in the starting gate—the type that is less likely to injure himself and others.

When the two-year-old is well conditioned, easily able to run a half-mile in 50 seconds, he should be taught to break from a standing start. In other words, break from the gate. No young horse should be broken from the gate until he has the strength and conditioning to make this effort without hurting himself.

A common method is to take the horse to the gate and break him away, trying for a straight rather than a fast start. The next day, the horse should simply be allowed to stand in the gate. Most trainers follow the practice of keeping the horse away from the gate after he has made two or three good breaks and his speed away from the gates has been increased to a reasonable level.

At this point, the trainer should have a fairly good idea of the class to which the two-year-old belongs. It is a good idea to keep daily records noting the work done by the horse, plus the weight carried and equipment used. After the plateau of the 50 second half-mile is well established, the fast, intensive work for racing usually begins.

Fast work is usually lengthened by a furlong or a sixteenth of a mile at a time, depending upon how the individual horse reacts to the work. The two-year-old is learning to fairly well lengthen and quicken his stride, but, if pushed beyond his ability, the horse can easily lose his stride or injure himself. Again, it cannot be over-emphasized, if the horse shows signs of strain or soreness, he must be rested until it clears up. As a rule, two-year-olds require more galloping than older horses. At least two days are generally allowed between fast work days. (Days of easy galloping and walking in between.)

Two-year-olds best suited to run short to mid distances, such as three to five furlongs, will generally be ready to race at this point. (If they are to be run as two-year-olds.) When the horse has proven that

Galloping in a group offers some valuable lessons to the Thoroughbred youngster.

he can run the distance in good time, it is probably time to enter him and run him. In general, two days had best be allowed between the speedy work and the race. The trainer doesn't want to "leave his race on the track."

Experience with the individual horse is the only way to determine how much time to allow between speedy workouts and/or races for the horse to be alert, with 100 per cent running ability. The trainer should always try to run the young horse in his class. Constantly being outrun can easily damage the competitive spirit of the young horse.

Mid to long distance two-year-old runners (five and one-half furlongs and up) will require conditioning for a longer time to gradually build up the endurance needed for the longer races. A good rule of thumb is to slowly lengthen the work until the horse can easily run an eighth of a mile farther than he has to go in competition.

There is much variation between individual horses in regards to building distance runners. Some horses may take as much time as nine months to be thoroughly conditioned to race over a distance.

It's usually not the racing that hurts a two-year-old, but *how often* he races. The trainer must be thoroughly familiar with the individual horse, being able to recognize what amount and type of exercise he needs to build and maintain peak condition. Also, one must know how much work a particular horse can stand; he should never be pushed beyond his capabilities.

The primary concern is to keep the horse sound, with the desire to run. A horse certainly won't run his best if it physically hurts him, or if he is discouraged.

Older Horses, Three and Up

Conditioning older horses to race is very similar to the programs followed with younger horses. However, the older horse often does not require as much galloping, relative to "works," as the two-year-old. Also, because of their maturity, older horses can be more easily conditioned to run distance races.

The conditioning programs begin with long, slow gallops to toughen up the horse. Gradually, breezes are added to the exercise, with speedy work coming only when the horse has had an adequate foundation of slow work. Obviously, previous injuries should be taken care of *before* any work begins.

Of course, it depends ultimately upon the individual horse and the care he has received during the "off" season, but short to mid distance runners (five to seven furlongs) usually require at least two to three months of conditioning before they are in good racing form. Short

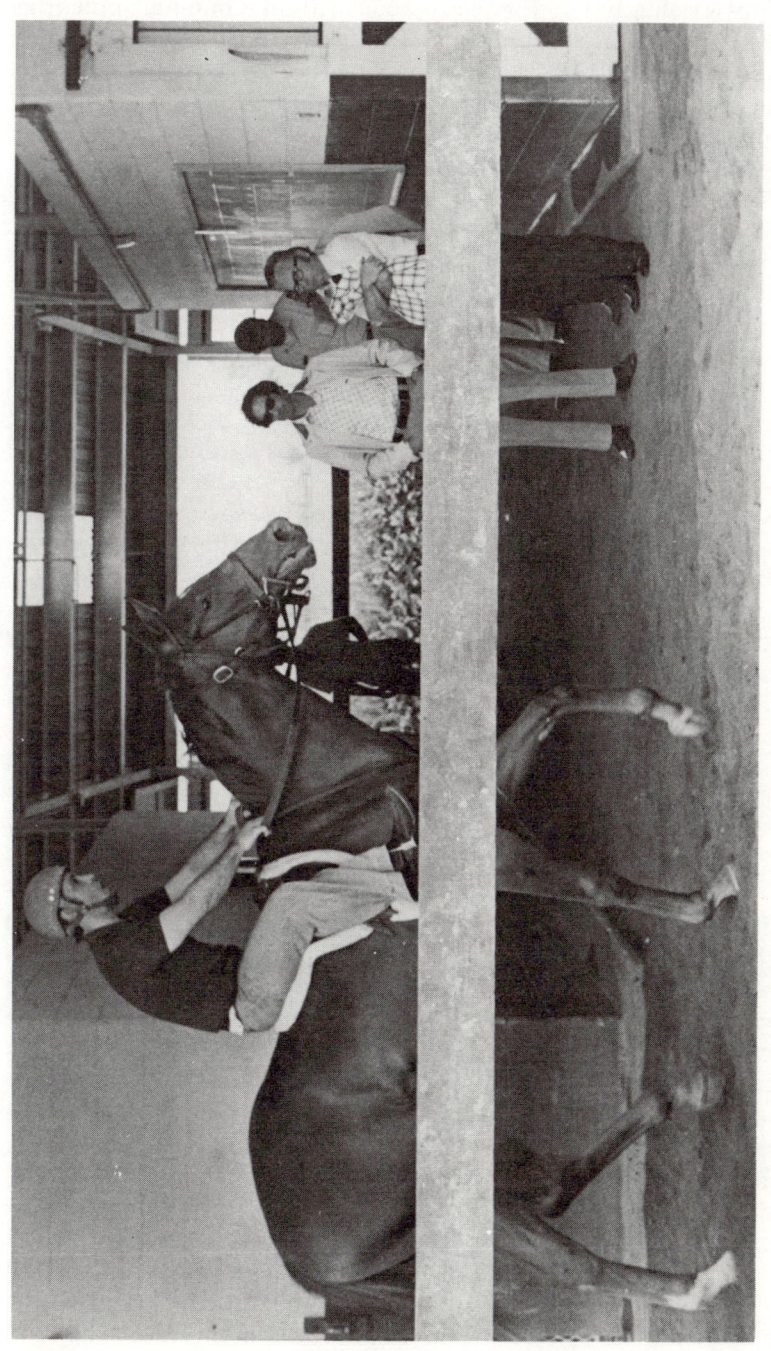

Mary Jane Gallaher, Inc.

A Spendthrift Training Center yearling receiving some beginning lessons in the shed row.

slow gallops gradually lengthened to about two and one-half miles are the beginning steps in the program. This early, daily exercise is only to toughen and condition the horse. No breezing is done until the horse can easily gallop this daily distance.

Depending upon the horse, it may take three weeks to two months to reach this initial level of condition. Slow quarter-mile, three-eighths and half-mile breezes are gradually incorporated into the exercise program. About a "two minute clip" is a safe speed with which to begin. To help insure the soundness of the horse during this stage of conditioning, it is a good idea to incorporate a short gallop as a warm up and then finish him out with a slow eighth after the breeze.

Between "work" or breeze days the conditioning programs of most trainers generally allow two to three days of easy exercise. Occasionally, exercise on the day following a breeze day consists of walking only. The work is slowly increased an eighth at a time as the horse develops the endurance and strength needed for the additional distance. As long work tends to dull the speed of sprinters, they are rarely worked over an eighth longer than the distance they will be required to run.

This length insures that the horse will be able to go the distance, but not "hold back" in anticipation of additional distance. The length of works is generally increased week by week as the horse develops the ability to take it. Before any really fast work is attempted, it is mandatory that the horse have a good, solid foundation of slow work so he won't hurt himself with the effort. After all, maintaining soundness is the most important element of any conditioning program.

When the sprinter reaches the level of condition at which he can breeze a half-mile on an average track surface in 50 seconds, work to sharpen speed is usually started. By increasing with slow moves, a horse with good speed should be able to go six furlongs in 1:18 to 1:20 before short, speedy works are started. Depending upon the distance the horse will be required to run, three to five furlongs is the average length for works to sharpen speed. Fast works, repeated two or three times before increasing the speed, are usually separated by two days of walking and galloping.

Many trainers make it a practice to have the horse break from the gate, preferably with other horses, on at least one long work before a race. When the race horse shows that he has the ability to go the distance, with the speed thought necessary, the trainer should enter the horse and try him. A race puts something into a horse that no amount of training can. The cliche is "one race is better than several works." The statement is only valid, however, if the horse is in adequate condition to withstand the physical strain of the race. The folly

The illustrious runner, Count Fleet, was the sixth Triple Crown winner (1943). Superb condition was instrumental in his longevity; he lived to the age of 33.

(not to mention the physical danger) of trying to "race a horse into condition" is too obvious to deserve mention.

The horse expected to race "over distance" (nine furlongs and up) is conditioned in much the same way as the shorter distance horse. However, the conditioning program for the longer distance runner involves gradually lengthening the initial slow gallops to about four miles. When the horse can gallop this distance with no effort, easy breezes of three-eighths and half-mile lengths are started.

Week by week, the distance is advanced in gradual stages as the horse is capable of taking it. With the distance horse, the works to sharpen speed are delayed until the horse is able to do a mile easily in a steady time of about 1:40. For the average horse, this shows good speed. Half-mile blow-outs are thought to be one of the best methods for increasing speed in the distance horse.

As in the conditioning program for the sprinter, the fast work for the distance horse is spread over the slow work, with easy gallops to increase distance endurance on the two or three days between fast works. When the horse has built up to the total distance that he will be required to run, generally four to eight works are needed to increase his speed. The distance horse *must* be in peak condition before any long, hard work is attempted because one race could easily ruin the horse for life.

Concerning the work just before the actual race, it is *generally* believed that a sharp, speedy move close to the race is better for the distance horse than a long-hard work. However, the ultimate decision must be left to the discretion of the trainer. He must know what the individual horse needs to be ready to race with total ability, fully recovered from previous work.

The distance horse should never be raced until he has proven that he can go the distance with the weight he will be required to carry, within several seconds of the time necessary. Again, it simply cannot be over-emphasized that one race before the horse is in really top condition can easily result in a permanently injured horse. Supreme effort on the part of the horse is required for distance racing, so the horse must have superb conditioning to withstand the strain of the race.

Older horses, because they have been previously raced, are frequently nervous when they first get to the track. As a result, it is a good practice to get to the track early enough for the horse to overcome his initial nervousness and get settled into the track routine so he will be able to race to his full potential.

All exercise for the race horse—whether old, young, sprinter or distance runner—must be followed with proper "cooling out." It may take only thirty minutes to cool a horse out after an easy exercise session, but at least one hour is generally required for cooling out after fast work or a race. At first the horse is usually walked rapidly for 10 to 15 minutes. Gradually the horse is slowed down to a slow walk. A few swallows of water are given to the horse at three to four minute intervals during the cooling out period. It is a good practice to check on the horse about 15 minutes after he is put up. Even the best groom can occasionally be mistaken about proper cooling out.

Many older horses are broken down because they are hurried through their conditioning program to prepare for a certain race. If the horse can't be ready for the race, the trainer should wait for a similar race later, when the horse is in top condition. It is also a good practice to avoid overmatching a horse. Just like the two-year-old, an older horse can easily become discouraged and lose that all important desire to win.

GENERAL REFERENCES

Burch, Preston M., **Training Thoroughbred Horses**, Lexington, Kentucky, The Blood-Horse, 1967.

Collins, Robert W., **Race Horse Training**, Lexington, Kentucky, The Thoroughbred Record Company, Inc., 1972.

7

Conditioning
Quarter Running Horses

As it is generally roughly stated, the Quarter Horse as a breed was developed primarily to run a quarter of a mile faster than the best representatives of any other breed of horses. The superlative burst of early speed, characteristic of the Quarter Horse, provides a natural sprinting ability.

The running Quarter Horse possesses natural "early" ability and commonly displays the desire to give his all every time he runs. Although some Quarter Horses are raced over distances up to 870 yards, the majority of Quarter Horse races are sprints ranging in distance from 220 yards to 440 yards. (The "recognized" distances for which the American Quarter Horse Association will allow official speed ratings are: 220 yards, 250 yards, 300 yards, 330 yards, 350 yards, 400 yards and 440 yards.) Obviously, at these distances the "all out" speed of the horse is the primary concern.

To successfully race in this manner the horse must be conditioned to his absolute peak, both physically and mentally. The slightest amount of pain or hesitation may add fractions of a second to the time, often the difference between winning or losing.

The 1974 All American Futurity at Ruidoso Downs, New Mexico (the richest race in the world, with a gross purse of $1,030,000) is a prime example of this case. The minute fraction of time (about 1/100th of a second) and distance (about 3 inches) between Easy Date, the victor, and Tiny's Gay, who ran second, made a difference in purse money of one hundred ninety-two thousand dollars!

Easy Date barely beats out Tiny's Gay to win the 1974 running of the All American Futurity at Ruidoso Downs, New Mexico. Her share of the purse was $330,000. Tiny's Gay collected $138,000.

Specific conditioning for the young horse usually begins in the fall when the horse is a long yearling. At this stage the horse is a baby, still growing. All efforts should be concentrated on keeping the horse sound and healthy. During the conditioning process one is building and developing the yearling, so exercise increases gradually, only as the animal grows in size and strength.

(At this point it is necessary to comment that this discussion is based on an assumption that the two-year-old year is the first year of racing. Yearling futurities, although increasingly prevalent, are too much of a strain on the young, immature horse. In essence, it is simply not physically possible to *properly* condition a yearling for racing.)

Most trainers allow a period of at least three to four months to properly condition an average young horse to race. Prior to saddle breaking, yearlings are exercised to begin muscle development. The methods vary widely, but ponying and longeing are favorites. Walking and jogging constitute the initial work until the young horse reaches the stage where he can easily lope for a short distance, such as a half mile up to a mile.

Every horse has a natural love of running and this should be preserved. The early conditioning is instrumental in building a good mental attitude in the horse. Logically, the young horse should never be overworked or allowed to become overtired. Ideally, he feels good at the end of an exercise session and is looking forward to the next one.

After about thirty days the average horse will be sufficiently conditioned for saddle breaking. Again, "average" covers quite a range. Many individual horses require a longer time to be physically ready for breaking. Examples are late foals, yearlings in poor health, excessively fat or high strung yearlings, etc. There are many exceptions and the state of the individual horse must be weighted against average standards.

Young horses are broke to ride gradually and gently to avoid frightening them or furthering any high strung tendencies they might have. The amount of riding is slowly increased only as the horse develops the muscle coordination, balance and strength to withstand additional amounts of riding. Quarter Horse trainers feel that it is important to get a fairly good degree of control on a young horse; no excessive amounts of reining, but the horse needs to respond willingly to rider commands. For example, the trainer may have to back a horse up if he crowds the starting gate, or a horse may get knocked off course coming out of the gate and the jockey must be able to straighten him up *quickly*. It is relatively easy to get disqualified in a Quarter Horse race for deviating from a straight course. The horse therefore, should be under control at all times.

An outstanding Quarter Horse broodmare. FL Lady Bug, dam of Barne's Ladybug, Go Bug Go, Lady Bug Leo, Lady Bug's Bar, Lady Bug's Moon, Lady Lasan, Leo's Showman, Miss Paula Bug, Rocky Bert and Top Ladybug.

Another outstanding Quarter Horse broodmare. Chicado V, dam of Anchor Chic, Chicado Chick, Successor, Table Tennis, The Ole Man, Three Chicks and War Chick.

The amount of riding is increased very gradually until the young horse can gallop one-half mile easily. Slow breezes are usually initiated at this point and the galloping is cut back to about once or twice a week. Often, young horses are galloped in groups to get used to others. As a rule, after Quarter race horses have learned how to run they are galloped only enough to maintain the endurance and wind needed for the distance they will be required to run. This is because long gallops tend to lengthen the stride, taking away from that early speed. The true sprinter gives his ultimate speed from start to finish, holding back nothing. As a result, gallops longer than necessary can work against the speed of the horse.

For the first breezes, young horses are generally jogged and galloped for about a hundred yards, then gently dropped down to a breeze. For about 200 yards the horse is allowed to run at his own speed, under control. The high speeds are reached very gradually to avoid injuring the horse by forcing him to exceed what he is capable of physically. The young horse should enjoy the breezing instead of being pressured. Again, it is very important to preserve mental well-being and desire. The young horse is usually breezed about once a week. Light galloping, exercise without a rider, walking and jogging constitute the slow work between breezes.

During this period the young horse should also be accustomed to the starting gate. He needs to learn that the gate is nothing to be afraid of. This is most easily accomplished by teaching the horse to stand calmly in the open and shut gate and walk through it. Eventually a young horse can be calmly jogged out of the gate, put into an easy gallop and then breezed. An average two-year-old is normally breezed, progressively faster, six or seven times over a period of about two months before he is ever taught to break from the gate. The early gate work is especially important for the running Quarter Horse as many races are *won or lost at the gate.*

The "all out" early speed of the Quarter Horse, coming out of the gate, from a standing start to full speed, involves a terrific amount of physical strain. (The power generated by the muscles driving bones is more than enough to cripple a poorly conditioned horse.) The two-year-old needs to be in the best possible physical condition before this is attempted. Also, if the horse has learned to be calm in the gate, not frightened by anything, the chances of injury are lessened.

Although the horse wants to run and is capable of greater speed, the speed should progress slowly, only as he physically develops. Ideally, breezes are far enough apart and progress slowly enough that the horse never learns to associate muscle soreness with the track. Again, the desire to run is extremely important.

Easy Jet's brother, Jet Smooth, winning the 1969 World Championship Quarter Horse Classic. Jet Smooth was bred, owned and trained by Walter Merrick.

Before the young horse actually runs he must be in peak condition. After three to four months of this slow building process the average horse will be ready to attempt some fast work. The fast work begins *only* when he is ready.

This means physically and mentally ready. Physically, the yearling (or early two-year old), should have developed adequate strength, muscles, coordination, balance and wind. Mentally, the horse should feel good and be ready to go. In other words, the young horse knows how, is capable, and wants to run.

As the horse progresses through the stages of development and legging up, most trainers can determine fairly accurately what distance he is best suited to run. For the most part, this is a matter of individual conformation and ability. The common divisions in the conditioning of two-year-olds are short distance (220 to 250 yards), mid distance (300 to 350 yards), and long distance (350 to 440 yards). These aren't hard and fast rules, only a common way many trainers divide their conditioning programs as to distance. Quarter Horse futurities usually range from 250 yards to 330 yards early in the year and lengthen out to 350, 400 and 440 yards by late summer and early fall.

Ideally, the young horse receives the best and most conscientious handling of his life when he reaches the stage in the conditioning program where he is ready to learn to break from the gates. There are so many new things for the youngster to learn and adjust to—many of which can have a permanent effect on his racing ability.

All work is concentrated on conditioning the young horse to naturally break fast and straight. It mustn't be overdone. When the horse gets the idea and does it right, the trainer should refrain from repeatedly breaking from the gate. Because breaking from the gate is such a strain, especially for the fast breaking Quarter Horse, the chances of injuring the horse are minimized if it is done as little as possible.

At this point, the conditioning is highly individualized with efforts consolidated toward getting the maximum amount of speed from the horse over the distance he will be required to run. *Only* when the horse has had an adequate foundation of slow work is he blown from the gates. Four or five times, at minimum intervals of a week, is the usual practice for getting the two-year-old ready to actually race.

Between fast works the regular exercise is generally easy, light sessions that maintain condition but do not take away too much of the racing "edge." Walking, jogging, light gallops and relatively slow breezes are the most frequently used methods of exercise. The nature of the sprinter requires that he be fairly "high" and really ready to run all out when asked to race. Therefore, after the initial state of peak condition is reached, exercise is kept to a fairly low level but

Considered by many Quarter Horse experts to be the fastest breaking horse ever, Vandy's explosive velocity is witnessed today through his offspring.

should always maintain condition and soundness.

Conscientious conditioning, progressing slowly as the stages become more difficult, can result in a sound and healthy two-year-old developed to his individual peak. The trainer has done everything he can to get maximum speed. The horse feels good and wants to run. It requires work, care and a watchful eye to reach this level with a two-year-old.

Because natural ability is such an important factor in the success of a sprinter, many horses, although superbly conditioned, are simply not able to consistently win. On the other hand, a sound, properly conditioned two-year-old puts most of the odds in the horseman's favor.

Older Horses

Older horses are conditioned in much the same way as younger horses, usually with the exception of slightly less galloping in the "getting ready" phase of conditioning. For the most part, success is simply a matter of the individual horse possessing the quickness and ability to run at superior top speed. Obviously, natural ability is a must, but so is proper conditioning.

Fundamentally, the horse needs to be maintained sound and wanting to run. The slightest degree of pain or lack of desire can easily cause a horse to hesitate that costly fraction of a second, or run with less than his total ability. Therefore, conditioning the older horse is aimed at keeping him physically able to go the distance, but mentally "high" and ready to run.

For the older horse, there is a delicate balance involved between keeping the horse physically capable but still bursting with the desire to run. It is a highly individualized type of conditioning depending solely upon the physical and mental requirements of each horse. Over-training can very easily rob a horse of his natural, quick speed. On the other hand, under-training or under-conditioning can result in physical trauma to the animal and financial trauma to the owner. Ideally, the older horse enters a race in a state similar to a tightly wound spring—he is tense and filled with explosive speed. Under-training can result in a horse being mentally ready, with the desire for bursting speed present, but lacking in physical ability. He easily may burn out during the first 100 yards or, worse, he may cripple himself.

With this type of horse, there is a very fine line between too much and too little exercise in the conditioning program. The trainer's only strong line of defense is to really know each individual horse and be thoroughly familiar with the requirements of every horse to achieve 100 per cent physical and mental performance.

For the novice, conditioning Quarter running horses can be a matter of trial and error with each horse. Again, the only hard and fast rule involved is to *know the horse.* Even so, individual conditioning requirements change from time to time as the horse runs different numbers of races with different time intervals between races, has slight injuries, occasionally runs at different distances, etc. Therefore, discussion of specific conditioning for the older Quarter running horse will be limited to generalized examples of common methods for conditioning the race horse.

The short distance horse (220 to 250 yards), that is raced fairly often, is galloped very seldom, if at all. Fast work (or a race) once a week is a common routine with only walking and jogging on the days between fast works. The walking and jogging is to keep the horse in condition, with only very limited galloping, in an effort to keep the horse high and wanting to run.

The mid distance horse (300 to 350 yards) again has exercise sessions of walking and jogging to maintain condition. Depending upon the individual horse, he will probably be galloped about one-half mile once or twice a week. The fast works take place about once a week—just enough to keep up the desire for bursting speed, without subtracting from it.

As a rule, even the longer mid distance horse (350 to 440 yards) is never galloped over one mile, if that far. However, this horse is often galloped twice a week, depending on his racing schedule. Walking and jogging are primary methods of keeping the horse at a constant level of condition if he has a rather busy racing schedule. Fast work, as in the other cases, is generally once a week. Each horse is usually worked over the approximate distance he will be required to run.

It cannot be over-emphasized: at any distance, the exercise is geared to the individual horse. The ideal level is an amount that maintains top condition but isn't enough to take away the slightest degree from running desire or ability. In other words, the horse is exercised enough to keep from straining himself when raced but not enough to take away the "racing edge." The fast work is dispersed at intervals throughout the conditioning program to keep the horse high—always bursting with energy and desire to run.

For this reason, walking and jogging are the methods of slow work heavily relied upon. In fact, on the day before a race, most Quarter horses are simply walked for thirty minutes to an hour. Most trainers agree that work above the amount required to loosen the horse up, on the day prior to a race, might take the edge off the horse.

Today the practice of racing Quarter Horses at distances beyond 440 yards (a quarter of a mile) is becoming increasingly popular. This type of racing demands a different type of conditioning, as it is a matter of balancing wind and endurance requirements with early speed. The distance Quarter Horse race (usually 510 up to 870 yards) requires an increase in wind capacity, endurance and length of stride. Slow conditioning, with additional distance added in small increments at gradual intervals, is required to develop such requirements.

For this type of race, since it certainly cannot be classified as a sprint (in Quarter Horse terms), the horse is conditioned more nearly like the Thoroughbred race horse. Specific conditioning methods are presented in the chapter entitled, "Conditioning Thoroughbred Race Horses." Logically, horses would be conditioned in the same way for the same type of race, especially since many running Quarter Horses are at least three-quarters Thoroughbred, as demonstrated by their pedigrees.

With the exception of the distance runner, the Quarter Horse is an extremely specialized type of race horse. As a breed, the horse was developed to give his ultimate effort over a short distance. This type of horse bursts with immediate, early velocity from a standing start and runs as fast as he possibly can from gate to wire.

Because of the short distance, natural ability is an extremely important quality of true racing success. When ready to race, the horse is sound, healthy, superbly conditioned and feeling good. The race horse is excited and burning with the early speed of which he knows he is capable. This type of horse must be sound and physically superior.

8

Conditioning Quarter Performance Horses

As an athlete, the Quarter Horse is extremely versatile. He was bred for quick bursts of speed over a short distance, hardiness and stability—mentally and physically. The result is a horse that can successfully compete in numerous events ranging all the way from racing to roping.

Each event requires some degree of specific conditioning for the horse to develop into a truly winning competitor.

Reining

Sound judgment on the part of the horseman is probably the most important consideration in conditioning the reining horse. Most leading trainers agree that reining horses are more easily burned out and over-worked than any other class of performance horses.

The American Quarter Horse Association Official Handbook states, "The horse shall rein and handle easily, fluently, effortlessly, and with reasonable speed throughout the pattern ... each horse will be judged on neatness, dispatch, ease, calmness, and speed with which it performs the pattern." (1)

To perform in the above manner, the reining horse simply cannot be bored and unwilling to work. Here is where the judgment comes in—the horseman must know his animal and be able to determine the amount of "reining schooling" that the horse needs to perform well and still be in good mental condition.

For the reining horse, the early riding as a two or three-year-old normally includes a lot of trotting in small circles. Along with strengthening the young horse this builds flexibility and maneuverability. The suppleness demanded of the reining horse is established in this manner.

As the horse grows in size and strength the exercise program increases. The average young horse will take the correct lead in the lope simply because it is easier for the horse to balance. Over a period of about thirty days of daily riding—no intensive reining—the average young horse will develop the ability and muscular coordination to change leads smoothly and quickly.

At this stage numerous trainers recommend allowing the young horse to rest for one to two weeks. Generally, it takes a young horse about a month of short sessions of riding every day to develop the ability to change leads in a smooth, easy manner and learn the basic rider commands.

However, this is only the *average* horse. Many young horses are not sufficiently developed physically or mentally to respond quickly to the initial conditioning. Others may simply learn and develop at a slower or faster rate than the average horse.

Usually six to eight months of patient, steady, time-consuming conditioning is required before a young horse can be expected to run any sort of a pattern with speed and confidence, and stop quickly and smoothly.

The conditioning interval between the green horse and the finished horse is aimed at building strength, maneuverability and a good mental attitude. The strength is important. Although it doesn't take long to run a reining pattern, the horse must possess sufficient strength and endurance to execute the pattern swiftly, in a collected manner, and finish without being winded. In other words, the horse cannot let down or give out at any point during the performance—he must perform with 100 per cent ability throughout the entire event.

Steady trotting and loping, with or without a rider, will help develop the strong leg muscles and lung capacity that the reining horse needs. However, rider control is so important in reining competition that a lot of exercise with rider is superior to riderless exercise. For example, the rider needs to develop his control to the point that he can freely and willingly lope the horse at different speeds. This obviously requires a good many "riding miles."

Conditioning for maneuverability and mental attitude go hand in hand. As the horse grows older, the amount of stopping, turning, spin-

The 1972 and 1973 A.Q.H.A. Honor Roll Champion Western Riding Horse, Log Cabin Rita, owned by David and Donna Foote, exemplifies the characteristic versatility of the Quarter Horse. Log Cabin Rita consistently places high in Western Pleasure, English Pleasure and Jumping, in addition to Western Riding.

ning and backing (the actual reining) is increased. The horse's capability to move, respond and handle himself is slowly built by gradually increasing the level of difficulty of the conditioning program. This segment of the conditioning is instrumental in building the all important mental well-being in the reining horse.

The horseman must take special care to provide variety in the conditioning routine to keep the horse from becoming bored. He also should be able to recognize the signs of boredom in his horse. The average horse will not work willingly when training is too intensive or redundant. In this case, the amount of time spent on actual reining should be cut so as not to push the horse so hard.

For variety in the conditioning routine, the horse may be worked in different areas, such as out in a pasture, and different things tried like working on parts of a pattern instead of actually running one.

In fact, variety needs to be incorporated into every conditioning program for reining as a precautionary measure to keep the horse from "souring." Every attempt must be made to not force the horse to do more than he is capable of doing. Also, once he learns to execute a maneuver well, the trainer shouldn't repeatedly force the horse to do it just because he can.

Common sense and sound judgment are mandatory on the part of the rider. Finished horses are seldom asked to run a complete reining pattern when not at a show. Conditioning a reining horse is a slow process, usually taking about a year to fully develop the horse.

In order to preserve the willingness to perform, the primary conditioning goals for the seasoned reining horse are overall physical fitness and a willing attitude. In other words, the finished reining horse is exercised regularly to maintain condition, but reined only enough to keep him sharp. With the younger horse, maneuverability, flexibility and subtle control are the fundamental objectives. Ideally, the reining horse is an athletic animal with superior muscular coordination. A superbly conditioned reining horse possesses the physical and mental ability to willingly execute maneuvers swiftly, fluently and calmly.

Western and English Pleasure

Many people are of the opinion that a pleasure horse does not require specialized conditioning. This is a false impression. Superior conditioning very often separates the consistent winners from the mediocre competitors.

The pleasure horse needs to rack up a lot of riding miles. Regular, daily exercise is very important to toughen up the horse. With the increasingly large pleasure classes at today's horse shows, many horses place low simply because they don't have the endurance to

Poco Troll, the 1973 A.Q.H.A. Honor Roll Champion Bridle Path Hack (Saddle Seat) horse, ridden by Joy Westrum.

perform consistently throughout the time required for judging a large class.

At the onset of the conditioning program, daily riding sessions of 15 minutes up to an hour are initiated. After about two weeks of this regular exercise, the average horse should be able to withstand riding for longer periods of time without muscle soreness or extreme fatigue.

It should be remembered that this is the "average" horse *only*. Many horses won't meet this schedule, especially if they were overly fat or in extremely poor condition when the exercise began. There are numerous other reasons, such as recuperating from injuries, parasite infestation, etc., that will cause a horse to build endurance at a slower rate.

By slowly increasing the length of the exercise sessions, the horse should eventually be able to withstand a two hour session without becoming overly tired. Walking is a good form of exercise for the pleasure horse. Because the walk is a uniform, four beat gait, the muscles and limbs of the horse are subjected to fairly equal amounts of exercise. Adequate amounts of walking will aid the horse in developing the free, ground-covering walk required of a winning pleasure horse. Trotting helps the horse attain the muscular coordination and "collected" look characteristic of a superior pleasure horse.

The lope should be bright—not gangly and strung out. Riding is the best method for developing the muscles, coordination and suppleness resulting in the free moving and physically balanced pleasure horse with stamina.

Endurance and stamina are fundamental, but the fine points designate true winning condition. The smooth, free gaits are one example of superior conditioning. Also, though it may sound ridiculous, many of the horses shown at pleasure do not travel in a straight line. As a check, the horseman can ride the horse along a fence, parallel to it, to see if he's moving in a straight path in all gaits. If not, the horseman needs to devise a system of leg aids and cues to teach the horse to travel along a straight line.

The pleasure horse must be conditioned to *always* take and maintain the correct lead. As basic as this sounds, numerous horses must be conditioned to take the correct lead—otherwise some horses will compensate and learn to balance in the wrong lead.

Subtle obedience is a must in a pleasure class. The horse should respond quickly and willingly to unobtrusive cues from the rider. A lot of time and patience must be spent to establish this kind of rapport between horse and rider.

Also, the pleasure horse must maintain the gait that the judge demands, stop easily and back without hesitation. Ideally, the pleasure horse backs in a straight line with his head tucked. The horse *does not* act like he is being pulled away from his front legs.

The rider should have adequate control to get his horse out of any bottlenecks with other horses—a frequent problem situation in pleasure classes. Obviously this requires sufficient "handle" on the horse to illicit a smooth, efficient response.

As with every other type of performance horse, the conditioning program mustn't be made a regime of daily drudgery. Variety may be added by riding the horse in different places and following different patterns. When the horse exhibits the need, he should be allowed to have a rest period. Above all, the rider doesn't want to bore the horse to the point that he plods along with no spirit or becomes "ring soured." The superior pleasure horse is always alert and receptive.

Barrel Racing

Barrel racing is an event that is extremely hard on a horse that has not been properly conditioned. The horse must run at top speed, check for the turn, turn hard, push away and turn at top speed again. The horse has to do this three times during one single event. The athletic ability of the horse certainly needs to be developed to full potential for the animal to be able to compete successfully and remain sound.

First of all, the prospective barrel horse must be well broke. In other words, the horse should rein well and respond readily to rider commands. This is important from a safety standpoint as well as speed. The horse also needs to have endurance and maximum flexibility. Plenty of riding, increasing in small amounts with each session, will help build endurance. Loping in fairly small circles helps to condition the barrel horse to keep his hindquarters gathered up and control his motion. It also aids in developing the maneuverability and flexibility required of a barrel horse.

All good trainers recommend proceeding very slowly when starting a horse on barrels. The endurance and flexibility are fundamental, later the horse has to be taught the barrel racing pattern and what is expected of him.

Initially, slowly walking and trotting around the barrels will teach the horse where he has to turn. Some trainers make it a practice to slow down or stop a horse before he gets to the barrel, at the point where he must check his speed and collect himself to get ready for the turn. A primary consideration is to go slowly and take special care not to frighten the horse by forcing him to do more than he is able to do. Also, one doesn't want to burn the horse out before he really learns what to do.

Although it varies considerably with individual horses, three times a week is considered to be about the maximum for working a horse on the barrels. On the days with no work around the barrels, exercise should be relaxed and aimed at building condition without a lot of mental stress on the horse.

When the horse reaches the point that he reins well and is under control at all times walking and trotting through a barrel pattern, the training proceeds to an easy lope around the barrels. Loping around the barrels will aid in developing the muscular coordination and balance mandatory at top speed later in the conditioning program.

Whether walking, trotting or loping through the barrel pattern, the horse should *always* be urged to speed up a little as he leaves the barrel. In other words, the rider is building an automatic reaction for the horse to come out of a barrel quickly, at all times.

The barrel horse also learns to collect himself and execute maneuvers with no wasted movements. In fact, many trainers will teach a horse to side pass, or walk sideways. Using both reins and foot cues, the trainer will teach the horse to keep his head straight, but walk sideways, with no forward motion. The purpose of teaching the horse to side pass is to condition the horse to bend laterally and respond quickly to leg cues—both aimed at establishing maximum speed when going around the barrels. The rider will have the control to move the horse's body closer to or farther away from the barrel swiftly, with no extra movement.

Any method that builds the capability of the individual horse to bend and maneuver well in small areas is the one to use. The barrel racing horse needs not only speed in the straightaways, but speed in the turns. Superior agility and suppleness, as developed by a good conditioning program, can shave those important fractions of a second off the time to result in a winning performance.

Speed can be gradually built up as the horse develops the ability to lope smoothly through the barrel pattern. Also, the horse needs to establish the capability to vary and rate his speed as too much speed going into a turn can slow the horse down. For this reason, the horse *must* be under control at all times. Also it is important that a bat or spurs never be used until they are really needed, even in competition. Constant flailing and spurring each time the barrels are run substantially contributes to the high number of "soured" barrel horses.

Coming to a sliding stop at the finish line is a bad habit for the barrel racing horse. Horses are smart and learn to anticipate the stop, often slowing down to get ready. This slight hesitation can add fractions of a second to the time and easily make the difference between winning and losing. If possible, the horse should be allowed to go well

Valeda Tretbar is shown riding Miss Pon Jo, a top barrel racing horse. Miss Pon Jo is also the 1973 A.Q.H.A. Honor Roll Champion Pole Bending horse.

past the finish line before stopping.

Barrel racing really tests the soundness of a horse. Because of this, periodic veterinary checks of the horse, with special attention paid to the legs, are an important part of the conditioning program. Naturally, a horse has to be in peak physical condition to be able to compete in a winning way.

The psychological part of conditioning a barrel racing horse can make a big difference in the way the horse performs. The horse may be a supreme athlete, but also burned out with no desire to run. Precautions must be taken to avoid "over-training" a horse on the barrels.

To keep a horse "tuned up," exercises can be devised to maintain agility, maneuverability and endurance without actually running the barrel pattern. Many people use figure eights, turning in corners, loping in small circles, etc. to avoid souring a horse on the barrels. Desire is very important; the trainer must keep the horse *wanting* to run.

Careful observation needs to be made of how the horse reacts to the conditioning program. Each horse will need a slightly different amount of work to perform at his best. Some may require special work for endurance, while others may need work on speed. The individual horse should be the main factor in formulating a conditioning program.

The first competition in public is a frightening experience for the average horse. There are so many people, horses and new sights. Before the event, the horse should be ridden around in the arena and given a chance to look at everything. Then the horse should be better able to smoothly run the barrels with his mind 100 per cent on what he is doing—not frightened by all he sees.

Most trainers prefer not to start a two-year-old in barrel training, much less barrel racing. It is usually felt that the physical and mental limitations of the two-year-old are too great compared to the demands of the event. In fact, many trainers won't enter a horse in barrel racing competition until he is four.

The ideal barrel horse is flexible, agile, strong and coordinated. He wants to run and is in superior physical condition, capable of superbly controlled speed. This state is *slowly* built by a consistent, common sense conditioning program. The conditioning of a barrel racing horse is a time-consuming process. It can often take as long as two years to develop a top flight competitor.

Roping

Over the years, roping has developed into a highly specialized sport and, as a result, the consistent winners are riding highly conditioned, tremendously athletic horses.

Typically, the event unfolds in the following manner. The horse is backed into a box-like enclosure with the calf shut in a narrow chute to the side. When the roper signals, the calf is released from the chute and breaks a cord stretched across the front of the box ("the barrier") when it runs a certain distance from the chute. The horse then must take-off at full speed to put the roper in position to rope the calf quickly. At the instant the calf is roped, the roping horse comes to a full, sliding stop. In the next series of moves, the horse backs up, keeping the rope stretched tight, always facing the calf, while the man throws and ties the calf. Properly executed, this should all be accomplished in a dozen or so seconds.

Obviously, the roping horse needs to be rugged, strong, fast and willing to work. Proper conditioning is critical to the success of any horse upon which such great demands are to be made.

In the early part of the conditioning program strength and stamina are built up. Plenty of riding, increasing as the horse toughens up, is basic. Many leading trainers like to just "use" the horse on a ranch to get the young horse accustomed to being around and watching cattle.

On the average, when the young horse is a late two-year-old to a three-year-old, if the horse is mature enough physically and mentally, easy work with cattle begins. The horse chases relatively slow cattle in a small, enclosed area. Gradually the novice roping horse learns to follow the calf and gauge the speed at which the calf travels—this is important because the beginning horse has to learn that he cannot race past the calf. Also, the horse learns to stop and back up when the loop is thrown.

Building the desire to work is a very important part of conditioning the roping horse. The specific lessons should always be short and within the capabilities of the horse. With the average horse, if it shows signs of impatience or unwillingness to work, the lessons are usually proceeding too fast. It will generally help the horse to slow down and go over familiar lessons, or possibly rest the horse for a few days.

During this time, when the horse is learning to work with cattle and building its strength, new lessons are slowly incorporated into the conditioning program. The horse needs to develop balance and coordination. Instead of always roping a calf, many trainers make it a practice to frequently tie the rope to a large rubber tire—the tire is a weight that doesn't fight back and is easier to work with for the novice horse. This method is used to condition the horse to brace against the weight of the calf and also learn to drag weight. It takes practice for the horse to develop the muscle coordination to balance while pulling against the calf.

Consistent practice, with the level of difficulty gradually increasing, is the only route to success in a conditioning program for the roping horse. The amount of actual roping must be geared to the individual horse in order to develop the proper mental attitude. In other words, the trainer is cautioned not to burn the horse out, but to keep him interested and trying.

Great strength in the roping horse's legs is an obvious necessity. The horse must be strong enough to come to a full stop against the weight and momentum of a calf, which might weigh up to 300 pounds, running at top speed. A lot of riding, and possibly pulling fairly heavy objects (like a log) with a rope from the saddle horn, are good leg muscle developers.

Conditioning the roping horse is a long, slow process. Muscular strength and coordination, along with desire, must be carefully cultivated. Regular exercise, most commonly in the form of riding and "just using," must be continued throughout the performance life of the horse to maintain the strength and agility needed for top condition. Also, the trainer must know his horse and determine just how much actual roping the horse needs to be in peak condition and ready to go after that calf with a 100 per cent effort.

Cutting

Cutting is a highly specialized event that demands a unique kind of horse to turn in a winning performance. The horse must have exceptional maneuverability and agility and, according to most trainers, that important inborn quality—"cow sense."

To be successful, the cutting horse has to learn to control his motions with superior ability. The horse should be collected at all times and work off his hindquarters to gain every advantage against the calf.

The superior cutting horse has the alertness, agility, speed and strength to watch the calf, anticipate its moves and "head" the calf either way it decides to move. The really top cutting horses are capable of coming to a smooth, sliding stop and pivoting a full 180 degrees, without ever taking their eyes off the calf.

Without excellent conditioning the cutting horse would not be able to develop and perform to the peak of his ability no matter what his genetic advantages might be. As with many other events, most trainers begin working with the prospective cutting horse as an already broke, late two or early three-year-old. Initially, the horse is taught the basic rider commands and exercised, usually in the form of riding, to begin muscle development. Some trainers like to put "a lot of handle" on a young horse and others feel that if "handle" is empha-

Two D's Dynamite, the A.Q.H.A. 1973 Honor Roll Champion Cutting Horse and the holder of several National Cutting Horse Association awards. Owned by Ray Walker, ridden by Sam Wilson.

sized too much the horse will be paying too much attention to the rider and not enough to the calf. This area is left to individual trainer preference.

After about two or three months, the average horse is relaxed enough and obeys the rider well enough to begin specific conditioning for cutting. However, it must be remembered that this is the *average* horse only. Some horses, because of their physical and mental development, may be able to proceed more rapidly with the conditioning process, while others may require that work advance more slowly.

Gradually the horse is taught to turn and stop smoothly. It is fundamental that the cutting horse keep his hind legs well under his body and *always* work off his hindquarters. This is what gives the horse the advantage against the calf and the ability to move swiftly and smoothly to hold a tough calf. Loping in small circles is considered to be one good form of exercise to condition the horse to collect himself. It also helps the horse develop strength in his legs and learn to maneuver with the hind legs tucked well under.

At the time conditioning for maneuverability begins, the horse usually experiences his first work with cattle. Most trainers initiate the young horse by simply driving gentle cattle with him. The horse watches the cow and learns to move when it does. In other words, the horse is learning what is expected of him. It is extremely important that the cow be slow enough so that the horse can easily watch it and follow its movements. One doesn't want to discourage the horse during his first experience with cattle.

The early work should always be within the capabilities of the horse. One major concern of the conditioning program is to preserve the desire of the horse—he should want to work and enjoy the challenge of "holding" a calf. Naturally, the individual horse is the only gauge for what amount of work is necessary.

As the horse expands his coordination and learns how to maneuver properly, more work with cattle is gradually brought into the conditioning program. Many trainers recommend that the horse be worked in a fairly soft area so that sure-footing is provided. Again, it is *very* important that the calf be one the horse can adequately hold without an extreme effort. At this point, the horse is simply learning to move like a cutting horse and watch cattle.

As with people, some horses are eager to work and others are stubborn. Many times a rest for a few days will help the horse that is not advancing as well as he should. Being familiar with the temperament and expression of the horse is one of the best methods to determine whether the horse needs a rest or more of a challenge.

Cutting imposes a strain on the legs of the horse. For this reason, endurance and stamina, along with strength, must be built up, as with horses in other areas of western performance. The cutting horse uses his hind legs as pivots, braces and balances. The front legs are used to reach so that he can rapidly make a move in any direction. The legs of the cutting horse are forced to take up most of the shock from the rapid movements. Therefore it is essential that the horse be well legged-up to be able to perform at his best. Flexibility and suppleness provided by superb coordination are characteristic of a great cutting horse.

The horse must be properly conditioned so that he can make the fluid, smooth motions required to prevent a calf from returning to the herd. After muscular coordination and agility have been established, the trainer should then be able to make a determination of how much "cow sense" the horse has. Not every horse is capable of becoming a really good cutting horse, no matter how well conditioned he is.

Specific conditioning of the cutting horse involves progressing at a rate gradual enough to keep up the desire in the horse while forcing him to execute tougher and tougher moves. It is a long, slow process requiring much individual attention. Attempts to rush a horse through cutting training almost always result in failure.

The well trained and conditioned cutting horse is expressive when faced with the challenge of holding a tough calf—his ears perk up and his front legs spread in anticipation of the calf's moves. He has style and enjoys his work.

Jumping

Like the human hurdler, the horse is not a natural jumper. The horse as a jumper and the man as a hurdler both must develop and learn to use muscles in an unnatural way to jump over obstacles. In the wild state, a horse jumped only when necessary to escape from enemies.

How does a horse jump? The first step, when the animal approaches the take-off point, is to check and shorten the stride, preparing to jump. With the hind legs well under the body ready to straighten and push forward and upward, the horse lifts his forequarters, stretching the head and neck out for leverage.

As the front of the body clears the obstacle, the head and neck come down to raise the hindquarters even higher. At this time, the forelegs are extended to take up the shock of landing and hind legs are tucked up to clear the obstacle. When the front feet touch the ground, the head again comes up. In the following movement, the front feet are again in motion before the hindquarters hit the ground.

As you can see, the movements of the horse's head and neck play an important part in balance and recovery after landing. The horse also must learn to judge distance and height.

The horseman strives for a smooth and collected jump, with a perfect arc over the fence. Ideally, the take-off and landing points are the same distance from each side of the fence.

Conditioning the jumper takes a lot of patience, work and time. The largest part of the conditioning program takes place on the ground, for to be a safe jumper the horse must be strong, sound, agile and confident.

Jumping places a considerable amount of strain on the horse's legs, so the conditioning program must be directed toward developing and maintaining the legs of the jumper as sturdy and sound as possible.

The general aim of the conditioning program on the flat is to develop the muscles, wind and balance of the horse. Initially, long walks and short trots are used to develop the horse physically. The trots become progressively longer as the horse builds endurance and strength, and cantering is incorporated into the regime.

Eventually, the horse should be conditioned to the point where he can easily sustain a controlled gallop for four to five minutes without being winded. During this time, the jumper is also worked with for extremely well-controlled mobility—such as stopping, turning and backing. To be a safe jumper, it is very important that the horse instantly obey the rider's commands.

The jumper *must* be in peak physical condition and the endurance requirements demand daily work on the flat as a part of the conditioning program. This daily work not only develops endurance and strength, but maintains them at a high level, once achieved.

Many trainers recommend walking and trotting the horse over a series of small, closely-spaced poles on the ground when beginning to teach the horse to jump. Two or three short sessions, daily, are generally advised instead of one lengthy training session at this early level. Common methods are to ride the horse over the initial obstacles, or execute the lesson riderless by leading the horse, using long reins or a longe line. Gradually the obstacles on the ground are placed farther apart and raised a bit.

This conditions the horse to lengthen its stride and stretch its neck. These exercises also develop neck muscles and proper shoulder movement for a jumper. Very important to a conditioning program is to progress slowly enough to develop confidence in the jumper.

To teach the jumper to lift his legs high and carefully when going over obstacles, numerous trainers will use a trotting lane. This looks very much like an extremely large ladder laid on the ground. The trotting lane is usually about eight feet wide, with the "rungs" about four feet apart.

Owned by John P. Kerek and ridden by Nancy Griffith, Mary's Surprise is the 1973 A.Q.H.A. Honor Roll Champion Jumping Horse.

The initial obstacles in the conditioning regime also aid in the development of the long, low stride demanded of a jumper. Also, the horse expands his ability to smoothly change stride length to accommodate the distance between obstacles.

A jumping lane is frequently used during this early training. The circular or oval enclosure is fenced on both sides up to a height of at least seven feet so that the horse cannot see out. The jumps are the same width as the jumping lane; 14 feet is a common example of width. In a jumping lane, the horse is free and is made to go around the lane by commands from the handler. The direction that the horse goes is alternated frequently. One single, low jump is the usual starting point, with the number and height of jumps increased gradually. A jumping lane is used to teach the horse to enjoy jumping.

The horse has a natural tendency to panic when faced with the prospect of jumping. Therefore, building confidence plays an important role in conditioning the jumper. *Never* should the horse be asked to do anything he isn't capable of doing. The jumper must learn to negotiate obstacles in a relaxed manner—confidently and willingly.

At this point, it must be mentioned that there are two distinct schools of jumping training. One training method incorporates the practice of never asking the horse to jump any obstacle with a rider on his back that the horse hasn't previously jumped riderless. The other school of training follows the practice of never jumping a horse without a rider, believing that jumping riderless will teach a horse to jump out of pastures, arenas, etc. and make the horse generally difficult to handle.

When the horse can execute low obstacles at a trot, gracefully, with its head down, specific conditioning at a canter and gallop begin. The low obstacles and their spacing develop variations in speed and stride length of the jumper.

At this level in the conditioning program, the jumper is ready for training and conditioning over higher obstacles. The time and patience taken with each horse while conditioning it to jump, better enables the jumper to cope with more complex obstacles—physically and psychologically.

The fences are raised gradually; but not until the horse clears them successfully and confidently. It is a general practice for jumpers to wear padded front bandages and over-reach boots to protect their front legs. When landing, the hind legs often over-reach and could easily injure the front legs.

Since jumping places fairly excessive physical strain on the horse, it is recommended that a horse be jumped only 10 to 20 minutes every other day. (3) In fact, the entire lesson including work on the flat, should not last longer than an hour. (4)

Ridden by Valeda Tretbar, Miss Pon Jo, the 1973 A.Q.H.A. Honor Roll Champion Pole Bending Horse, is also a top barrel racing competitor (see photo on p. 119).

By slowly increasing the levels of difficulty, the horse is conditioned to jump a variety of obstacles and combinations of obstacles at a variety of angles and spacing. The jumper judges his pace, obeys willingly and instantly, and jumps obstacles only where and when asked.

When the horse develops balance, suppleness and control, as demonstrated by the ability to change direction in mid air by shifting the hindquarters while propelling the body forward and stretching properly over a jump, etc. many different kinds of jumps can be introduced in the conditioning program.

Conditioning the jumper is a long, slow process. Stamina strength and wind must be conscientiously developed along with superior balance and mobility. The good jumper possesses the qualities of instant obedience to rider commands and excellent body and muscle control.

The conditioning program eventually turns out the kind of animal that can judge distance, height and pace, smoothly adjust stride length and speed, obey immediately, change direction in the air, and—most importantly, enjoy jumping.

Other Events

There are many other performance events approved by the American Quarter Horse Association which provide the horseman and horse with the opportunity to demonstrate their ability to perform. The AQHA also provides standards so that the quality of a performance can be judged.

Western riding, working cowhorse, pole bending and working hunter are only a few examples of the many other performance events. These events have not been presented in detail because the horses that compete in them require conditioning so similar to horses in events presented elsewhere in this book.

The Quarter Horse is an extremely versatile animal—an all around horse in every sense of the word. He is a talented athlete, and properly conditioned, has the capability of performing in many different events.

REFERENCES CITED

1. **Official Handbook of the American Quarter Horse Association**, Twenty-Second Edition/January 1, 1974, Amarillo, Texas, The American Quarter Horse Association, 1973.
2. Coggins, Jack, **The Horseman's Bible**, Garden City, New York, Doubleday and Company, Inc., 1966.
3. Edwards, H. and Geddes, C., Editors, **The Complete Book of the Horse**, New York, New York, Arco Publishing Company, Inc., 1973.

9

Conditioning Harness Racing Standardbreds

Harness racing Standardbred Horses are bred for speed. Originally, to qualify for registration, the horse had to be able to go a mile within a standard length of time—hence the name "Standardbred."

The harness racing entry consists of one horse and a lightweight sulky with one driver; the standard distance is still a mile. Trotters and pacers are the two types of harness racers. The difference between the two is a matter of gaits used while racing.

The trotter moves with diagonal support. In other words, the front leg and the opposite hind leg move in unison. Because the gait is diagonal, the horse is always balanced. The center of gravity of the horse stays down the middle of the body. The trotter moves forward with an up and down motion. On the other hand, the pacer moves with lateral support—the legs on the same side of the body work in unison. Because of this lateral support (or the legs on the same side of the body working together), the center of gravity of the pacer shifts from side to side. As a result, the pacer moves forward with a rolling motion, rocking from side to side.

Among the Standardbred Breed, specific family lines are noted for producing superior trotters or pacers. For the most part, however, the gaits are a matter of training and shoeing. (1) The pace is considered to be a slightly faster gait than the trot.

The Standardbred's speed comes from the long forearms and long, narrow muscles which give the horse the ability to extend into extremely long strides. These long strides are repeated very quickly when the horse is racing—in fact, the superior harness racer can give the appearance of practically "flying."

In many cases, harness races are heat races. In other words, the horse is required to run two or three races on the same day. For this reason, conditioning the trotter or pacer is aimed toward building superior endurance, strength and lung capacity. The Standardbred must be capable of performing with 100 per cent ability throughout *each* race.

Basically, trotters and pacers are conditioned alike. For this reason, specific conditioning of the harness racing Standardbred will not be broken down into trotters and pacers.

Young Horses

The Standardbred is generally broken to harness as a long yearling or a two-year-old. Before the specific conditioning regime is initiated, the young horse is thoroughly ground broken and taught to obey fundamental driver commands. Although no two harness racers are conditioned identically, the basics are similar. Time and patience, in vast amounts, with an understanding of "horse psychology," are required to introduce a young horse to the equipment and fundamentals of harness racing. The early work should proceed slowly, taking plenty of time for the horse to become comfortable with each piece of equipment and thoroughly learn each lesson.

When the young horse becomes accustomed to the harness and responds to the driver's commands, the work for endurance begins. To develop the young horse's muscles, he is usually jogged daily. One and one-half miles to three miles every day is the routine distance for the initial, slow jogging.

The specific length and speed of the daily jogging sessions are determined solely by the way the individual horse reacts to the conditioning regime. To assure maximum soundness in later life, the jogging must not be too strenuous.

During this time, the two-year-old is taught to turn, maneuver and handle himself confidently with the sulky. Again, the difficulty of maneuvers demanded of the young horse increases only as the horse develops the confidence and ability to execute them. The early conditioning, consisting of jogging only, usually lasts from one to two months. At this point the young Standardbred should have sufficient strength and wind to begin with slow, mile heats. However, this is the "average" horse, only; depending upon the initial condition of the colt, some may require a longer period of early conditioning. Examples are

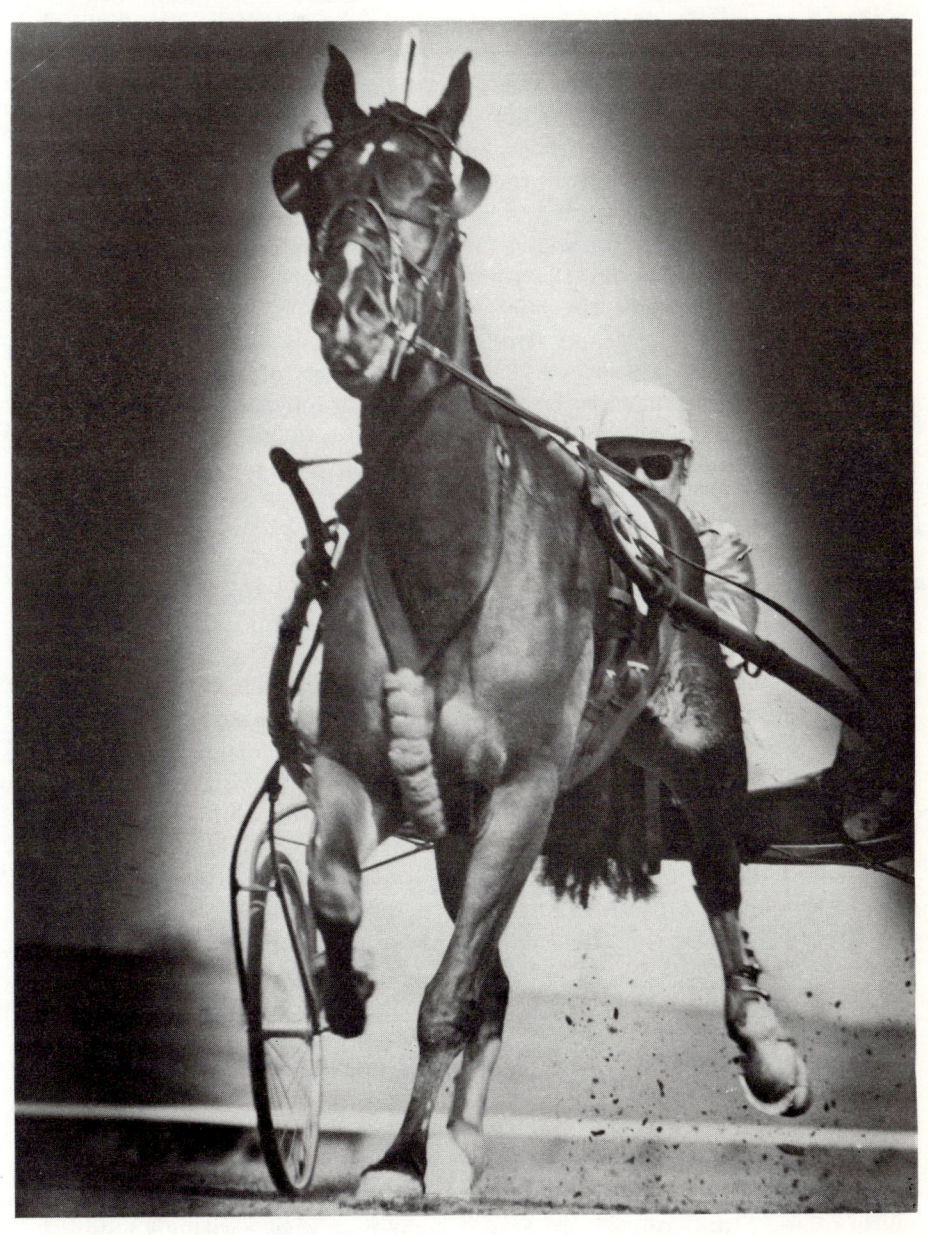

A trotter in action; notice the diagonal movement of the legs.

an extremely young or immature horse, an overly nervous horse, a horse recuperating from illness or heavy parasite infestation, etc.

The heats are gradually initiated into the conditioning regime. As a general rule, Standardbreds are worked on the track two days a week. These two days are usually spaced as evenly as possible throughout the week. (For example: Monday and Thursday.)

With the beginning trotters and pacers the mile is usually worked in 2:50 to 3:20. (2) The ordinary practice is to start with two heats twice a week. These beginning workouts help the young horse to establish the rhythm of its gait. They also are an aid in developing muscular coordination. While conditioning the young horse by method of mile heats, it is important not to get the horse too tired—the horse should *always* finish its mile willingly and strongly.

Proper leg care is another important segment of the conditioning program. The legs need to be gradually conditioned in an attempt to avoid future lameness problems. Specific attention must be paid to the action of the horse. With the extended gait, it is common for trotters and pacers to interfere and injure themselves.

As the conditioning program develops strength, endurance and wind, speed will progress naturally. When the two-year-old reaches the level of condition to easily work a mile heat in 2:40 to 2:30, many trainers go to workouts of three heats twice a week. During these stages, the young horse learns to follow the starting gate and other practices required in racing.

The time of the two-year-old gradually works down as the horse establishes his gait and learns to extend. While developing the stamina and strength needed for harness racing, conscientious care should be taken to change the routine from time to time to keep the young horse fresh and willing to work. Instilling the will to race in a two-year-old is part of conditioning the horse. Young horses are easily bored by constant routine. For variety, different practices should be instituted into the conditioning routine at intervals when the horse begins to be bored. For example; walking substituted for jogging, resting the horse for a day, etc.

The harness racer should *never* be allowed to slow down at the end of the mile. It must learn to move out when the end of the race is near.

Shoeing is a critical segment of conditioning the harness racer. The action of the horse needs to be free and level. Eighths of an inch and ounces in weight can alter the gait of the horse drastically. Few harness racing Standardbreds go longer than four weeks without having their shoes reset. The angle and length of the hoof are always measured meticulously.

In the pace, the legs on the same side of the horse move in unison.

These minor adjustments are crucial because of the extended gait of the trotter and pacer alike. Again, interference can be a very serious problem. As a rule, trotters are more likely to have interference between the front and hind legs on the same side of the body. Scalping, speedy-cutting, shin-hitting and hock-hitting are examples. With the pacer, cross-firing is the most common type of interference. In this situation, the hind foot and the front foot on the opposite side of the body come in contact with each other. Correct shoeing is a critical element in conditioning a perfectly balanced and gaited horse.

Six weeks to a month before the first race, the conditioning program really intensifies on building endurance, stamina and speed. Numerous trainers even go to four heats on the days of race conditioning to get a colt really toughed up. On a race training day, the three or four heats that the two-year-old runs get progressively faster with a little more speed at the end.

During this last "toughening-up" period, care must be taken to avoid getting the young horse too tired and discouraged. The psychological portion of the conditioning program plays a big part in future racing ability. The young horse should *want* to race, not dread it. The proper conditioning regime provides the physical well-being and endurance required of the harness racing horse to race with confidence.

The colt's first race is where the conditioning program really pays off. All of the constant, gradually increasing early work results in a strong, sound horse that has the physical qualities required for harness racing.

Older Horses

The physical demands harness racing places on a horse are different from those in Thoroughbred or Quarter Horse racing. Racing with a rider aboard, at a gallop, places strain most severely on the front legs of the horse, while stress is more evenly distributed in the harness racing Standardbred. (3) This is because of the trotting and pacing gaits used as opposed to running. The Standardbred pushes its entire body forward with one hind leg at a time, instead of both hind legs working together to push the body forward. As a result, in the Standardbred, lameness of the hind limbs usually occurs as often as lameness of the front limbs.

The Standardbred horse needs extremely strong legs, and superior condition is very important in maintaining this strength. The conditioning program is a year round proposition. Recently, changes have taken place in the harness racing world and horses are beginning to be raced more and more months out of the year.

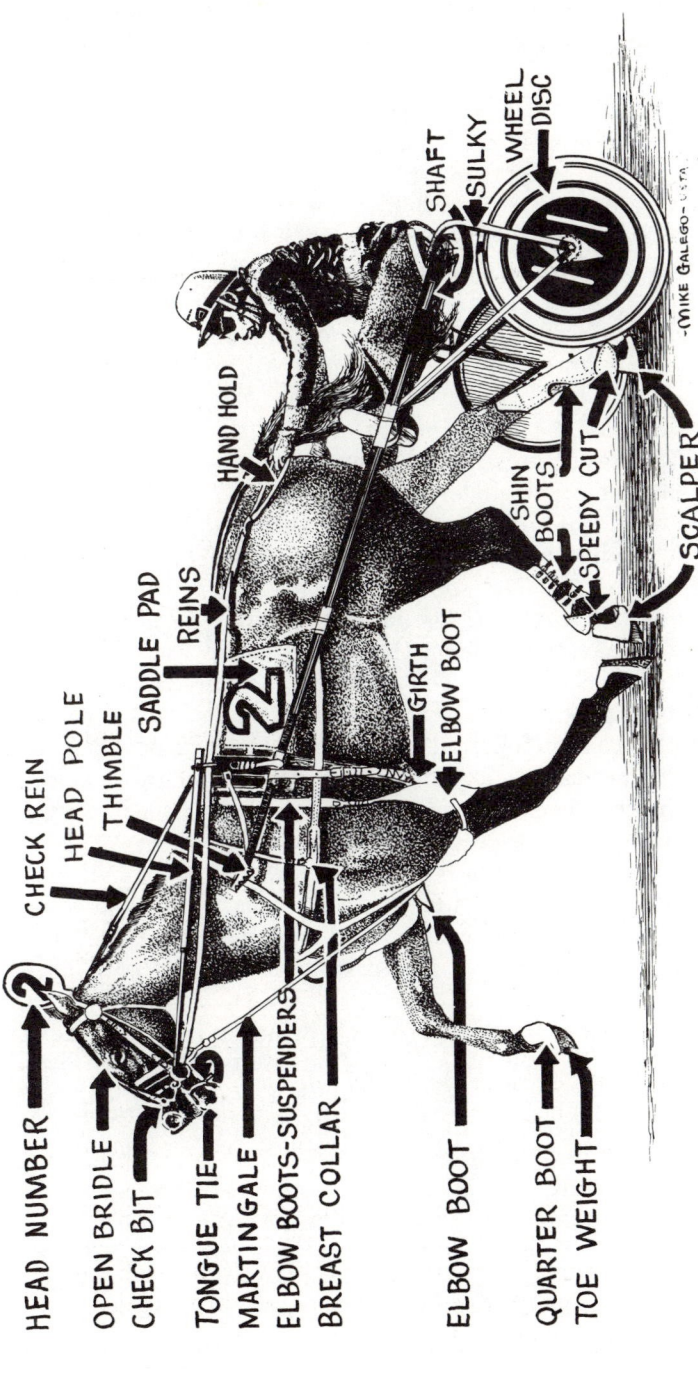

Conditioning the finished horse primarily concerns keeping strength, endurance and wind at a superior level. When the horse is in superior condition, naturally, the chance of injury will be lessened and the horse will be adequately prepared to race to the best of his ability.

In general, the program of daily jogging with two days a week of race conditioning is continued throughout the racing life of the horse. Frequently, the two days of race conditioning are divided into "slow" and "fast" workout days.

Particular attention must be paid to the length of time between race heats. About three-quarters of an hour is considered to be the optimum interval between heats. (4) This allows enough time for the horse to regain its strength, but not cool out entirely. To maintain superior physical condition, the horse must be completely stripped of all harness racing tack and all of the equipment must be thoroughly cleaned between heats. This practice is aimed at cutting out sources of chaffing and irritation that could hinder the horse while racing.

The speed and length of the daily jogging sessions depend solely on what the individual horse requires to maintain condition. Two to four miles is an average length. The speed of the jogging is critical when warming a horse up for a race. If the jog is too slow, the horse won't be ready to race. It takes away from the racing speed and endurance of the horse if the jog is too fast. The general procedure is to warm a horse up at the best jogging rate for the individual horse for two to four miles. This is usually followed by one to three relatively slow heats ending thirty minutes to an hour before the actual race. Again, this depends upon what each individual horse needs to be adequately warmed up and prepared to race at his best.

The manner in which the horse is cooled out after a race or a race conditioning session is extremely important. It usually takes at least an hour of walking, rubbing and well-spaced sips of water before the horse is cool and dry and can be put into a stall without the possibility of gorging on water.

When the harness racing Standardbred is in winning condition, he is tight—always in shape to race. This type of horse needs regular exercise; but rest periods, when the horse exhibits a need for them, are also an important consideration in a conditioning program. When a horse has an injury, major or minor, or is not performing with his full ability, a rest is normally indicated. During the rest intervals the horse will usually get an adequate amount of self-exercise on his own.

Proper shoeing to maintain balance and the best gait is mandatory when conditioning the harness racing Standardbred. The feet and legs of the horse must receive specific attention daily, checking for any sources of future problems. Because trotters and pacers do have a

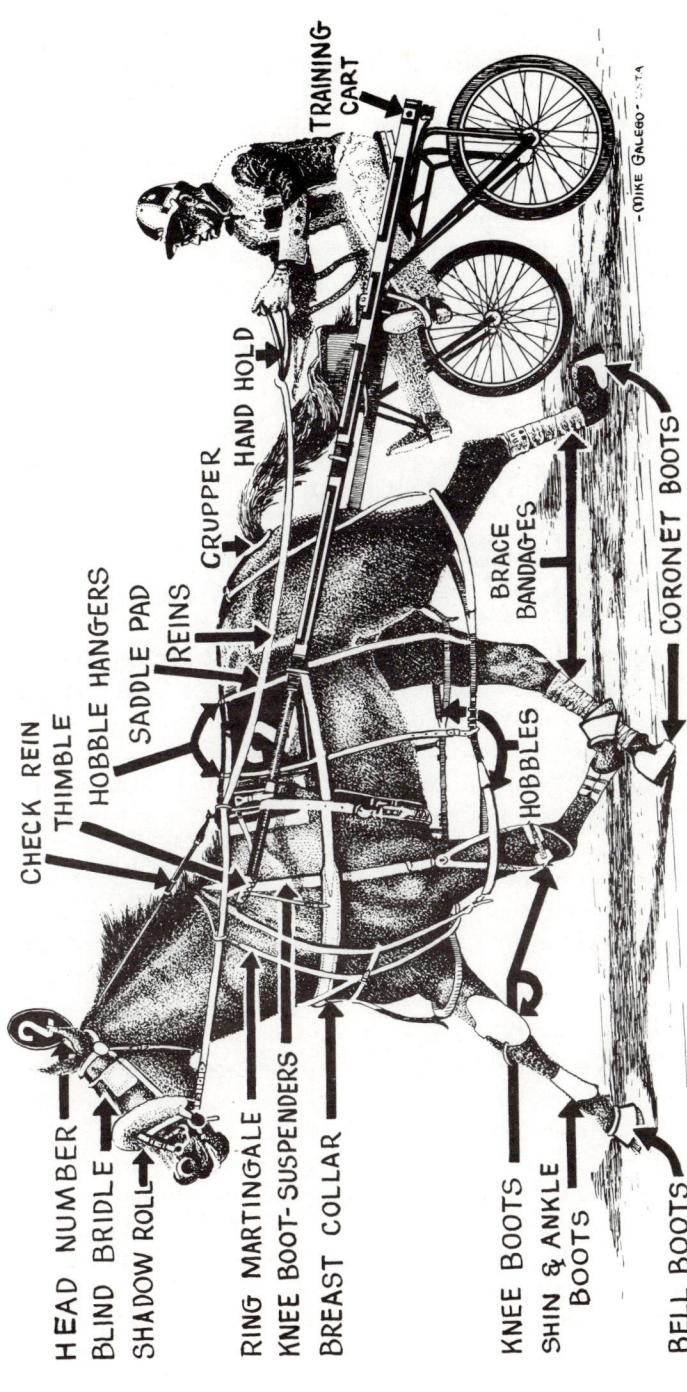

EQUIPMENT COMMONLY WORN BY THE PACER

courtesy of The United States Trotting Association

definite tendency to interfere and hurt themselves, due to the extended gaits used, protective equipment is often required. The variety is extensive, but elbow boots, arm boots, knee boots, shin and tendon boots, ankle boots, scalpers and bell boots are examples of equipment for protection of the front legs. Equipment such as shin boots, ankle and speedy-cut boots, coronet boots and scalpers is designed to protect the hind legs of the harness racer.

Proper conditioning is vitally important for the harness racing Standardbred. The stamina and endurance demanded by harness racing are developed only by consistent, carefully planned conditioning programs. When properly conditioned, the harness racing Standardbred is willing and able to go the whole distance with total physical effort.

REFERENCES CITED

1. Ensminger, M.E., B.S., M.A., Ph.D., **Horses and Horsemanship**, Danville, Illinois, The Interstate Printers and Publishers, Inc., 1969.
2. Harrison, James C., **The Care and Training of the Trotter and Pacer**, Columbus, Ohio, The United States Trotting Association, 1968.
3. Harrison, James C., Op. Cit.
4. Harrison, James C., Op. Cit.

Other Breeds and
Other Competitive Events

Many breeds of horses were not presented in the preceding discussions of specific conditioning for particular events or tasks. A breed of horses has a common origin and some distinctive characteristics to distinguish this particular type of horse. In some cases color is the distinctive characteristic. The Appaloosa, Palomino, Pinto and American Paint Horse are examples.

Within themselves, each breed approves and promotes a special set of performance events, but in numerous cases the similarities outweigh the differences between these events. It simply would not be possible to present every single event found in the horse world today.

Specific conditioning for many varied competitive situations has been presented. The horseman, supplied with the basic material in the early portion of this text, the specific material which followed, plus the interview section, should find himself with ample working knowledge to recognize and provide for the unique conditioning needs of his individual animal.

10

Conditioning Breeding Animals

Obviously, peak physical prowess aimed at athletic achievement is not the goal in a conditioning program for breeding animals. Conditioning practices aimed at building superior health, fertility, and breeding soundness should be the goal. Without a peak state of physical health it is unreasonable to expect breeding stock to produce winning offspring.

BROODMARES

In many cases, by trying so hard to produce winning colts, the horseman has created several problems for himself. He often does too much and goes against the "way nature made the horse." Common examples are: interfering with the natural breeding season in an attempt to get early colts, suppressing heat in the performance mare with hormone shots, keeping a mare too fat, hand-breeding, etc.

Before any mare is ready to breed, she should be in top condition, including good physical health. Sound sanitation procedures, worming and immunization schedules, dental examinations, regular foot care and exercise are all important considerations for healthy broodmares.

Without proper exercise, mares have a tendency to get fat and lazy, age quickly and decrease in fertility. Ideally, broodmares are kept out where they can move around and get plenty of self exercise. Horsemen often run into trouble when they try to keep broodmares in stalls or in pens.

Free exercise in safe, good quality pasture is essential in a proper conditioning program for mares and their foals.

Large, clean, well maintained pasture provides ideal broodmare environment. However, self exercise, as allowed by a large paddock will help broodmares maintain their weight and build good condition where good pasture is unavailable. A large paddock helps minimize the chances of a pregnant mare getting kicked or otherwise injuring herself.

Surroundings conducive to well-being, mental as well as physical, are important in any breeding establishment. Mares that, for some reason, must be kept up should be kept in clean, large, comfortable stables with a regular program of exercise. Time in a large paddock, hand walking, ponying or possibly light riding are common methods of forced exercise for broodmares.

Quality colts and a high live foal rate are what every horseman is working for in a breeding program. Superior health of the broodmares is a must. If the mares aren't in peak physical condition, foaling can place quite a stress on both the mare and the foal. The breeding potential of the mare and the performance potential of the foal may both be drastically hampered. Excellent mare care and conditioning helps produce foals with the potential to win, for the mare carries the foal during one of the most important phase of his development.

Every mare is an individual, but on the basis of general characteristics, they can be categorized. Many veterinarians and breeders refer to mares in three groups (1): maiden mares, or those who have never been bred; barren mares; and foaling, or pregnant mares. The following discussion will be broken down into these three categories.

Maiden Mares

Conditioning practices to get maiden mares ready for breeding vary greatly depending upon the initial state of the individual mare. There are two general types of maiden mares; the filly that has not been trained and the filly coming out of intensive training, especially race training.

The filly that has not been in training is generally used to running with other horses and fits easily into the broodmare routine. As a rule, few problems are encountered with this type of mare.

Racing and performance fillies, coming out of training, have a tendency to be tight and nervous. They are accustomed to exerting a lot of energy and usually need a "let down" period to relax. It normally takes from one to three months for this type filly to calm down and fit into the broodmare routine.

At first, a filly coming out of training should be kept in a stall until she relaxes and can be safely turned out with a few gentle mares. Because of the competitive drive instilled during training, this type of filly is often afraid of other mares and may need especially gentle handling to adapt. After an excessively nervous filly has been stalled for a few days, a day or two in a small paddock with one or two older, extremely gentle broodmares will often help the filly get used to being around other horses in a relaxed situation.

It just takes time for this type of mare to adapt to a lifestyle without keen competition. Some mares may require a longer period, often as long as six months, to get used to the relaxed routine of a broodmare.

Aside from relaxing, the let down phase of conditioning also gives the maiden mare a chance to adjust to a new ration. In addition to psychologically "coming down" from the competitive situation, during this same period the mare needs to be gradually accustomed to a new diet more suitable to the comparatively sedate broodmare routine.

For example, the new ration should include relatively more hay. If the mare were left on the same "hot" ration she required during her days of competition, she would likely be too "high" when it came time to turn her out into the broodmare pasture. Depending on how demanding her competitive schedule was, she may also be underweight. This period gives her an opportunity to regain this lost weight before she is turned out.

On the other hand, mares that have been on the show circuit, especially halter mares, frequently need to lose weight to attain breeding condition. While in training, the mare may have received hormone injections to suppress heat and the let down period also allows time for normal cycling to begin again (if ever!).

Some horsemen feel that a maiden mare can be safely bred without an examination for breeding soundness—if the mare is in relatively good condition. However, if the horseman is paying a high stud fee or has a valuable mare, it certainly makes sense to have a veterinarian examine the mare before breeding.

An exam for breeding soundness will turn up any problems that might be present. The breeder can then possibly correct these problems before the breeding season starts. There are many conditions affecting breeding soundness which can only be detected by a veterinary exam. Uncovering them early can save quite a bit of time and money. With the growing expenses facing today's horseman it benefits the breeder to take advantage of any efficiency aids available to him.

In planning and following a sound program for conditioning broodmares it helps the horseman to have a fundamental knowledge of the reproductive cycle of the mare. He can more easily plan programs for his individual mares, recognize signs of trouble and optimum breeding times when equipped with this foundation of basic knowledge.

The estrous cycle and activity of the ovaries in a nonpregnant mare are related to the season of the year. Length of daylight and temperature are the major seasonal influences. For this reason, many breeders use heated and lighted barns in a breeding program planned for early colts. The majority of mares go through three specific reproductive phases during the year. These are a dormant period, a period of adjustment and a true breeding season. For individual mares the dormant period, or anestrous, varies greatly—all the way from 40 days to eight months. (2)

Usually, anestrous occurs in the late summer or fall. The ovaries of the mare are not very productive during this phase and she seldom shows signs of estrus, or heat. Even if possible, breeding the mare at this time very rarely results in conception.

The adjustment period, the phase between anestrous and the true breeding season, also varies widely among individual mares. It can be very short or last as long as three months. Most mares go through this phase during late winter to early spring. Reproductive cycles are usually irregular and the heat periods are unusually long. As a rule, mares are not fertile during this period because ovulation doesn't occur at regular intervals.

In this country, the true breeding season is usually considered to be from early March through late July or August. (3) The cycles occur regularly and last about 21 days. Reproductive cycles are divided into two distinct phases—estrus (heat) and diestrus.

Characteristics of estrus in the mare are sexual receptivity and growth of follicles on the ovaries. Estrus periods become progressively shorter near the end of the true breeding season. Five to seven days is the common length of estrus during the middle of the breeding season. Ovulation usually occurs near the end of the heat period (4) and, ideally, breeding takes place at this time. During estrus the mare readily accepts the stallion, normally.

Ovulation initiates diestrus, or the period between heats. During diestrus the mare will normally actively resist the stallion. In the middle of the breeding season this period lasts about 15 days, but often ranges from 11 to 18 days. At the end and beginning of diestrus the mare is said to be "coming in" and "going out" of heat, respectively.

The conception rate in mares is influenced by many factors which can easily lower it. However, a good teasing program can help the breeder turn the odds in his favor. A teasing program simply involves subjecting a mare to a stallion at regular intervals to detect any signs of heat in the mare.

Because young mares are often afraid of the stallion, the maiden mare should receive special attention during teasing. Any unnecessary roughness can cause the mare to develop a bad mental attitude toward the stallion and result in a "problem broodmare." Keeping complete, detailed records of the mare's reaction is a very important part of a teasing program. These records are a great aid in any conditioning program for broodmares—they can be used for future reference to determine the best breeding times and for information regarding any physical problems that may develop.

It is a common practice to tease mares about twice a week during their adjustment phase. By March or April, most mares will have settled into regular cycles and are generally teased daily or every other day. Because of the short and intense heats during the middle of the breeding season, close observation and faultless records will help the breeder work with his individual mares in the best way.

Large breeding establishments often use both teasing and palpation schedules to insure the most effective breeding program. The palpation schedule provides information about follicle presence and size. Every time a mare is teased, a teasing form is filled out as part of the record keeping system.

The form contains information such as the mare's name and number, date of teasing, heat intensity and comments about the mare. Heat intensity is commonly scored on a scale of one to five, to provide a standard for comparing different heats. A common set of heat scores is as follows:

1 Rejects stallion, irritable in his presence.
2 Doesn't fight or accept stallion; either coming in or going out of heat.
3 Slowly accepts stallion with interest and urinates.
4 Accepts stallion and gives off small vulvar secretions.
5 Accepts stallion with great interest; profuse vulva secretions and activity.

(Texas A&M University, College Station, Texas)
Breeding operations using coinciding palpation schedules will also record that information at this time.

There are many teasing techniques in practice today. Three of the most common are pasture teasing, stall teasing and pen teasing.

Pasture teasing is used most often with small operations since it wouldn't be practical with a large operation. The stallion is taken to the pasture where the mares are kept and led through the mares. Each individual mare should be observed while the stallion is being led through and for a few minutes after the stallion has left. Best results are obtained with the type of stallion that gets excited around the mares, even when no contact is made.

The stallion is brought to the mare's stall for stall teasing. He can make contact with the mare and discover any signs of estrus. Frequently, more visible signs of estrus can be detected by this method. A competent stud handler is needed in this situation.

Many people believe that pen teasing is the most efficient method. With this technique, the stallion is put in a small pen adjacent to the mares and allowed to make contact with them. If mares are showing signs of heat, they will usually seek the presence of the stallion. Conditions are most like the natural state with this teasing method. Also, a stallion can tease quite a few mares at the same time. With this method, a longer observation time is required to carefully observe each mare. In most situations, about half a day is allowed for observation.

The breeder needs to decide which teasing method best fits his needs and put it into regular practice. No matter what kind of teasing technique is used, a good teaser is a major consideration. Ideally, the teaser can be handled easily by one man and shows a continued interest throughout the entire breeding season. Vasectomized stallions or geldings on hormone shots are animals commonly used as teasers.

The main purpose of teasing is to help determine the optimum time for breeding the mare. Physical conditions are ideal for breeding just before ovulation. Congestion of the mucous lining of the vagina protects against injuries and infection and the opened cervix enables direct projection of sperm into the uterus. (5)

To help insure a live foal and minimize the risk of infection to either the mare or the stallion, good breeding hygiene is a must. The reproductive organs of both animals should be washed with mild soap and rinsed *thoroughly*. It is a good practice to wrap the mare's tail in disposable gauze. Some mares may have to be hobbled to prevent injury to the stallion.

After the mare has been bred, teasing should continue for at least 21 days to determine if the mare comes into heat again. The majority of pregnancy tests aren't accurate until 30 to 40 days after conception. One good method of pregnancy diagnosis is rectal palpation. A competent, experienced veterinarian is needed to make a safe, accurate diagnosis.

It usually isn't practical to diagnose pregnancy until 40 days after breeding since resorption of the embryo, if it is going to happen, usually occurs between the 25th and 35th days after conception. The accuracy of rectal manual palpation is 98 to 100%. (6). There are quite a variety of other pregnancy tests in use today. Several chemical and hormonal tests, with good accuracy, are frequently used. With any pregnancy test, the main consideration is to find out which mares are *not* pregnant rather than which are pregnant. This is important to the breeder so that mares proving barren can receive special care and conditioning to induce heat again and be rebred. Otherwise the mare may fail to show a normal heat period for several months, possibly resulting in a barren year for the mare—and one less foal for the breeder.

Barren Mares

Barren mares represent lost time and money to the breeder. Failure of a mare to become pregnant can be due to either one or several causes. First of all, the mare must be in good physical condition. A mare shouldn't be too fat, but in an active, thrifty condition.

Nutritional deficiencies can cause barrenness. Supplementation of vitamins A and E has been shown to improve fertility in mares (7) and supplementation of vitamins and minerals can possibly improve breeding performance. Any nutritional deficiencies can certainly result in reproductive failures and poor health. For complete nutritional requirements, refer to **Feeding To Win.**

Heavy parasite infestation can also be a cause of infertility, so a sound program of health management is essential to the conditioning of broodmares. Primary causes of infertility in the mare are infections, hormonal imbalances, anatomical and psychological factors. With the mare, psychological causes are relatively unimportant and are usually remedied with proper handling and rest. (8)

The first step is to call a veterinarian for a thorough examination of the mare. Before a barren mare can be successfully treated, the cause needs to be determined. Uterine infection is probably the greatest cause of infertility in the mare. (9) There are many causes of genital infection in the mare, but the most common are "windsucking", foaling, foaling complications and poor breeding practices. Nearly all causes can be related to poor health and sanitation management.

Cervical and uterine infections are usually localized, i.e., the mare doesn't show any other signs of illness. Veterinary assistance is required to diagnose, identify and treat the infection. Often, treatment of such infections is long, tedious and unrewarding. In all cases, the mare should not be bred until it is *certain* that the infection is completely cleared up. The infection could easily be spread by the stallion to other mares.

In some cases, mares with poor reproductive conformation or poor muscle tone of the reproductive organs will continually suck air in and out of the vagina when in motion. This type of mare is termed a "windsucker." This defect provides a perfect entrance for bacteria and a resulting infection. A Caslick operation, to suture the vulva of the mare, may be required to prevent continual infection. After this operation healing is complete and rapid, but one heat period is usually allowed before breeding so the reproductive tract can return to normal.

Hormonal imbalances frequently result in abnormal estrous cycles. Anestrous, silent heat, split heat and false pregnancy are all examples of hormonal imbalances. These conditions generally require veterinary treatment to get the mare in breeding condition.

Anatomy can also be a cause of infertility in the mare. Imperforate hymen and vaginal septum are both examples of anatomy as a cause of infertility. Both conditions are easily treated and remedied by a veterinarian.

Foaling and breeding can both injure the mare and cause her to be barren. In some cases, one of the foal's hooves will tear the walls of the vagina and/or rectum of the mare. Immediate surgery is called for in this situation because the mare will be sterile until the tear heals.

Young mares are often injured during breeding. Most common are perforations of the vagina. This condition bleeds considerably, but is not serious. Sexual rest and antibiotic injections are generally all the treatment that is required.

There are many, many factors that can cause a mare to be barren. Aside from obvious poor condition, a veterinarian is needed to diagnose and treat most causes of infertility. Barren mares require special care and conditioning to become healthy and productive.

Foaling Mares

When the broodmare is proven to be in foal, the next consideration of the breeder is, "When will she foal?" The average gestation time for a mare is 336 days (10), or a little over eleven months. With individual mares this figure can vary all the way from 320 days to 370 days.

Because of this individuality of mares, a "normal" gestation period is any time that the mare delivers a normal, healthy foal. During pregnancy the breeder needs to do everything he can to keep the mare in foal. Specific conditioning for the foaling mare includes those practices aimed at keeping the mare healthy and preventing abortion.

During pregnancy, a broodmare needs regular exercise to stay healthy. Broodmares on quality pasture will get plenty of exercise just roaming and grazing. During the last one-third of pregnancy free-choice exercise is preferable to forced exercise.

However, if conditions require that a broodmare be stalled, she should be afforded the opportunity for self exercise in a paddock. If this is not possible, the mare needs to be led at a walk for about an

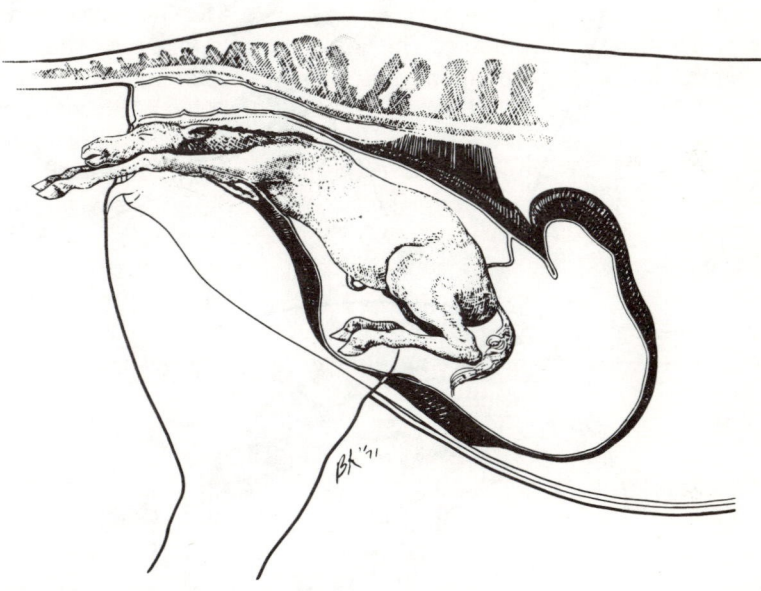

courtesy of Batvin Kramer, Senior Medical Illustrator, College of Veterinary Medicine, Ohio State University

In a normal birth the foal is presented in this manner with the forelimbs, head and neck fully extended.

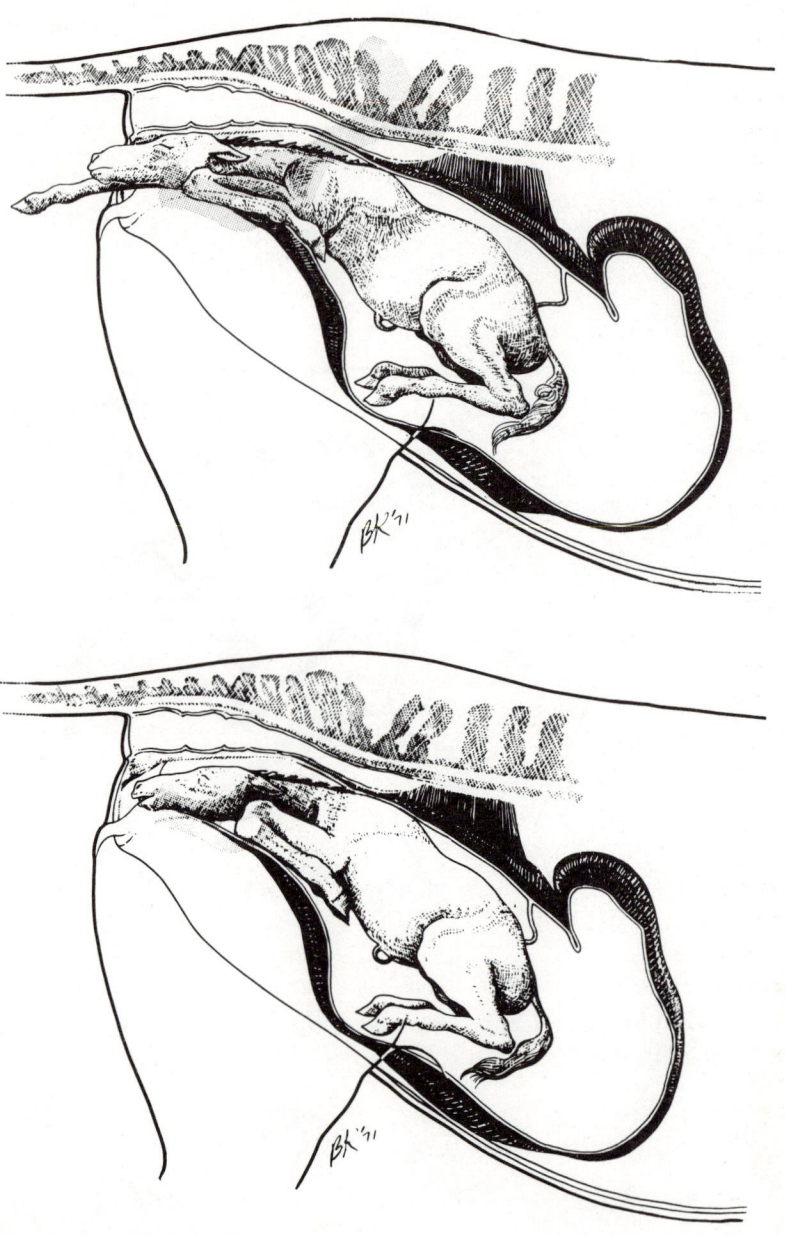

In some cases of abnormal birth, a fetus can be presented with one or both forelegs flexed.

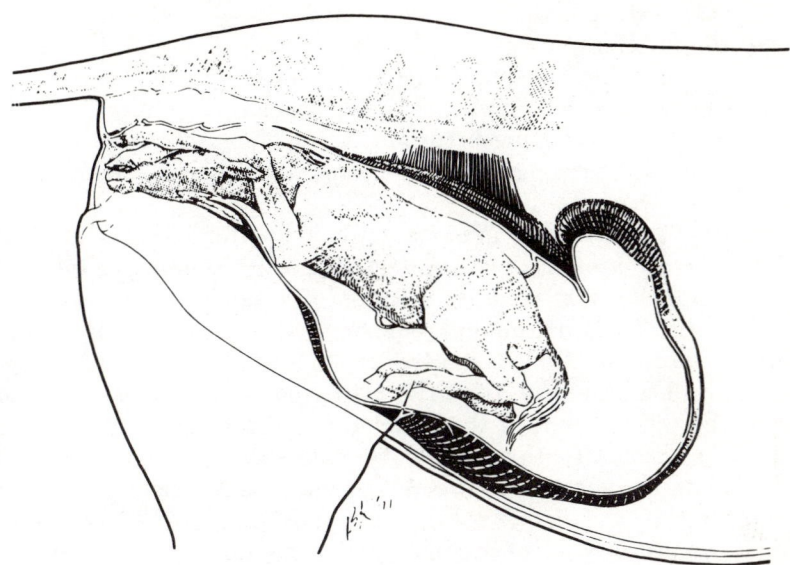

Abnormal presentation with both forelegs crossed over the head and neck.

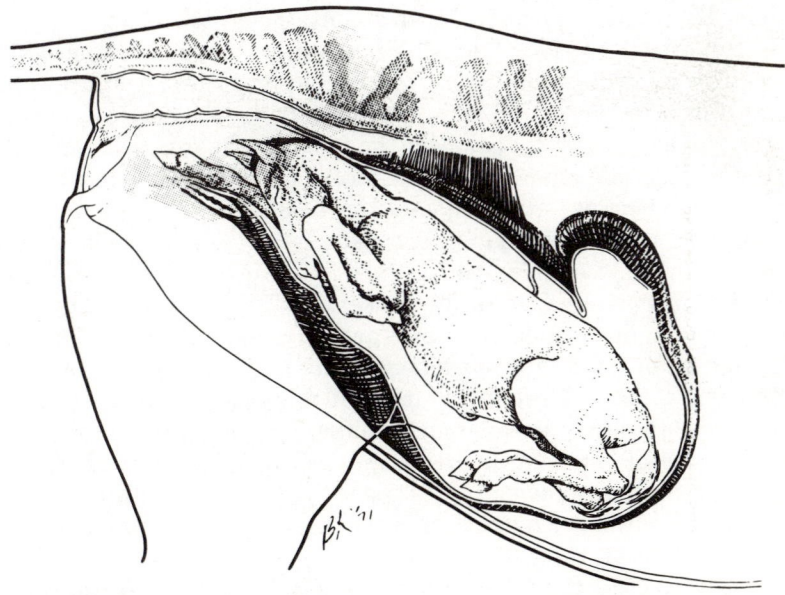

Abnormal presentation with head and one foreleg not extended.

hour *every day*. Again, for the broodmare, free exercise is considered to be the better choice.

Young, excitable maiden and barren mares should be kept away from those mares heavy with foal. Mares close to foaling tend to be calmer and quieter. Undue disturbances could possibly upset their pregnancies. Mares carrying their first foals are generally most likely to become overly excited.

Nutrition is extremely important for a pregnant mare—inadequate nutrition is a major cause of reproductive failures occuring today. Like other mammals, the greatest amount of fetal growth occurs during the last third of pregnancy requiring additional nutrients for the mare. Because of this, the seventh to eighth month of gestation marks the beginning of the critical period. It isn't necessary to increase the total volume of the broodmare's ration, she shouldn't be too fat, but special attention should be paid to the amount of protein, vitamins and minerals. The amount of vitamin A, calcium, phosphorus and protein in the diet of a pregnant mare will need to be increased during the last 90 days of pregnancy. Specific nutrient requirements of pregnant mares are covered in **Feeding To Win.**

With foaling mares, abortion is always a possibility to be considered by the breeder. For this reason, the breeder should be able to recognize abortion and take quick measures to determine the cause of the abortion. Some types of abortion are contagious (they can be spread by contact with secretions from the mare, fetal membranes, etc.) and will require immediate attention to prevent the spread of the abortion-causing infection to other mares in foal.

Rarely, if ever, does a foal born one month before full term live. Because of this, abortion generally refers to the delivery of a fetus, dead or alive, between the first and tenth months of pregnancy. (11)

Abortions early in pregnancy are usually *not* due to a disease-producing organism. Common causes are hormonal imbalances, nutritional deficiencies and natural causes. Many of these abortions, because they happen so early in pregnancy, go unnoticed by the breeder. In fact, he often is left wondering if the mare was really in foal in the first place. Many large farms make it a practice to re-check mares around the 80th day of pregnancy to make sure they are still in foal.

Physical factors causing abortion include falls, kicks, twisted navel cords and twin pregnancies. The breeder should *never* dispose of the aborted fetus without first determining the cause. A laboratory examination to find out the direct cause is always called for; veterinary consultation is essential. If the abortion was due to an infection it can easily be spread by contact with the aborted fetus and infected mare and increase the loss to the breeder.

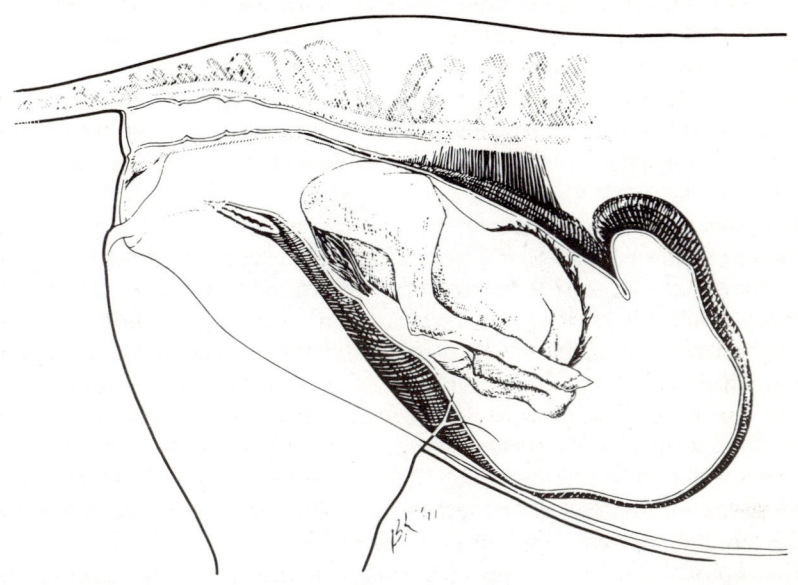

courtesy of Batvin Kramer, Senior Medical Illustrator, College of Veterinary Medicine, Ohio State University

Breech presentation of fetus with head and knees also flexed.

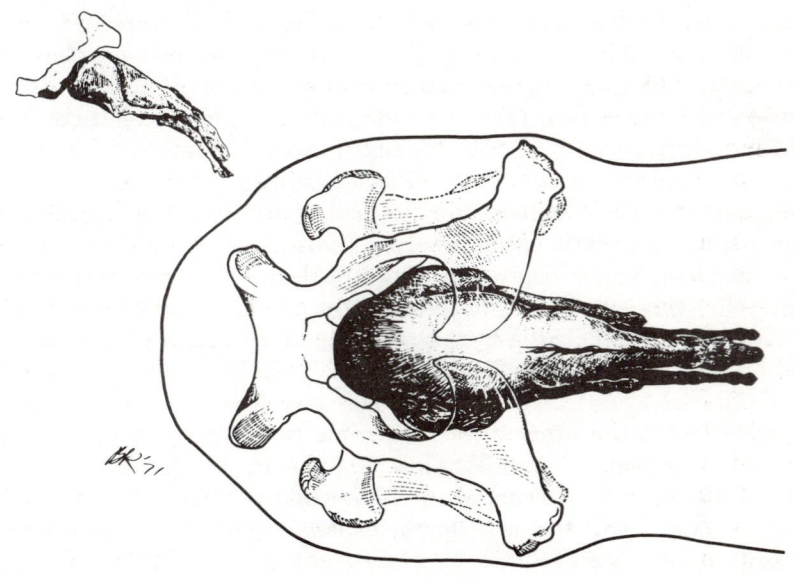

courtesy of Batvin Kramer, Senior Medical Illustrator, College of Veterinary Medicine, Ohio State University

Top and side view of breech presentation.

Viral and bacterial infections are the most common type of abortions. Two viral diseases can cause abortion in the pregnant mare. Viral arteritis, sometimes wrongly called "pinkeye" or "Equine Influenza" (12), and viral rhinopneumonitis (viral abortion) can both result in a pregnant mare aborting. There are vaccines for both of these diseases, so the breeder should consult his veterinarian to see if his area is a "hot spot." If so, the immunizations can be included in the health management program.

There are many kinds of bacteria that can cause abortion. One specific example is salmonellosis (contagious equine abortion), caused by the bacteria *S. abortus equi*. There is a killed bacterin immunization for mares that can be included in the health management program of the breeding operation, if needed. The same organism that causes cervical and uterine infections in mares is responsible for numerous abortions. Good sanitation practices and breeding hygiene are the best insurance against infection.

Many miscellaneous factors can cause a pregnant mare to abort; eating moldy feed, estrogen overdoses and opening the cervix are a few examples. Some mares just habitually abort, for no apparent reason that the veterinarian can determine.

The breeder's best defense is to include *prevention* in his conditioning programs for broodmares. Common sense health and sanitation practices can be very effective in preventing abortion. For example, only healthy mares should be bred, and all barren mares should be examined by a veterinarian. It is also a good practice to enforce strict breeding hygiene and have a lab examination of *all* aborted fetuses. Immunization and worming programs, fitted to a specific locale can also help insure the best health for broodmares.

When a pregnant mare doesn't abort, foaling is the next consideration. Birth is a critical time for both the mare and the foal. Their future condition is often determined by the processes during birth.

Birth is a very natural process. The breeder should not try to help the mare deliver, except in the event of obvious difficulty. When the time of birth is near, the external reproductive organs of the mare should be washed with a mild soap.

In the first phase of birth, the muscles and ligaments of the birth canal relax. Then the uterine muscles force the "water bag" through the cervix, releasing the fluid. This is followed by abdominal contractions, lasting from ten minutes to two hours, that expel the foal. The mare then expels the afterbirth, usually within two hours after birth has taken place.

Inducing labor in mares is a relatively new idea that shows a great deal of promise. It is important to remember, however, that *only* a qualified veterinarian should use this procedure. Research with this technique has shown no problems with normal foals, uterine infections or complications after birth. (13)

After the mare has foaled, an attendant should recover the afterbirth and make certain that the mare hasn't retained any of it. A missing piece as small as a hand can cause acute laminitis or even death of the mare. If she hasn't passed the afterbirth within three hours, maximum, the veterinarian should be called immediately.

Foal founder (acute laminitis due to foaling complications, such as a retained portion of the afterbirth) can be extremely difficult to treat and early treatment is very important. A veterinarian should be called with utmost haste.

Fortunately, the majority of mares aren't prone to foaling complications. However, "foal colic" is one of the most common complications following birth. This isn't classified as a true colic because pain is due to the contraction of uterine muscles instead of abdominal muscles. If the mare has foal colic, the signs of pain will usually appear within ten to thirty minutes after birth and generally disappear within about the same amount of time. For prolonged pain, a veterinarian's assistance is recommended.

A mare that has foaled easily, with no complications, needs a reasonable amount of easy exercise. Moderate exercise, such as half hour sessions of walking and trotting, helps restore the tone of the uterus and speeds recovery of the reproductive system. Few mares will be in condition to breed during foal heat if they have been stalled for the entire period after foaling. With good weather, a normal mare and foal can be turned out within a day of foaling.

There is a lot of disagreement concerning ninth-day or "foal heat" breeding of mares. Even though this is a short heat, generally the mare will accept the stallion and can conceive. One advantage of this practice is simple—the mare is kept pregnant. With registration systems setting age at January 1, breeders want early foals of considerable size by late summer or early fall.

Many people breed a mare at this time because, following foal heat, some mares may not cycle regularly for up to two months. Much time is lost in this case, especially if the mare has foaled late in the breeding season.

To be bred during foal heat a mare must be in good breeding health and have experienced *no* foaling complications. Many breeders won't breed a mare at foal heat because the possibility of infection and unnoticed tissue damage is highest at this time. The minor injuries heal rapidly, but the danger of spread of infection and abortion are somewhat greater.

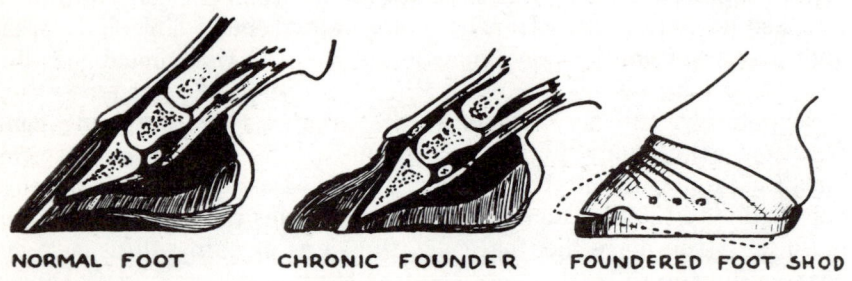

NORMAL FOOT CHRONIC FOUNDER FOUNDERED FOOT SHOD

GROOVING OPERATIONS TO RELIEVE LAMENESS OF CHRONIC FOUNDER (AFTER FRANK)

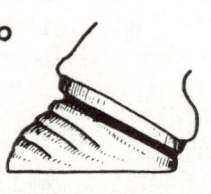

GROOVES ¼ INCH DEEP

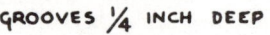

CHRONIC LAMINITIS (FOUNDER)

*Taken from **Horseman's Veterinary Guide**, The Western Horseman, Inc., 1963*

If not promptly diagnosed and treated, foal founder can progress to the extremely serious chronic condition illustrated above.

The individual mare is the only deciding factor. Is she in good breeding condition? Does the mare have a history of failures to settle, abortion, foaling complications, abnormal cycles following foaling, etc.? Accurate and detailed records on each mare are the breeder's best tool for making this decision. Each and every mare must be considered as an individual—no hard and fast rules apply.

In a group of mares foaling in a pasture, a mare will normally isolate herself during foaling and stay separated from the herd for a while. In nature, herd stallions seldom breed a mare during foal heat. (14) He may come over and tease the mare—this helps her clean out and begin to cycle regularly again.

Foaling mares don't usually present a problem to the breeder. The conditioning program for broodmares, however, should include *year round* planning, with good health programs and veterinary assistance when needed.

STALLIONS

A conditioning program for the breeding stallion includes all the factors necessary to develop good physical and mental well-being. Nutrition, health management, exercise and psychology should all be considered by the breeder. The object of a conditioning program for the breeding stallion is to develop a superb state of condition to help insure that a high percentage of the mares get in foal and that outstanding offspring are produced.

A stallion needs to be in top physical health to perform at his peak in the stud. Health is a major factor in the fertility of the stallion, and maximum fertility is what the breeder wants. A fertility level of anything less than the animal is capable represents a loss in time and money.

Health, physical fitness and psychological well-being are indications of a properly conditioned breeding stallion. Generally, a program for building peak condition is started two to three months before the breeding season begins. The length and type of conditioning program varies widely with individual stallions.

The initial condition of the stallion is a primary factor in determining the kind of conditioning program the stallion needs. In other words, what has he been doing? Stallions coming out of training, especially race training, will need a "let down" period similar to the broodmares. It takes time for the stallion to adapt to a relaxed routine in comparison to the stress and excitement of competition.

Stallions that have been turned out to pasture during the off season will more easily fit into a conditioning regime. Young studs being used

Pictured here at twenty-three years of age is Leo with owner, Mrs. Bud Warren. His record as a sire and as a maternal grandsire of Quarter running horses has made him one of the most famous horses of all times.

for their first season will require special attention and extra care. It is very important that they develop a good mental attitude; young horses mustn't be allowed to become discouraged or subjected to overuse.

The conditioning program must be developed to use the right combination of high quality nutrition and exercise to maintain the stallion in active, thrifty condition. Many stallions are kept too fat and this definitely has a depressing influence on fertility. Regular, daily exercise is very instrumental in developing peak condition in the breeding stallion. Most horsemen are firm believers in continuing a daily exercise regime throughout the entire breeding season. Exercise aimed at maintaining good all around physical fitness helps the stallion maintain fertility, health and psychological well-being.

The type and amount of exercise is governed by the individual stallion. Self exercise, usually in a paddock, and/or forced exercise are the usual alternatives. The stallion should certainly be provided with a clean, comfortable stall and a large paddock.

The paddock, where possible, is several acres in size and, ideally, sown with grass so the stallion can graze when he is outside. Except in the case of bad weather, most stallions should be allowed free access to the paddock so they can exercise at will. Obviously, a stallion paddock should be free from dangerous obstacles, with safe, sturdy fencing of at least five feet in height.

Free access to the paddock will depend upon the individual horse. Some stallions may get too much exercise on their own and have a tendency to "run weight off." In such a case, limited access to the paddock would logically be better. Other stallions may tend to be lazy and need forced exercise in addition to free access to the paddock to build and maintain good, athletic physical condition.

The most common methods of forced exercise are riding, longeing, forced jogging in a round pen without a rider, ponying and either hand or mechanical walking. The amount of daily exercise depends on what the individual animal needs to maintain fitness, but usually ranges from thirty minutes to two hours a day. Combinations of strenuous work (usually riding), trotting and walking need to be devised to fit the requirements of the individual horse.

In an average situation, the exercise sessions should be regulated so that the stallion finishes a session cool enough to be brushed off and turned out in a paddock or corral, without a lengthy "cooling out" period. But it is important to remember that the amount and type of exercise should be designed to fit the specific needs of each individual.

Every conditioning program for a breeding stallion should include provisions for maintaining good psychological well-being in the horse.

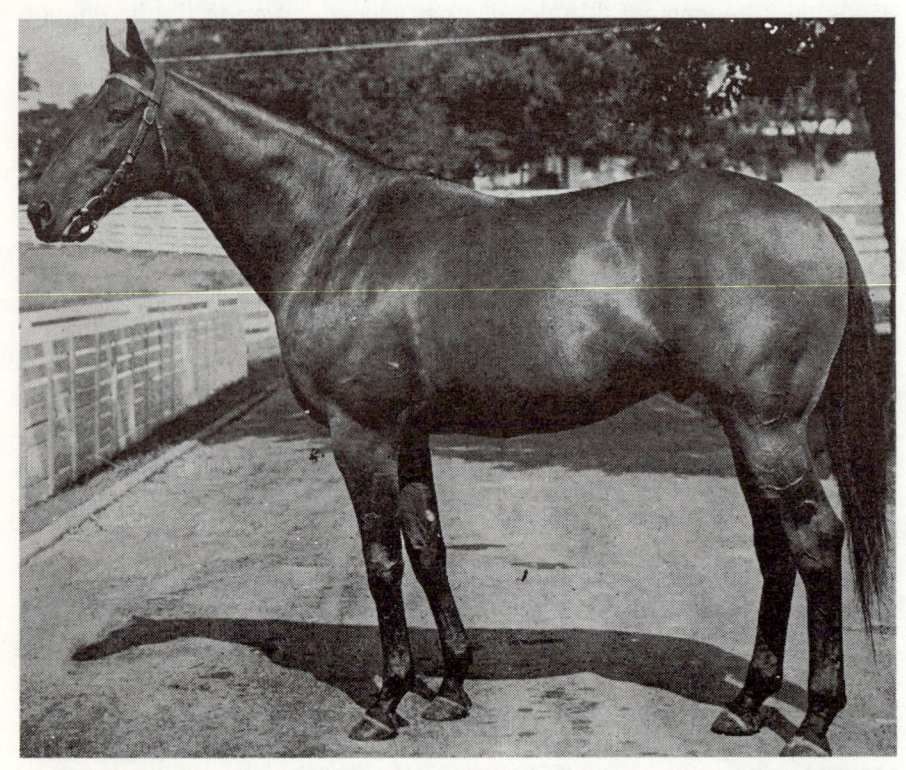

Ribot, an international stakes winner, was undefeated in 16 starts. Equally impressive is his ability as a sire.

Combinations of stimuli from the nervous system of the stallion play an important part in his participation in the sexual act. The way a stallion performs will also greatly reflect previous experiences and changes in mood and habits.

The young stallion particularly needs special handling during his initial use as a stud because it will have a permanent influence on the animal's ability to breed. A patient, experienced mare should be used. Even with this precaution it may take several clumsy and awkward attempts over a period of several days for the young stud to successfully breed the mare.

The job of the handler is to encourage and coax the stallion at the proper time and discourage him, *in a proper way,* when needed. The young stud that is mildly interested in the mare, but doesn't attempt to breed her may present a real potential problem. This situation demands an exceptionally docile mare. If the mare fights, squirms, kicks or is vicious, permanent psychological damage to the young stallion may result.

The stallion needs to have confidence in himself, as developed by careful handling and also respect for the stud handler. Each stallion is an individual and has to be treated as such, so there aren't any hard and fast rules that apply to the handling and disciplining of stallions.

Most horsemen agree that stallions shouldn't be "picked at" continually. The constant irritation can only build up resentment in the animal. When it is needed, punishment should be administered swiftly and soundly so the horse knows that he is being punished and why. Definite departures from acceptable behavior should not be tolerated. A "spoiled" stallion is an irritation at best if not outright dangerous. On the other hand, picking at him for any and every small infraction of perfect "parlour manners" can destroy his psychological well-being. In short, no one but a *highly* competent horseman should be allowed to handle a stallion.

The temperament of the individual stallion is the best guide for the severity of disciplinary measures. Some may require only a threat, while others will require that a more severe measure be taken. After punishing the stallion he should be shown the respect and gentleness that every horse needs until his actions again become offensive.

The temperament of the stallion is very important as it has been proven that this has a definite effect on the day to day quality of his semen. (15) The temperament of the stallion is dependent to a large degree upon the attitude of the handlers and his environment. The moody, vicious or extremely nervous stallion is almost always the product of poor management.

To help develop and maintain a content, secure mental well-being in the stallion, it is best that he be handled by only one man, especially at the time of service. Also, stallions are usually most content when they are not isolated. Large quarters, from which he can see other horses, can greatly aid in keeping the stallion calm and contented. In some cases, the stallion is even allowed to run out with a few mares he has bred. This situation emulates a natural state and many horsemen feel it is good for the mental and physical health of the stallion.

Before the breeding season actually begins, it is a good idea to have an examination of the stallion for breeding soundness. One reason for the low reproductive efficiency of horses today is that many horse owners fail to recognize the importance of the stallion in situations involving infertility.

A breeding soundness exam will usually include a good general physical examination, examination of the external and internal genital organs, a semen sample and observation of sexual desire (demonstrated while the stallion breeds a mare). It is also helpful to provide the veterinarian with the breeding history of the animal. The breeding history of the stallion should be included in the record keeping system of the owner. Each year he should record the number of mares serviced, percentage settled, numbers of services per conception, when the mare foaled, etc.

The purpose of the examination is to uncover any abnormalities which could affect the fertility of the horse. However, the only certain evaluation of fertility is the proven ability of the stallion to settle a mare. Although microscopic examination of semen by an experienced person is a good indicator of fertility, it can be misleading. Again, the purpose of the initial examination is to discover any abnormalities so they can be corrected before the breeding season starts.

There are many factors which can affect the fertility of a breeding stallion. For this reason, it is important that the breeder be able to recognize some of the things that can go wrong. With this information, the breeder can better plan a conditioning program to develop the maximum health and fertility of his stallion.

A definite relationship exists between nutrition and fertility. Inadequate nutrition can result in decreased sexual desire and semen quality. For complete nutrient requirements of breeding stallions, refer to **Feeding To Win.**

Bacterial and viral infections are common causes of stallion infertility. Bacterial infections can be the result of a general infection, such as strangles. The infection can become so painful that the stallion will refuse to breed a mare. Mares bred by an infected stallion usually abort or deliver extremely weak foals with slight chance of survival. Complete sexual rest and administration of antibiotics will

courtesy of The Complete Book of the Quarter Horse, Arco Publishing Company, Inc. of New York, Nelson C. Nye

The famous King, outstanding foundation sire of the modern day Quarter Horse, possessed prepotency which crossed well with the speed lines to produce smooth combinations of racing, show and performance horses.

often clear up the infection. Viral infections, such as coital exanthema, are highly contagious. A veterinarian can easily diagnose this condition and will prescribe treatment, including *absolute* sexual rest.

Genetic factors can result in infertility. The cryptorchid is one example. In this case either one or both of the testicles fail to descend into the scrotum. This inherited defect is fairly common and, although the horse may not be entirely sterile, he should not be used as a breeding animal because the defect is hereditary. (16) Because of the higher temperature in the abdominal cavity, sperm is not produced by the testicles which have not descended. Generally the cryptorchid is difficult to handle, so gelding the animal is often a wise decision.

The defects predisposing to hernias (protrusion of an organ or tissue through an abnormal opening) are inherited, so the animal with a hernia should not be used for breeding purposes. Hernias can cause a decrease in sperm production and veterinary assistance is usually required for treatment, depending upon the severity of the condition.

Size and position of the genital organs is determined by genetic factors and has a definite effect on fertility. Some stallions have testicles positioned close and horizontal to the abdomen, instead of being down in the scrotum, slanted away from the abdomen. This fault in anatomy is highly undesirable and can diminish the fertility of the stallion. Testicle size and weight, also inherited, is related to sperm production and can make a difference in fertility.

Abnormal hormone regulation results in lack of sexual desire or failure to produce sperm. Both cases can cause sterility. Unfortunately, the response of stallions to hormone therapy is frequently erratic. (17)

Psychological factors play a complicated role in stallion fertility. A lack of psychological well-being often results in abnormal sexual behavior. This is most commonly caused by bad management of the breeding stallion. Common examples of abnormal stallion sexual behavior are failure to attain or maintain erection, incomplete intromission, dismounting at the onset of ejaculation and failure to ejaculate. Conscientious, experienced management will usually be able to correct or prevent these psychological problems.

Stallions have numerous individual quirks in their natures such as refusing to breed a mare of a certain color, biting the mare, preferring certain surroundings or a specific handler, etc. It is the responsibility of the handler, along with veterinary assistance, to recognize and treat mental problems like these. Stallions that are in good physical condition and psychologically well adjusted will rarely have problems regarding the sexual act. There are specific practices that should be avoided. Overuse of stallions is an extremely poor practice. Although it varies greatly with the breed and individuality of the stallion, Ensminger (18) recommends the following guide:

Age	Hand-Breeding
2-year-old	10 to 15 mares per year
3-year-old	20 to 40 mares per year
4-year-old	30 to 60 mares per year
mature horse	80 to 100 mares per year
over 18 years old	20 to 40 mares per year

Studs should be allowed to be aggressive, but not to endanger the handler or the mare. However, unnecessary roughness while handling the stallion during breeding should definitely be avoided. Other bad practices include forcing a stallion to breed a mare he doesn't want to breed and isolating him during the non-breeding season.

There have been recent studies to determine the seasonal influences on stallion fertility. Although sexual behavior in the stallion is not very well understood, efforts have been made to relate behavioral patterns to the season of the year. Results of these studies certainly suggest that a stallion's fertility is considerably decreased during the natural non-breeding season. (19)

There are many miscellaneous factors that can result in lowered fertility of the stallion. The act of mounting a mare places a great deal of stress on the hindlimbs of the stallion, so physical defects, such as ringbone, spavin, etc., will have a direct bearing on the breeding ability of the animal.

Each stallion will require an individualized conditioning program to be developed and maintained at his best—both physically and mentally. It is most important that the horseman be familiar with his animal and devise a unique program for each stallion.

REFERENCES CITED

1. McGee, W.R., D.V.M., **Veterinary Notes for the Standardbred Breeder**, Columbus, Ohio, United States Trotting Association.
2. Hughes, J.P., D.V.M., Stabenfeldt, G.H., D.V.M., Ph.D., and Evans, J.W., Ph.D., "Estrous Cycle and Ovulation in the Mare," Journal of the American Veterinary Medical Association, Volume 161: 11, 1972, pp. 1367-1374.
3. Catcott, E.J., D.V.M., Ph.D., and Smithcors, J.F., D.V.M., Ph.D., Editors, **Progress in Equine Medicine**, Volumes One and Two, Wheaton, Illinois, American Veterinary Publications, Inc., 1969.
4. Catcott, E.J., D.V.M., Ph.D., and Smithcors, J.F., D.V.M., Ph.D., Editors, **Equine Medicine and Surgery**, Wheaton, Illinois, American Veterinary Publications, Inc., 1972.
5. Catcott and Smithcors, **Equine Medicine and Surgery**, Op. Cit.
6. Catcott and Smithcors, **Equine Medicine and Surgery**, Op. Cit.
7. Stowe, H.D., "Reproductive Performance of Barren Mares Following Vitamin A and E Supplementation," Proceedings of the 1967 Convention of the American Association of Equine Practitioners.
8. Catcott and Smithcors, **Equine Medicine and Surgery**, Op. Cit.
9. Catcott and Smithcors, **Equine Medicine and Surgery**, Op. Cit.
10. Ensminger, M.E. B.S., M.A., Ph.D. **Horses and Horsemanship**, Danville, Illinois, The Interstate Printers and Publishers, Inc. 1969.
11. Catcott and Smithcors, **Equine Medicine and Surgery**, Op. Cit.
12. Siegmund, O.H., Editor, **The Merck Veterinary Manual**, Rahway, New Jersey, Merck and Company, Inc., 1967.
13. Purvis, Alan D., D.V.M., "Inducing Labor in Mares," The Blood-Horse, Volume XCIX: 12, 1973, pp. 1024.
14. Ommert, William, D.V.M., "Help Mother Nature Increase Your Live Foal Rate," Horseman, Volume 17:7, 1973, pp. 14-23.
15. Rule, Fred, D.V.M., "Breeding Soundness in Stallions," The Quarter Horse Journal, Volume 24: 3, 1971, pp. 53.
16. Catcott and Smithcors, **Equine Medicine and Surgery**, Op. Cit.
17. Catcott and Smithcors, **Equine Medicine and Surgery**, Op. Cit.
18. Ensminger, M.E., Ph.D., Op. Cit.
19. Pickett, B.W. and Voss, J.L., "Reproductive Management of the Stallion," Proceedings of the Eighteenth Annual Convention of the American Association of Equine Practitioners, 1972, pp. 501-531.

GENERAL REFERENCES

Miller, W.C., F.R.C.V.S., F.R.S.E., **Practical Essentials in the Care and Management of Horses on Thoroughbred Studs**, London, England, The Thoroughbred Breeders Association, 1965.

Prickett, M.E., D.V.M., "Abortion and Placental Lesions in the Mare," Journal of the American Veterinary Medical Association, Volume 157: 11, 1970, pp. 1465-1470.

Sager, F.C., D.V.M., "Care of the Reproductive Tract of the Mare," Journal of the American Veterinary Medical Association, Volume 149: 12, 1966, pp. 1542-1545.

Worthington, William E., D.V.M., "Management of Stallions, Considerations of Feeding, Health and Fertility," Lectures given at the Stud Managers Course, Lexington, Kentucky, Stud Managers Course, 1973, pp. 86-96.

11

The Art and Science of Conditioning
(Expert opinions and practices)

This chapter consists of interviews and written contributions from respected persons in all phases of the horse industry. Leading breeders, trainers and owners throughout the world present the "art," or practical aspect, of conditioning while highly respected veterinarians and scientists present conditioning from a scientific viewpoint.

The format of this chapter varies slightly from that of the companion publication, Feeding To Win, in that several notable professionals are represented as contributing authors. We feel that these persons, recognized as experts in their respective fields, could better present their ideas in this form rather than the regular interview method.

The editorial policy of Equine Research Publications is not to comment on the material presented, but to simply choose high-ranking individuals from the many areas of the horse industry and make their knowledge and practical experience available to the reader. It is our hope that the reader can draw his own conclusions and thereby benefit from this type of presentation.

R. Gordon Greeley
D.V.M., M.S.

The following section, "Conditioning the Feet and Lower Limbs," was contributed by Dr. R. Gordon Greeley who has written several books and numerous scientific articles on this subject. Dr. Greeley worked as a farrier prior to receiving his B.S. and D.V.M. from the University of Missouri in 1953. After this he was involved in a Large Animal Practice in Missouri for seven years. Dr. Greeley then continued his studies at Texas A&M University where he received his M.S. in 1966. At this time Dr. Greeley is a Professor in the Department of Veterinary Anatomy, College of Veterinary Medicine, Texas A&M University. He is a widely recognized authority in this field and also noted for his illustrations.

Conditioning the Feet and Lower Limbs

by

R. Gordon Greeley

The athletic prowess of the horse is no accident of nature, his body is that of a specialized athlete. He is endowed with a large heart and capacious lungs. His muscles are distributed on his bones in such a way as to attain maximum leverage, and the action of each muscle or group of muscles is integrated with the action of other muscles to produce superb coordination. Bone and muscle are reinforced by a remarkable, in some ways unique, system of ligaments. It is not inappropriate to credit him with having a ligamentous skeleton that complements the bony skeleton and muscle system. The resulting power and precision of movement culminate in the performance of the feet and lower limbs.

Equine feet and lower limbs are, mechanically and physiologically, a tribute to the wisdom of the forces that govern the adaptation of species for survival. They are quite tolerant of the awesome stresses and strains imposed upon them in the course of normal movement. The better one understands the extremities of the horse, the more impressed one is that such an apparatus can be contrived from the ingredients available—mortal, vulnerable flesh and bone.

Normal movement for a horse could be defined as that which takes

Dr. R. Gordon Greeley, highly regarded scientist, professor, lecturer, writer and equine medical illustrator.

place in his normal habitat, plains and foothills. When the horse is confined by man the surfaces on which he moves and the actions he performs are modified, sometimes to his detriment. Therein lies the value of conditioning and a challenge to the trainer.

Ligaments and Tendons

Ligaments may be described as structures that connect bones with bones, although some ligaments are quite specialized and, at first inspection, would hardly seem to fit such a simple definition. Tendons are structures that connect some of the muscles to bone. Ligaments and tendons are made of the same substance, collagenous connective tissue, commonly called gristle.

Gristle, like muscles, deteriorates with slothfulness and responds to exercise. It neither possesses nor needs a great blood supply, a scant blood flow is enough. Gristle, like any other tissue, is dependent on quality nutrition.

As tendons cross joints they must slide freely in very restricted quarters. Tendon sheaths are provided to lubricate their passage. To illustrate the structure of a tendon sheath one may wrap a pillow once around a post—the free edges meet on the far side of the post. Consider the surface next to the post as being firmly glued to the post. The tendon sheath is built this way except that it is hollow—not stuffed like the pillow. The inside surface of the resulting closed cavity is lined by a membrane that secretes a substance more viscous than water but not as heavy as oil. As the tendon slides, the slick surface attached to the tendon rubs on the slick unattached surface of the "pillow." This type of stucture is called a synovial membrane and the contained fluid, synovial fluid. Synovial membranes are also found in joint capsules and bursas.

Consider a man who works at his desk all week by day and entertains himself in the evenings with television. Saturday morning he may ambitiously grab a handsaw and set about trimming all the vegetation in the yard. About mid-morning his wrist begins to swell and become sensitive. In an effort to finish the task rapidly he exerts on a high branch when a twinge of pain stops the morning's work abruptly.

It is probably accurate to guess that the unconditioned tendon sheaths of this wrist were stretched beyond their capacity. The delicate synovial membranes become mildly inflamed, to which they responded by an over-production of synovial fluid (swelling). As work progressed the quality of the fluid secreted by the membranes deteriorated; it became abnormal, not especially slick. Tissue debris sloughed into the cavity, and possibly light hemorrhage from overstretched vessels. Now debris and blood clots roughen the passage of the tendon.

The pain that discouraged further labor could well have been caused by a tendon stretching and fraying at its attachment. Unfortunately, this pain will persist.

With this day's labor terminated but the weeks' pent-up energy unexhausted, this same man may turn his thoughts to recreation. He saddles his horse, who has spent an indolent week in the stall. A wild, prolonged canter through the countryside does wonders for the man's spirits, but Sunday morning will quite likely find the wrist of the man and the fetlock joints of the horse in a similar painful, swollen condition.

A similar sequence of events takes place when a joint is sprained except that the onset is usually abrupt, being the result of injury to a ligament of the joint. Since the synovial membrane of the joint capsule is attached to the ligament, it is almost invariably injured, too. While conditioning cannot insure against trauma, it is true that tough conditioned ligaments are less subject to trauma.

Hoof

The structural material of which the hoof is made is called horn (peculiarly, it is never said that horn is made of hoof). The horn of the hoof is of several types; the hoof wall, the sole, the frog and the white line. Each possesses qualities peculiar to itself.

Hoof is manufactured by specialized cells of the skin (corium) which lines the hoof. It is apparent, then, that production of horn is a metabolic process as surely as are digestion, hair growth, or salivation. Growth of healthy hoof reflects the state of health and plane of nutrition of an individual no less than is indicated by a glossy hair coat, pliable skin, mental alertness and other well-recognized criteria.

The point is well illustrated by the ring that may appear on the hoof following a period of fever, indigestion, infected tooth or other circumstance capable of disrupting the state of health or nutrition. The hoof of a foundered foot grows chronically inflamed skin; everyone is familiar with the consequent grooves, ridges, bulges and poor horn quality.

Encircling the upper extremity of the hoof wall and growing down on the surface of the wall for a short distance is a special skin structure called the periople. The function of the periople is to secrete a waxy substance on the surface of the wall. The function of the waxy substance is to retain moisture in the hoof. Microscopically, the wall is not a homogeneous mass of horn, but a mass of closely packed, vertical hollow cylinders. The skin that produces the horn supplies moisture to fill the cylinders, which maintains the texture and strength of the horn. Rasping, nail holes and deep sand are some of the hazards to retention of a waxy seal on the wall. When the seal is lost the horn tends to dry out, become brittle, break and crack.

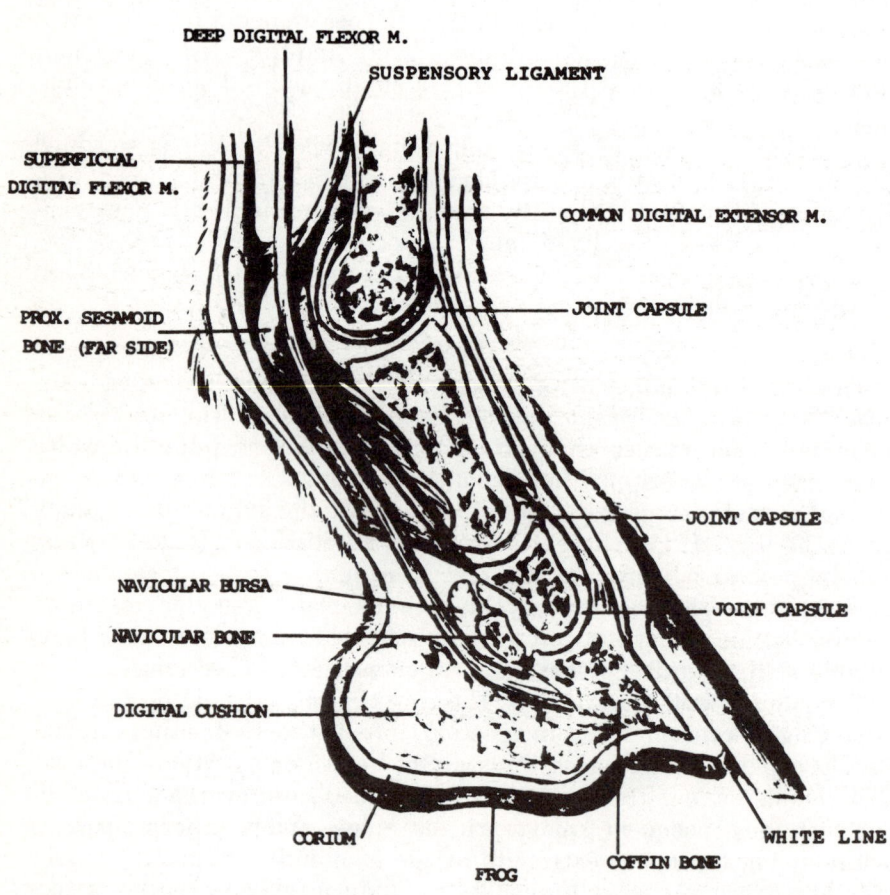

DEEP DIGITAL FLEXOR M.

SUSPENSORY LIGAMENT

SUPERFICIAL DIGITAL FLEXOR M.

COMMON DIGITAL EXTENSOR M.

JOINT CAPSULE

PROX. SESAMOID BONE (FAR SIDE)

JOINT CAPSULE

NAVICULAR BURSA

JOINT CAPSULE

NAVICULAR BONE

DIGITAL CUSHION

CORIUM

FROG

COFFIN BONE

WHITE LINE

Drawings by R. G. Greeley, D.V.M., M.S.

Many ways have been found to replace the lost periopic wax. Home concoctions, such as engine oil and kerosene mixtures, are plentiful. Several commercial products are available for this purpose. The shine and texture linseed oil provides when rubbed on a fine walnut rifle stock promises similar results on hooves. The important thing is that one chooses a material to his liking and uses it conscientiously when needed.

Time is often lost when the care of an animal's feet is delayed until the start of training. Misshapen hooves may have a deleterious effect on the proper development of joints; this is best handled as growth progresses, not when maturity is nearly reached. Too, splayed hooves broken away at the quarters are not receptive to well-fitting shoes when shoes abruptly become necessary.

Circulation

Heart and lung development are as vital to the well-being of the horse's feet as to the maintenance of speed over long distances because the feet require a surprising volume of blood flow. Besides nourishment of the tissues blood flow must maintain warmth in the extremities. At the opposite pole, blood flow must be adequate to dissipate accumulation of heat in the tissues. Pounding concussion, stretching and movement of tendons and ligaments, bone sliding on bone, and turbulence of synovial fluid within joints and tendon sheaths all generate heat.

Horses upon whom great demands are never made may not experience foot ailments, but those of whom strenuous performance is required are vulnerable to many breakdowns. Heat accumulation in active tissues can do much to deteriorate those tissues. Navicular disease, sidebone and other common ailments of horses' feet may often be directly traceable to inadequate circulation.

Blood flows rapidly into the feet and must vacate the feet at an equal rate. An elaborate structure exists to accomplish this. Pressure on the frog is transmitted to a gristly pad (digital cushion) between the heels; the pad, while protecting the inner bones and tendon, exerts pressure on the heels and cartilages of the heels causing them to expand. Concurrently, an amazingly extensive complex of veins is compressed, forcing their contents up the limb. When the internal pressure in the heels is interfered with, circulatory insufficiency is likely to develop.

Pure inactivity can be one cause for slow blood through the feet. When the feet are not alternately picked up and put down the forced return system is inactivated. Nails in the heel inhibit the elasticity and ability of the heels to expand. High heel caulks remove the frog

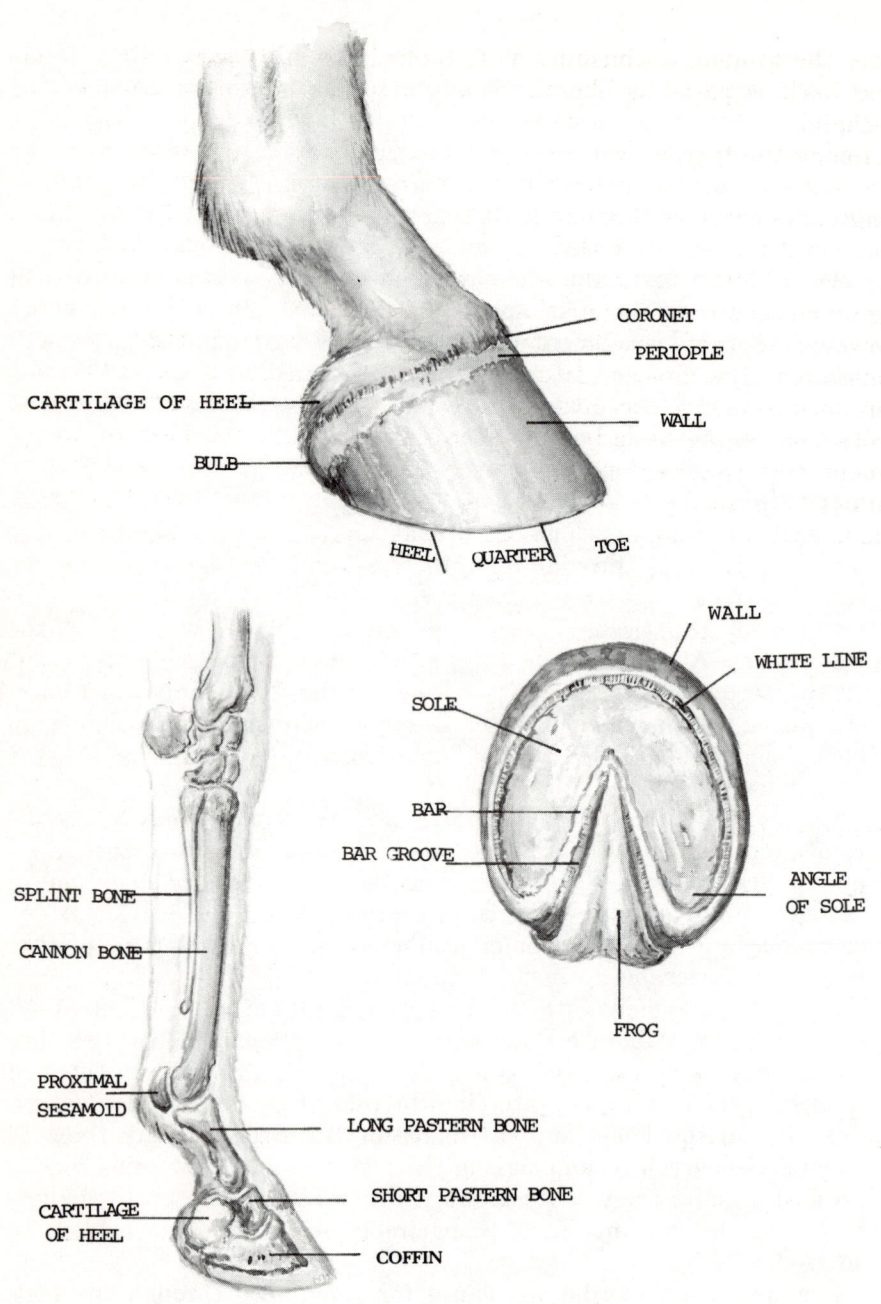

CORONET

PERIOPLE

CARTILAGE OF HEEL

WALL

BULB

HEEL QUARTER TOE

WALL

WHITE LINE

SOLE

BAR

BAR GROOVE

ANGLE OF SOLE

FROG

SPLINT BONE

CANNON BONE

PROXIMAL SESAMOID

LONG PASTERN BONE

SHORT PASTERN BONE

CARTILAGE OF HEEL

COFFIN

Drawings by R. G. Greeley, D.V.M., M.S.

from the ground, diminishing the internal foot pressure. Often the frog itself is pared so liberally that its contact with the ground is negligible.

Among the farriers who shoe running horses it is the rule to part the frog and sole until shiny new horn is exposed. Probably the running horse survives this handicap because at the moment before the foot breaks over, the fetlock is driven close to the ground and the pastern is almost level; the short partern bone puts pressure on the digital cushion from above just as surely as the frog could from below. However, another consequence of this frog and sole trimming must be considered. The distance from the ground to the sensitive, vascular corium has been reduced to a small fraction of an inch. Mechanical protection of the underlying skin isn't much, and the heat of the ground surface plus that generated by the concussion of fast motion cannot help but have an unfavorable effect upon the very skin (corium) itself.

Walter Merrick

(Interview by Barbara Wright)

Walter Merrick has garnered the unique distinction of being the only breeder-owner-trainer in the history of Quarter Horse racing to win two All American Futurities. Easy Jet, in 1969, and his daughter Easy Date, in 1974, are Mr. Merrick's two All American winners. This amazing feat serves to amplify his enormous abilities in all areas of Quarter Horse racing.

Mr. Merrick currently serves as President of the Quarter Racing Owners of America, Inc., on the Board of Directors of the American Quarter Horse Association and also on the AQHA Racing Committee. His numerous accomplishments include being listed by the AQHA as a leading money-earning owner, a leading breeder of money-earning horses, a leading breeder of winners (by both number of wins and winners), a leading money-earning trainer and a leading breeder of Register of Merit qualifiers.

This veteran horseman makes his home on the sprawling 14 Ranch near Sayre, Oklahoma. During his 35 years in the business he has had success after success, unmatched by others. He is widely recognized for his important role in Quarter Horse history, especially in the development and expansion of both the breeding and racing industries. Three Bars, Revenue, Blob Jr., Midnight Jr., Grey Badger II, Tonto Bars Hand, Jet Smooth and Easy Jet are only a few of the many, many notable Quarter Horses Mr. Merrick has owned, leased or trained.

"Conditioning covers a pretty wide field," Walter Merrick explained. "Several things enter into it. You have to get a horse's physical condition to its highest peak using exercise, feed and blood count. Any race horse, to give his peak performance, needs to have a fairly high blood count—this is extremely important and can be achieved by high quality feed and, when necessary, vitamin shots."

When asked if he has a regular conditioning or exercise program for weanlings, Mr. Merrick replied, "No, we always let our foals run out, we don't keep them confined. We like for them to have plenty of exercise so they can learn how to run and take care of themselves. When the foals are still nursing—at about three months of age, or as soon as they begin to eat—we start creep feeding them."

Before being broke, Mr. Merrick's yearlings also run on pasture. "Yearlings have the opportunity for free exercise when they need it, and they do take a lot of exercise. Yearlings will run and play, giving

Walter Merrick, the only breeder-owner-trainer of two All American futurity winners.

themselves about the right amount of exercise—that is, if they are out where they have enough room," he cautioned.

On halter breaking foals Mr. Merrick says, "We try to halter break them when they are weaned, but sometimes don't get around to it quite that quick. We definitely like to have them halter broke before they are a year old."

In answer to a question concerning breaking to saddle, Mr. Merrick said, "Twenty months is the average age for breaking young horses to saddle, but it ranges from 18 to 22 months. Most of the young horses are put right into training at this time." He then explained, "We usually drive a colt for a couple of days before we put a boy on him. This is a gradual way to teach the young horses to get the feel of the bit in their mouths and to learn to handle a little, also they can get used to the saddle on their back at the same time. This method eliminates quite a few problems. As for equipment, we use a light stock saddle and a snaffle bit.

"We always use a light boy when breaking colts," he added, saying, "I personally prefer a boy weighing 120 pounds or less—if possible. Of course, it is always a problem to get light boys. I hardly ever put a man weighing over 130 pounds on a young horse and I'd certainly prefer one weighing 120 pounds!"

When asked if young horses are broke to saddle in groups or separately, Mr. Merrick replied, "We handle them individually, but usually work with five or six yearlings at the same time. However, they all get individual care and training, but I can't really tell much difference in the way colts and fillies handle or train at this early point. Sometimes when a colt gets older though, you have to change your tactics a little bit."

At this stage in the conditioning process Mr. Merrick's young horses are ridden in pastures. "We like for them to have pasture experience. In other words, we ride them out through the pastures here quite a bit and get them handling fairly well. We don't put a neck rein on the horses, but they are ridden enough to learn how to travel out across the country and also learn to easily guide and stop. When young horses reach this point we start galloping them on the racetrack."

All young horses' knees are X-rayed before they go into training on Mr. Merrick's ranch. "But we will go ahead with a colt to a certain extent if he has a B knee. We put him into light training, but you certainly need to be careful with one before his knees are closed. For example, you wouldn't want to set the horse down and let him work really hard until you are positive that those knees are solid. I don't think light training such as slow gallops will damage one."

Mr. Merrick was asked about the initial racetrack work for young

Easy Date just after winning the 1974 All American Futurity.

horses and replied, "We usually gallop a colt about half a mile a day, a half a mile at one time. However, we alternate walking one day and galloping the next day. Sometimes certain colts will need more galloping. In fact, each horse in training is a little bit different—you can't set a pattern on a group of colts and follow through exactly with it. Some will just naturally require more training than others. For example, a tougher colt will demand more training and exercise."

During the conditioning program, "A half a mile is about the maximum amount we gallop a horse. Again, some colts may need to be galloped three-quarters, but half a mile is the average figure for us." Mr. Merrick commented, "Many people will put more galloping than that in young horses, but we've had a pretty successful program with this amount of galloping. We often jog; what we call a jog is a long trot, about a half-mile first and then let the horse go into a gallop for another half a mile."

After the young horses have had about sixty days of galloping, breezes are initiated into the program. Concerning physical preparation of young horses for breezing Mr. Merrick says, "A colt has to be tightened up, have his muscles tight and be well conditioned before you start breezing him. If not, you are apt to hurt him. It's very easy to pull a muscle or shin buck a young horse. Many times a colt will get body sore, especially if he isn't up to the work. I firmly believe in putting plenty of slow work into a colt before he is ever set down and breezed. In addition, these horses are never breezed more than once a week."

Other special precautions to prevent training injuries include frequent use of a turbolator, plus several different kinds of tighteners and bandages. "After a leg has been rubbed down well with tightener, it is bandaged and left for 12 hours. This practice and the turbolator with ice and epsom salts are all we use," he explained, then added, "I have had very good luck with the turbolator and use it often."

When asked how he gets young horses accustomed to being around other horses, such as in a race, Mr. Merrick replied, "That doesn't seem to be much of a problem if you allow them to run together in the paddock before they go into training. They get used to other horses and don't mind being around others. This is one of the major reasons we don't separate our yearlings. We do separate the colts and fillies, but they all run in groups in paddocks. I firmly believe this helps a great deal in that the young horses learn to protect themselves and be around other horses."

In order to accustom young horses to the starting gate Mr. Merrick's operation keeps the gates on the tracks and rides the colts through them every day during their routine work. "When they are getting ready to run, we stop and stand them in the gates for short periods. Also, we usually make a little bit of noise by slamming the gates to get them accustomed to the noise and motion. The first several times we break them from an open gate. At this stage they are getting eager to run and will simply break out and run the best they can. Before his first race, a young horse will average about six trips out of the gate."

Getting a young horse used to crowds is often a problem, Mr. Merrick said. But he added that "We have a little track in town here and it is pretty good to get one acquainted with the crowd."

As to the time for entering a young horse in his first race Mr. Merrick commented, "I don't like to run a colt before he is 24 to 26 months old at the minimum, and prefer that they be 30 months old. Some of the futurities are so early now that it's hard to stay off them that long. In fact, there are some yearling futurities across the country which I am definitely against.

"If you are going to run in those early futurities, you have to prepare young horses earlier, but if people would just leave them alone until they are 30 months old we certainly would have a lot more sound horses.

"If a horse is started as a two-year-old, naturally he's more likely to break down. In the past I've had a few horses that weren't raced at all as two-year-olds and they came on to make some of our best horses as three-year-olds. But, if a horse is handled properly as a two, I believe he'll be as good as a three-year-old as he will anytime in his life."

According to Mr. Merrick, the amount of Thoroughbred blood a horse has doesn't make any great difference in the kind of conditioning he requires. "For instance, Easy Jet is $7/8$ths Thoroughbred and Jet Smooth, too, but there were no problems at all. We trained them exactly as we do an average Quarter Horse." However, he further remarked, that "Possibly they have a little more desire to run and pick it up a little quicker."

"I believe the breeding is more important than the conditioning, but you need to put the two together to be successful and develop a good colt," Mr. Merrick observed when asked which has the greatest influence on the ability of a horse. "They really go hand in hand," he said, adding "You can take the best colt in the world and if he isn't conditioned right he won't perform well. On the other hand, if he doesn't have the right breeding he won't do well either."

Mr. Merrick was asked what conditioning measures can be used to get the most speed from a horse. He laughed and said, "Well, that's kind of a tough question—the procedures I've described are my idea. I've been around the tracks for years and it seems like there aren't many trainers who train alike. Even though they all do it different, they all win races, so it's hard to establish a permanent, solid training program. Different trainers, using different practices, all have a certain amount of success—you can't really say that any way is the best way."

On building desire to run Mr. Merrick said, "After about the second time out of the gate our colts naturally have the desire to run. Any colt, if he has the proper bloodlines, will come to it at about that point. Once in a while a colt that doesn't have strong race breeding might be a little 'dead-headed'—possibly he won't have much desire until after he has run some, but our colts generally come around pretty fast."

At the time of this interview, Mr. Merrick's filly, Easy Date, had recently won the 1974 All American Futurity with the unique distinction of being the only All American winner sired by a previous winner. Easy Jet, winner of the 1969 All American Futurity, is also owned by Mr. Merrick, so the logical question was, "As young running prospects, were Easy Date and Easy Jet similar?"

"They were a good deal alike," Mr. Merrick remarked. "However, Easy Jet was a little more hard to manage than a filly would be. He didn't have any bad habits. Easy Jet felt so good all the time, he was more aggressive than Easy Date. He was just jumping, bouncing and playing all the time. Easy Date is quieter in that respect, she doesn't play quite as much as he did.

"Other than natural aggressiveness, their training habits were very much the same. Of course, Easy Date hasn't run near as much as Easy Jet did when he was a two-year-old. Easy Jet started running in January of his two-year-old year and didn't quit until December—he ran nearly a full year. I don't think there is one horse in a thousand that would stand the training and take as much racing as Easy Jet did as a two. In fact, I believe we ran him 26 times when he was two and that's a lot of running for any two-year-old. We came along quite a bit slower with Easy Date and didn't try to peak her out until All American time, around the first of September."

Mr. Merrick was then asked how long it takes to tell that you have a really superior prospect and he replied, "It usually takes about 90 days in training, but it didn't take us that long with Easy Jet. He came around quicker than most colts do and by the second time we worked him we knew that he was really a runner.

"Easy Date developed slower, we really didn't know that she was a top filly until she ran in the Kindergarten Stakes in California. That day she beat a real good field of colts and we felt like we had a real runner then.

"We start our two-year-olds slower than our other horses," Mr. Mer-

Easy Jet, winner of the 1969 All American Futurity and sire of Easy Date, the 1974 All American Futurity winner. Both were bred, owned and trained by Walter Merrick.

rick said as the interview turned to conditioning older horses. "I believe older horses need more exercise than younger ones do to stay in condition. The older horses are better developed—their bones are set and they aren't apt to sore up. They might need to be galloped as far as a mile, a slow gallop. As I explained before, we gallop every other day, alternating walking with galloping. Our stable is split up, with half of the horses in training galloping one day and the other half the next day.

I haven't used a mechanical walker much," he answered when questioned about the walking sessions. "I try to stay away from them as much as I can because I've had some bad luck with one. They are good labor-saving devices, but aren't as safe as they could be for a high-priced colt. I just don't like to take the chance of putting one on a walker."

When asked about specific amounts of exercise for older horses, Mr. Merrick replied, "it depends a great deal on how often you run the horse. In the later part of the year, if you have been running a horse quite a bit during the season, he will more or less run himself in shape and won't need any increase in work. But, if one isn't running very often, he will need increased amounts of exercise.

"When a horse isn't getting enough exercise he has a tendency to fill up. You can look at a horse and tell if he needs more work—his muscles aren't hard and tight. Horses will also let you know if they aren't getting enough exercise—they become listless and tired looking."

Mr. Merrick was asked what he thinks about swimming as a conditioning technique and recounted this experience. "I had a two-year-old with sore ankles and we couldn't put the proper amount of track work in him. We swam this horse quite a bit. If a horse has sore legs, you can get the proper amount of work in one with swimming instead of galloping. But you have to build up to it." He cautioned, "For example, the swimming pool we used at Ruidoso was circular, 50 feet across. The first time or two, once or twice around the pool is enough. A horse has to be watched closely and taken out when he begins to tire. After several sessions, the horse usually builds up the endurance to go around the pool eight to ten times.

"I wouldn't recommend swimming for a sound horse, you can get them more physically fit by regular exercise. But, for sore horses, swimming can keep the weight off their backs and still give them fairly good exercise."

Under Mr. Merrick's supervision, stallions, mares and geldings all receive about the same amount of exercise. He hasn't found that the sex of a horse makes nearly as much difference as the individuality of the horse. When asked how long one can expect a running horse to stay sound, he commented, "That varies quite a bit depending upon the horse, the care they've had, and luck. Bad luck can knock you out in just a minute, but if a person is careful and lucky with a horse there is no reason why the horse shouldn't stay sound until he is eight or ten years old."

Mr. Merrick added that he has not had a problem with horses developing bad habits, but that natural nervousness can be a problem. "You can use Vitamin B_1 to calm a horse and this is used quite a bit at the track, but we don't have much trouble with nervousness. I have had a few horses that would 'wash out in the paddock'—that is, in the paddock before a race they would become nervous and begin to sweat. To help, a vet can give the horse an injection of Vitamin B_1 the night before the race and this usually takes care of the problem.

"We have had a few horses that were extremely nervous in the stall and had success putting a goat in the stall with them. In most cases the horse takes up with the goat and settles right down."

When asked if he takes special efforts to keep people away from his horses in the barn area at the tracks he said, "I like to keep the crowds away to let the horses rest as much as possible. I don't like a lot of noise in the barn area."

To warm up before a race, Mr. Merrick's horses usually work "three-eighths of a mile, with an eighth of that at a two-minute clip and a slow gallop for the other."

As for equipment during a race, he said, "I make a practice of using the minimum amount of equipment. Some horses go to the track with a shadow roll, blinkers and everything else that can be put on one, but I believe you are better off using the least amount possible. However, quite a few of our two-year-olds run in blinkers because they don't see quite as much and tend to be less nervous about the crowd. A nose band, D-bit and French blinkers make up the main equipment we use. With some horses it is necessary to use a breast harness to keep the saddle in place, but I have never had one like that.

"Depending upon the horse, we might tie one's tail up on a muddy track. When it is muddy the horse's tail should be braided and taped up if it is long enough to get wrapped around his legs. But, most of our horses have fairly short tails and it really presents no problem."

Mr. Merrick's horses are given a bath with warm water first thing after a race. After the bath, the horses are rubbed down with alcohol, walked for an hour and put into the turbolator for 35 to 40 minutes. "Sometimes we do their legs up that night and in other cases we wait until the next morning, but I have found that it is a good practice to go right into the turbolator with them after they run. It takes any heat or soreness out of the leg.

"If a horse is having any kind of leg problems we many times use cold water bandages. After a race we bathe the horse and then cool him out in the cold water bandages. In some cases the bandages are used before a race and kept on for five or six hours before he runs."

Mr. Merrick commented that he prefers a blister to firing a horse's legs. "I believe you get the same results if you stay off the horse long enough to allow him to heal properly," he explained. "The time element is the big factor and I like to stay off one at least six weeks. Some trainers go back to work with one much quicker, but I believe that they are defeating their purpose.

"You bring a horse back the same way a new colt is started," he said. "Begin with slow gallops and gradually build up, galloping a little farther each time. The proper feed, vitamins and conditioning are very important."

For the type of horse that doesn't have enough wind Mr. Merrick recommended not to run him until he gets more work in him—"the proper amount of work and exercise will develop the wind."

On lengthy trips Mr. Merrick follows the practice of making rest stops every five to six hours to allow the horses to walk around and relax. Also, he makes certain that they are fed lightly in an effort to prevent one from going off his feed. The altitude change on trips can be a problem, so Mr. Merrick explained his solution.

"After going from a low altitude to a high altitude we put the horses on oxygen for 20 minutes each day. A plastic muzzle, attached to an oxygen bottle by a long tube, fastens to the horse's halter allowing it to breathe the oxygen. It takes 30 to 40 days for the horse to get acclimated," he commented. "horses adjust to a low altitude much sooner, usually within two or three weeks, but the thinner air at a higher altitude is quite a shock for the horse."

Mr. Merrick describes his method for "letting a horse down" as follows: "We have small runs, about 90 feet by 20 feet, and walk the horses for an hour before turning them loose in the runs. If horses don't show excessive nervousness and energy, they will 'let themselves down' in this small area. In the situation where a horse runs too much, he is put in a stall every night for a week and walked by hand during the day, before being turned out in the run. Naturally, some horses are more of a problem to let down than others."

Concerning breeding animals, Mr. Merrick's broodmares have constant opportunity for free exercise. "The broodmares run in large pastures year round, usually 20 mares per pasture (300 to 400 acres per pasture). All of the mares foal in stalls, with a man there all the time. There is just less danger of losing a foal, so we like to be there when a mare foals and lend a hand if needed. I firmly believe that being on hand at the time of foaling saves quite a few foals.

"Usually, a mare with a strong, healthy foal is turned back out the first day after foaling. However, if the foal is a little weak, they are kept up until the foal is strong enough to travel well—usually three or four days."

Conditioning and exercise programs for Mr. Merrick's stallions are similar during the breeding season and the off season. He explained, "Every stallion is provided with a paddock; they are put in the paddocks every morning and back into the stalls at night. The stallions exercise themselves with this free exercise. I know of people who do ride their stallions, and gallop them some, but our horses seem to take their own exercise."

When asked if he employs special practices to keep older breeding animals in good condition, Mr. Merrick said, "We don't have too many old mares, but those we do have require special care such as ground feed and extra feed. Also, some of these mares are timid and won't get their fair share of feed, so we have to 'baby' them a little.

"We don't have any old studs," Mr. Merrick added and then quietly related, "I did have Three Bars a few years ago. In fact, he died here. We did everything in the world for him that we thought might help. For example, we fed him ground feed all the time plus lots of raw eggs in his feed at night—anything we thought might help, he got. He was 28 when he died."

Concerning feeding, Mr. Merrick stated, "Our race horses, of course, are fed individually, three times a day. At night they get what we call a hot mash. It is a mixture of oats, sweet feed, bran and several different kinds of vitamins. The oats are cooked for three hours and mixed with the rest of the feed. Each horse is fed about three and one-half gallons of this hot mash. In the morning and at noon they are fed three quarts of dry oats. The stallions are fed in the same way as our runners."

Explaining that the quality of the native pasture varies with the season of the year and becomes especially dry in the hot summer, he said, "We feed the broodmares quite a bit in the summer and then don't feed as heavy when the pastures are good—usually in early spring and fall. The creep feed for the colts is a half and half mixture of oats and sweet feed, with vitamins added."

As to the type of hay he prefers, Mr. Merrick said, "We feed more alfalfa than most breeders do, but I've found that we have very good results with it. In this country we are fortunate enough to have especially good alfalfa. In some situations we use Oklahoma prairie hay, but feed alfalfa basically. I don't put much emphasis on which cutting the alfalfa is—the way the hay is put up is extremely important. Many people have a tendency to bale it too green and this certainly is bad for horse feed. The alfalfa needs to cure properly and be baled when there is just enough dampness to hold the leaves on. If a bale contains any mold or dark hay it cannot be fed."

In answer to a question about health practices, Mr. Merrick said, "This is dry country and we don't have a very large parasite problem. We do worm twice a year, by tubing, but there just isn't enough rain to create a very big parasite problem. With our horses at the track, fecal exams are used periodically to check for specific parasite problems. Also, once a month blood tests are taken. Hemoglobin is the main factor we check.

"As for trimming and shoeing, our foals in pasture usually don't need trimming until they are halter broken." Mr. Merrick explained that at this time a regular program of trimming every 30 to 40 days is initiated. The young horses are first shod about the time they go into training, with shoes being re-set every four weeks. Broodmares in pasture are also trimmed regularly, at 60 day intervals.

Mr. Merrick explained his grooming routine. "15 to 20 minutes is spent grooming a horse each day. We use a soft brush and rub rag—what we call a rub rag is a large rag that resembles a face towel. The rag takes all the dust off and puts the shine to their hair. In the spring, when a horse is shedding, we do use a rubber curry comb because it helps pull the hair and slip one off a little faster.

"We pull a mane and tail—take a half a dozen hairs at a time and wrap them around your comb, then pull them out. After the mane is thinned properly you can pull the ends to even it, and it will look pretty nice.

"Every day we use a hoof dressing to keep the horse's hooves soft and flexible, but we rarely use a coat dressing.

"We don't follow the practice of clipping horses all over. Years ago if I had the race horses here in this cool country and went to a warm place like south Texas or California, I would clip them, but I haven't done it lately."

For an adequate stall size, Mr. Merrick advised, "Twelve by twelve feet, or larger. I believe a stall could be 20 by 20 feet, if you could afford it. With a larger stall the bedding is the worst drawback—it takes so much. Wheat straw is the type of bedding used here and our stalls are cleaned and re-bedded every morning.

"We use both solid stall walls and those with spaces between so horses can see each other. In some cases, if a horse is put in a stall where he can't see other horses he will fret and get nervous, but I don't believe it's a big thing. Most horses will become accustomed to being by themselves within a few days."

Mr. Merrick recommends one helper for every three horses. When asked what qualities he looks for in help, Mr. Merrick smiled and replied, "Oh boy, that's a problem! In the horse business, especially, it's extremely difficult to get experienced help. Today quite a few people are using girls—it seems like the girls just take a bigger interest in it than the boys do and you see quite a few girl grooms around the racetracks.

"I haven't worked many girls, but really think they make a better groom than a boy does," he commented, "because girls take more interest in the horses, are easier with the horses and are more particular about keeping the equipment cleaned up. As for hiring help, if a person is inexperienced but responsible and willing to learn, I'd have quite a bit of patience with him and try to teach him what he needs to know."

In summary, Walter Merrick's horses are provided with ample opportunity for free exercise when not in training. Young horses and broodmares are kept in large, safe pastures with feed made available. Stallions are provided with individual paddocks and allowed to exercise at will.

While in training, individualized conditioning schedules are devised to meet the needs of each horse. High quality feeding programs and health practices are followed, again designed for the environment and particular performance situation of the horse.

Elliott Burch

(Interview by Mary Jane Gallaher)

Elliott Burch, head of Paul Mellon's Rokeby Stables, has achieved unprecedented success in the Thoroughbred business. His credentials include four Horse-of-the-Year Champions: Sword Dancer (1959), Bowl Of Flowers (1961), Arts And Letters (1969) and Fort Marcy (1970).

Burch is the grandson of Hall of Fame trainer William Preston Burch and the son of Preston Burch, a famous equine conditioner. Preston Burch headed Brookmeade Stables until his retirement in 1957. Having understudied his father there after college, Elliott assumed command for a short time. Then in 1962 he went to the Rokeby Stables in New York.

Burch is considered by turf experts to be the best modern day conditioner of horses that excel at one and one-half miles (considered the true classic distance). The Belmont Stakes, third leg of the Triple Crown, is America's showcase in that respect.

Burch has captured three Belmont trophies, meeting Sword Dancer, Quadrangle and Arts And Letters in the winner's circle after their fields crossed the finish line.

It is Louisville's Kentucky Derby, however, that has always presented the greatest difficulty to Burch. The same three that triumphed in the Belmont under his handling let him down in the famed "Run For The Roses."

As a Thoroughbred trainer, Burch is a strong believer in racing two-year-olds, if they are mature.

"Many of my father's best horses were started at two in three-eighths of a mile baby races. Most of them lasted through more racing years than the average horse. Fillies in particular are more precocious than colts. If a colt is big and promising, you don't start him early in the year. But nature often takes care of that because he's usually a big green dummy.

"My two-year-olds often start in July. Even if you just get one race in them at two, it is a big help as it shows them what racing is all about. In New York, two-year-olds usually come to hand in August during the Saratoga meeting.

"Key To The Mint is a good example. At two he looked like three; at three, like four. He made ten starts at two, three of them in stakes.

Elliott Burch (left) shown with Paul Mellon, owner of Rokeby Stables, for whom Burch has trained some of this country's most notable Thoroughbreds.

Midway of a horse's two-year-old season you should have a pretty good idea of his racing ability."

In training, Burch determines how a horse is doing by his eating habits, his coat condition and his attitude. In like manner, Burch says a horse will tell you when he is ready to run.

"I'd rather train them into condition than race them into shape. Every horse needs not only individual but constant attention to his work program. Fillies don't take as much work as colts, light geldings don't need as much as stud colts. Two-year-olds often require more work than older horses. Older horses need less and less, then tend to get sour if they are honed too hard. The most important thing with older horses is getting them to a peak, then holding them there. Two-year-olds are the most honest; older horses tend to cheat. After awhile they figure out that they don't have to run their heart out every time they race.

"One thing I don't want is a horse that's too intelligent. If they have too much smartness about them, they figure, 'To hell with you, I'm going to run when I feel like it.'

"Lots of horses require a great deal of work. You simply find out by trial and error. For instance, I realized afterwards that I, and I alone, was responsible for Key To The Mint's terrible race in the Belmont Stakes. (Ed.: Riva Ridge was a seven-length winner; Key To The Mint placed fourth, beaten by 13 lengths.)

"I made a bad mistake in hooking another horse in with him before the Belmont and he just went so fast he had nothing left for the race.

"Each horse is different as to his exercise needs before he is to run. Some want a light blow-out the morning of the race. Some may need this work a week before they run. With others, if you plan to run on Saturday, try to give them a light work-out on Wednesday.

"If a horse comes back from the track blowing, you know he is not fit and that you must work him until he is fit. If he's lighting up on you, I back off on exercise until I find out why. If he shows lameness, slow down until you find out the trouble source. Some fillies you can walk, then just blow-out and run.

"I believe a horse actually peaks at the end of his three-year-old season, just as he turns four. He should hold that form about a year. There are, of course, exceptions to every rule."

When asked if young horses are disturbed by the racetrack noises, Burch commented, "When it comes to distractions such as crowd noises, I find they aren't really bothered by it. I usually take them to the paddock several times and go through the whole pre-race routine there except for saddling. You can stuff their ears with cotton which makes a dramatic difference (also can be used if a horse objects to being clipped). Most horses are so busy running, they don't pay attention to the crowd. I think the Kentucky Derby with its hordes of people, all that hoopla plus a closed paddock, is the worst experience for a horse."

Burch believes that the New York system of stabling at Belmont, then vanning to Aqueduct to run, often unsettles horses. As he says, "You have to remember that every race is a new experience for a horse. For all the above reasons, we try to keep it as quiet around our barns as is possible—I don't want any yelling around. Also, I send horses that are to run that day to the track early so they can get through their exercise and relax. I also cut their rations back the night before, mainly hay, as nearly all of them will overeat if given a chance.

"I use different methods when a horse is to leave my barn to go elsewhere, whether it's when we move the stable to Florida, or send a horse to Mr. Mellon's farm in Virginia for rest or treatment.

"The biggest change is to take a horse from New York to California to run. The best plan is to ship in, run, ship right out. If he has to stay, it will take him a month or more to get acclimated. The reverse does not seem to work shipping West to East.

"I think if you plan to point for France's Arc de Triomphe, you'd ship right after the Belmont Stakes, go over and let him get used to the water and the different style of running. If possible, if a horse is to ship a lot, put him on bottled water and take your own hay. Oats are fairly consistent throughout the country but hay is not."

With today's strenuous racing and with tracks wanting only horses ready-to-run using stall space, large stables such as Rokeby shuttle horses back and forth to its Virginia farm almost on a commuter basis. Consequently, a whole new concept has come into being for turning out and/or sending home for repairs. Since Rokeby is one of the largest stables in New York, Burch is in a position to have definite ideas on that subject.

"If I send a horse to the farm, the ideal way to prepare him is to gradually decrease his exercise. Sometimes they're too lame even to do this. It really takes from three weeks to a month to unwind a horse.

"Once at Rokeby, they are first turned out in a very small paddock so they have no opportunity to rip and run. When the horse is back in light training at the farm, I don't mind him being jogged or ridden. When it comes to any strenuous work under saddle, as breezing, I prefer it to be done under supervision. If the horse is turned out, I caution the farm people not to let him get too fat. Trying to get that fat off when I get him back often causes him to break down.

"When a horse comes back to me after a lay-off, what I do depends on how long he's been away. I usually begin training him from scratch using short gallops that get longer and longer, slow works which are gradually quickened. If he's been gone six months, it likely will take two months to get him fit again. And then he'll probably have to run two or three times before he returns to his best form."

Rokeby representatives, like most others of the New York racing fraternity, and like all professional athletes, are much in the hands of medical men. Since soundness plays such an important role in the Thoroughbred racing game, Burch spends many hours trying in humpty-dumpty fashion to put his blue-blooded charges back together again. His vast experience gives him a special insight into what veterinary medicine can and cannot do.

"We X-ray all the knees of our young horses so as to find those that are 'open' and those that are mature and filled in. The veterinarian grades them on a A-B-C basis—this year we were pleased to find only one C."

In answer to many of the more frequent questions aimed at trainers concerning horse conditioning, Burch cited the following practices:

"After a race, we get all the sweat out of a horse's coat by washing him, then he is walked at least an hour. I know he is completely cooled out when he stops blowing and drinking water. We never put a horse away wet. I prefer hand-walking to a mechanical hot-walker. I think the machine can get a horse hurt and by hand you can control the amount of water he drinks.

"After a horse has run, we use a good brace on his legs, and likely bandage him. Every time one of my horses races, his feet are packed with mud to take away the sting of running. Sometimes feet get so bad they have to be packed every day. In any case, we often X-ray to make sure there's no trouble.

"In feeding, I would if I could, feed straight clover hay. As it is, my hay is about 75% clover. If I have a fat horse, I put him on timothy which tastes good but contains less nutrition. If I get a horse that's eating his bedding, I change to shavings or something else inedible.

"When it comes to feeding, if you don't know about nutrition, get a nutritionist to check to see what your horses need. I do use supplements but am not sure of their effects—I suspect that people who use many supplements are trying to compensate for lack of minerals in a horse. By the time a horse is in serious training, there is no putting in minerals that should be there in the first place.

"We give vitamin shots, have blood tests made regularly and check for worms about every six weeks. Some horses never have worms, others do every time we test. I leave this to our veterinarian but I don't use the same worm treatment each time and we worm only when necessary.

"As to legs and feet, time is the best cure of all. With a horse with sore shins, we blister after the heat is gone from his legs. If we're going to severely blister shins, knees or ankles, we send them to the farm as time is the major factor.

"A bowed tendon needs time for nature to heal it. If you can give a horse a year or even two, he will come back, but there's always the chance he'll re-bow.

"I don't believe in firing. I think it's barbaric. I've only fired one shin in all the time I've been training. The only firing I approve of is for a splint—I think it will kill its growth.

"As to windiness in a horse, there is no way I know of to cure this—long gallops will help develop strong wind.

"When it comes to swimming your horses, I believe as my father always told me that swimming and jumping are natural to the horse, but I do not use it as I think it requires a different set of muscles. It seems likely to me that you may be building up the wrong muscles for racing.

"Bad habits are trainers' bugaboos. Once a horse gets a bad habit, it's hell to break him of it. They so often pick up such things as poor gate behavior, lugging in or bearing out, from bad riders. Many times they've been cut in the mouth, they'll lug in or bear out—a bit should not be used again until the place has healed. I don't think exercise per se causes these troubles. I know a horse may get high on himself and hurt himself. This is where exercise helps.

"A change of equipment often helps. Sometimes I use a more severe bit. Blinkers will help keep a horse's mind on his business—many are so curious they want to see everything going on around them. I use a shadow roll during training hours and in the afternoons, too. Shadow rolls not only keep them from seeing too much, but help keep dirt out of their faces. I believe 80% of race horses hate dirt in their eyes and faces.

"Sometimes habits are so bad you just have to turn them out, then start training them all over.

"As to clipping, some horses have thin hair and don't need it; the others I clip all over when we ship to Florida; if we van them, I clip under the legs and belly. If we go by air, I wait until we get South to do it.

"We keep a shoeing list—horses in active training should be shod every three weeks. As to bandages, we mostly use them to prevent a horse from running down. The abrasions caused by contact with the track are one of the sorest things for a horse. We don't use run-down bandages on first-time starters but we can usually tell if they're going to 'run-down' when they come back. Give the sore places plenty of time to heal and don't run a horse with this tendency on an 'off' track.

"As for stable management, I like stalls 12 feet by 12 feet and the walls 8 feet high. This gives a horse plenty of room to move around freely—and I like windows between stalls so horses can see each other.

"We clean and re-bed every day while horses are out at work. The stall is 'picked up' again in the afternoon—a dirty stall promotes disease.

"I allot three horses per groom and three per exercise boy. That's the most a man can handle efficiently, but they can do four or five if they have to. When I hire, I put horsemanship first, then cleanliness, sobriety, and kindness to horses. A groom or rider should like horses and like what he's doing. I don't want my horses abused.

"The main quality you look for in a race horse is heart which is something you can't tell about until you've raced him a few times. He may win a maiden race easily, but then you put him with better stock and you can't find him.

"I make it a practice never to get high on a horse until he shows grit and determination. A good jockey can usually tell you if he has the will he needs to win."

Peter F. Haynes
D.V.M., M.S.

Studying at Colorado State University and the University of Minnesota, Dr. Peter F. Haynes established himself as one of the country's leading veterinarians. "Adaptive Physiologic Changes of Horses in Training," his masters thesis, provides a firm foundation for his authority in the field of equine conditioning.

Dr. Haynes, born in Honolulu in 1944, grew up in the Hawaiian Islands where his family raised and bred horses for pleasure. During this time the Haynes family was involved in most horse related activities including equestrian sports and showing horses.

After graduation Dr. Haynes specialized in equine medicine and surgery, although he has been involved in nearly all areas of equine practice. Research on race-training in Thoroughbred horses has been a major concern of his. Currently, Dr. Haynes is an Assistant Professor of Veterinary Surgery at the School of Veterinary Medicine, Louisiana State University.

*Instead of the interview format, Dr. Haynes chose to contribute in-depth discussions of specific topics of his selection. Because of personal experience and comprehensive studies in these areas of conditioning, Dr. Haynes felt that this type of answer would be most helpful to **Conditioning To Win** readers.*

Miscellaneous Notes on Equine Conditioning

by

Peter F. Haynes

Heritability, or the "genetic pool", plays a very important role in an animal's success, and here I refer to athletic success or potential. We all know that the product of two champions does not necessarily lead to a champion, however, the chances are certainly a lot better.

Heritability will account for conformation, body size, the proper musculo-skeletal system conducive to speed, coordination and the "desire to win" that some horses have. Thereafter, the success of the animal is a man-made quality and the role of proper conditioning techniques cannot be over-emphasized.

Dr. John Faulkner of the University of Michigan once related the following comparison: During the last 50 years human athletes have improved their ability to run by some 10 to 15 per cent in given Olympic events while the equine athlete has improved its ability less than five per cent.

Human athletes are not selectively bred on the basis of performance. On the other hand, intense breeding programs would appear to provide the equine racing industry with a highly selected athlete.

Why then have the human athletes increased their ability to perform? Proper conditioning programs would appear to be the single most important factor.

Management of Young Horses

Prior to weaning, colts should be halter-broken. The earlier this is done the better, for it greatly facilitates later handling of the young animal. Traditionally, foals are grouped at weaning time according to age and, on occasion, sex, if the facilities permit.

A specific conditioning or exercise program is usually not necessary as long as these foals have adequate room to exercise in a large and safe pasture. I would think that most foals, as playful and energetic as they are during this time, would self-exercise at least four or five miles per day if the confinement area is large enough. This would far exceed the economics of a structured exercise program. In cold climates, it may be beneficial to stable foals at night and turn them out in the day for their self-exercise.

The weaning of foals is quite stressful and typically a time when they are affected with upper respiratory disease. To minimize disease conditions during this period it is most beneficial to vaccinate foals prior to weaning.

Newborn foals are given immunity through the colostrum or "first milk" of the mare. The protection that foals obtain from the colostrum is termed passive immunity. This means that the foal receives antibodies from the dam for protection against diseases to which the dam is immune.

With this in mind, it is necessary to maintain a mare's immune status as current as possible prior to foaling (especially tetanus and encephalitis), so that these antibodies will be imparted to the foal. The life of these passive antibodies is somewhat questionable, so the preferred practice is to vaccinate foals at a young age.

Thereby, they may build up their own protection against common disease entities. The vaccination program can start as early as three weeks of age and should include the following biological products ad-

Dr. Peter F. Haynes, a leading authority in the field of equine conditioning.

ministered at intervals recommended by the manufacturer:

Streptococcus equi bacterin (strangles)
Equine Influenza Vaccine
Equine Rhino-pneumonitis Vaccine
Tetanus Toxoid
Encephalitis (sleeping sickness) Vaccine

Dr. Marvin Beeman and associates in Littleton, Colorado have used this program for a number of years and our experience at Colorado State University agreed with the beneficial results of vaccinating foals at an early age. By no means does it eliminate upper respiratory disease in the weanling, but does greatly reduce the clinical picture and make it a lot less stressful on the animal.

A conscientious parasite control program should be begun when foals are 60 to 90 days old. Emphasis should be placed on control of both roundworms (Ascarids) and bloodworms (Strongyles). Depending upon the time of the year, Bots should also be considered. Routine administration of anthelmintics (deworming medication) should be done at 60 day intervals.

For the yearling, the same routine health program, including parasite control and boostering the vaccination series, should be carried on. Yearlings also should be given the opportunity to self-exercise.

One factor that obviously determines whether a long yearling will be trained or not is when the animal is going to be raced as a two-year-old. If economically feasible, I feel that two training periods should be conducted prior to racing in the two-year-old year.

The first, 45 to 60 days of riding, should start during the fall. By no means are these horses worked hard—only give them an early feeling of race track galloping. After this session, a turnout of two to three months should occur prior to the start of full-fledged training. This allows the horse a self-exercising and non-stressed growth period that presents a better candidate to the pre-race training to follow.

As to the subject to racing two-year-olds, if one looks at the statistics involving two-year-olds that remain sound throughout their two-year-old year, fewer horses would be raced at this age. There is no doubt that some horses are extremely successful and remain very sound during two-year-old racing. However, the percentage of breakdowns is far higher for this age group than it is during subsequent years. These breakdowns are extremely costly to the equine racing industry—both time and money are lost when an animal is injured and has to be laid up. Some horses are more suited to racing at this age than others, but identification of these animals is not a simple task.

Radiography of the distal radial epiphysis ("X-raying knees") in yearlings and early two-year-olds, I think, is a very good practice. The philosophy behind this is to determine when a youngster is "skeletally mature". The radiographic determination is relatively simple. This growth is a very dynamic and progressive process until the epiphyseal line is completely closed. Therefore, when we grade these animals A (closed), B (closing) or C (open), the division between these categories has to cover quite a large range.

Understandably, people get over-anxious because of the time and money involved in training these young horses and have a tendency to work them too hard, too fast and too young. If one refrains from heavy race-training until the animal's epiphysis has closed, the chances of breakdown are markedly reduced.

Obviously, this delays the onset of hard work until the horse is older, thereby reducing injuries related to immaturity. Those who try to speed up the maturation process by dietary and horomonal measures are doing an injustice to the individual. I prefer to let nature take its course and decide for us when this animal is ready for intense work.

I feel that trimming the feet of young horses is a routine part of their care. Under ideal circumstances, it would be best to trim at sixty day intervals starting when the foal is three to four months old. Environmental surroundings can be a factor in determining the frequency at which feet are trimmed, for on a hard and dry surface this interval may not be necessary. Certainly, in the foal with any limb abnormalities, trimming should start at a very young age and at more frequent intervals.

I see no reason to shoe an animal until the exercise program is initiated. Even at that time it may only be necessary to keep the colt well trimmed, depending on the track surface and the intensity of work. Yearlings, in may cases, can get by without shoeing for their first 45 to 60 days of training, but as the intensity of exercise increases in the third and fourth month of training, I think, it is advantageous to have a set of plates on the horse.

Preventive firing, in my opinion, would be parallel to a professional football player having knee surgery prior to his rookie year in the NFL season to reduce the chances of knee injury at a later date. Those who feel that firing is an advantageous practice base their judgment on the fact that the scar tissue resulting from such a technique leaves the part fired stronger. In my opinion this is questionable. Fortunately, the animals that are fired are given a rest, which is probably the single most important part of the entire procedure. By the time firing holes have healed and the swelling subsided the animal has usually had 90 days of rest and is much more capable of going back to his previous exercise routine than at the time he was fired.

Conditioning and Exercise Measurements

We did a study at Colorado State University that included heart rate as an indicator of training adaptation during the initial phases of race-training in Thoroughbreds. Our results concurred with other investigators and other breed data from similar studies. There is no doubt in my mind that the length of time that it takes an animal's heart rate to return to pre-exercising levels is an index of the degree of fitness that horse has achieved. One must realize, however, that the heart rate is controlled by a variety of inputs of which exercise is only one. Also there are differences between individual animals which must be considered.

The post-exercise heart rate decreases rapidly immediately after the exercise is completed. This makes it necessary to be very exact regarding the times the heart rate is taken after the exercise. It appears that the single best times to take the heart rate are between one and five minutes after exercise.

It is also very important to exercise the animal over a standard distance in a given time period to obtain information valid for comparisons. The exercise effort should be stressful enough that a heart rate of greater than 200 beats per minute is achieved. As the animal increases in fitness, the exercise will naturally have to be stepped-up in order to adequately stress the individual. Only exercise efforts of a given distance and speed can be compared. All other factors being equal, the animal with the lowest heart rate one minute after exercise should be the best conditioned animal.

The single most important aspect to consider is that two animals of identical conditioning may not be able to run at the same speed. The outcome of a race is determined by many things, among which is the fitness of horses. Other variables can be even more important in determining who gets to the finish line first. Greater use of heart rate determinations by trainers might allow this single measurement a more serious evaluation and lend tremendous information to its use.

With a little understanding and practice, the heart rate can be counted by anyone. Persons wanting to determine the heart rates of their horses during the post-exercise period could either use a stethoscope or manually count the heart rate at the girth of the horse on the lower left side. The facial artery under the horse's jaw is most commonly used to take heart rate in the resting state, but many animals will be moving around enough after exercise to make counting the heart rate by this method very difficult.

The heart score concept, as a basis for determining an animal's athletic capability, was first developed by Steele and co-workers in Australia in the mid 1950's. Recently, many people have doubted the validity of this concept. The basis for the concept is: the larger the animal's heart in relation to his body size, the more capable that animal may be of delivering blood to tissues utilized during exercise. Supporters of this concept feel that the heart score complex can be used to give a relative index of heart size.

At Colorado State University, I conducted a small clinical trial utilizing this concept and was unable to substantiate the findings of the original investigators. I personally feel that determination of a horse's potential performance capability is best determined on the stressed (exercising) animal rather than the resting animal.

Swimming as a "Conditioner"

Asheim and co-workers from Sweden reported on heart rate values on horses while swimming. From these heart rate values it would appear that horses can obtain a degree of cardiovascular fitness with swimming as their sole conditioning program. However, there is a tremendous physiological difference between swimming and running. Swimming is an exercise that is concussion free. We all know that injuries associated with performance and racing are due to stress, strain and concussion. Therefore, it would seem that swimming alone is inadequate for preparing a horse for performance activities.

The swimming of horses probably has a very good place in the convalescent patient that would further injure himself by running exercise. This would allow that some degree of fitness be maintained during the convalescent period, hopefully shortening the training necessary to obtain previous levels of fitness. Similar muscles are used in swimming and running, but the muscular emphasis is different.

I think it is important to distinguish between the cardiovascular fitness that swimming can maintain versus the cardiovascular *and* musculo-skeletal fitness that running can maintain. The best way to get an athlete in top condition for a given event is to train him in such an event. Therefore, one must be cautious in using swimming as a method to condition for racing.

Routine Health Management for The Equine Athlete

Respiratory disease in the race horse is probably the most important contagious disease from which they suffer. These animals should be maintained current on all vaccinations series started as youngsters. The control of parasites in stabled horses is not as difficult as in horses that are grouped. If an animal has been on a good parasite control program prior to racing, deworming may be done at 90 day intervals.

In any event, parasite control at 60 day intervals would most likely be adequate. One consideration in deworming horses at frequent intervals is that the medication be changed occasionally to minimize resistance that parasites may develop to the drug therapy.

As to the method of deworming horses, the drugs are equally effective when put in the feed as when administered with a stomach tube. The problem is that many animals may refuse to eat feed adulterated with anthelmintics. Therefore, rather than holding a horse off feed or decreasing his feed consumption during the time of feed additives, it may be easier to have the horse stomach tubed.

Fecal examinations can provide a reasonable index of the effectiveness of the parasite control program. These exams, however, can be misleading, and the fact that a few parasite eggs are seen does not always correlate with the degree of infestation. I would have a tendency to de-emphasize the fecal examination and re-emphasize the routine use of anthelmintics, as modern drugs are safe when properly used.

Recognizing that racing horses involves a considerable economical investment, I can understand why "blood tests" are run as frequently as they are. However, I would question whether these tests are as necessary as people would like to think. The veterinarian uses blood tests in a diagnostic capacity with diseased animals. I feel that the blood test is utilized on race tracks to find reasons for poor performances and that the tests are seldom as informative as most would believe.

The principal emphasis of a blood test is placed on the number or amount of circulating red blood cells commonly known by terms such as hemoglobin or hematocrit (packed cell volume). These is no doubt that adequate numbers of circulating red blood cells are necessary for a horse to perform at his maximal capacity. Unfortunately, when a horse is at rest, this evaluation is under considerable influence of factors that are difficult to control.

An indication of low red cell mass is probably a fairly accurate determination. The opposite is not true, as excitation, dehydration and external stimuli can greatly increase the hematocrit giving one a false assurance that his horse has "enough" red blood cells. The horse stores a large number of red blood cells in the spleen and the degree of splenic contraction that is present at the time of sampling will directly influence the red blood cell count.

It becomes obvious that, to eliminate such an influence, the spleen should be maximally contracted. Exercise is the easiest way to cause maximal splenic contraction, and, in fact, immediately after exercise of adequate intensity, one will find that the red cell blood count is the most accurate (reproducible) for that horse.

Performance Related Injuries

There is no specific amount of time that a horse should be "laid off" after an injury; the convalescence associated with racing injuries is directly related to the injury and the functional loss involved with that injury. Basically speaking, one would rest the horse long enough for the inflammatory and repairative process of the injury to totally subside.

The tendency is to try to get horses into training too rapidly by overtraining to make up for lost time after an injury. I think what is most important is that an accurate diagnosis be established at the time of the injury, thus allowing the best determination of the convalescence period necessary.

Over-exertion and under developed muscles can be causes of interfering in horses, but the key factors are conformation and conditioning. Regardless of how well conditioned and muscled a poorly conformed horse is, interfering can still occur when the conformation is a predisposing factor.

Horses that are considered racing prospects are seldom so poorly built to interfere at a slow pace. But the speed at which these horses run, coupled with the fatigue experienced at race's end, can be disastrous for the animal that has a tendency to interfere. The best example I have seen of this fatigue is in horses on competitive trail rides.

In these athletic events, high speed is not a problem. The factor in these events is fatigue after going 40 to 50 miles in an eight or ten hour period. The horse with poor conformation can start interfering, and quite severely, under these circumstances.

Navicular disease is often a problem with the horse as an athlete. Two factors play a role in the origin of navicular disease: 1) The conformation of the animal, and; 2) its use; both of which can predispose the navicular area to excessive concussion. The navicular disease syndrome is a very complex lameness problem and one that has received much attention in recent years.

A number of conditions involving the foot can look like navicular disease. Frequently, other abnormalities co-exist or complicate the clinical picture. The disease has varying degrees of severity from mild cases to "cripples" and is usually progressive in course and irreversible.

Therapeutic measures for navicular disease and the duration for which such measures will be beneficial to the horse depend on the severity and progression of the disease. In some cases, corrective shoeing can provide a marked improvement in the animal. However, if the use of the horse remains the same, since the conformation will not be changed, it cannot be expected that a horse will be kept sound for a prolonged period of time.

Posterior digital neurectomies ("nervings") are used in animals for which shoeing programs are insufficient to maintain soundness. The relief is permanent, but not without its potential complications. Posterior digital neurectomy is the only means I know of that will give long-term relief to the animal that is used extensively, for, as the disease progresses, the animal is incapable of recognizing its presence.

(Ed.: Dr. Haynes has a refreshingly scientific approach to equine conditioning. Perhaps all horsemen can take optimistic note of this as a possible trend toward increased scientific interest in the fields of developing and evaluating the horse as an athlete.)

Matlock Rose

(Interview by Barbara Wright)

Matlock Rose is a real winner. The success of his conditioning program has been proven time and time again at major horse shows across the nation.

As a western horseman, Matlock Rose has trained and shown winning horses in all areas of competition—reining, roping, cutting, halter and so on. His reputation ranks with the best in the field.

Matlock has been associated with the top Quarter Horses in the nation for more than twenty years. Among his numerous accomplishments are not one, but two National Cutting Horse Association World Champions which he trained and rode—the famous Stardust Desire, 1966, and Peppy San, 1967.

Making his home near Gainesville, Texas, this native Texan has a well-planned and practical horse training establishment.

Matlock is a strong believer in really knowing one's horses. His conditioning program involves no strictly regimented schedules for horses in training. The conditioning programs are always individualized to fit the needs of each particular horse. He firmly states "If you don't know your horse, you haven't got any business showing him."

Matlock Rose doesn't take much stock in generalizations—each horse is the sole determiner for the type and amount of work the individual needs to achieve and maintain winning condition.

Foals are weaned when they are five to six months old. They are also halter broken at this time. Under Matlock's care they usually receive forced exercise until they are broken to saddle. As for methods of exercise during this period, he prefers to jog them in a round pen and use a walker.

If weanlings and yearlings are not being shown at halter Matlock likes to leave them outside rather than stall them until they are broken to saddle. In the event that a young horse must be kept in a stall, it is turned out into a large pen several hours a day for self-exercise.

During the spring of their two-year-old year the youngsters are broken to saddle. They are ridden with a hackamore and a snaffle bit. The riding is always small amounts at a time until the colts start going. Then the young horses are turned out until the next fall.

When asked if he handles colts and fillies differently Matlock replied, "Usually your colts are a little stronger and can take a little bit more work than fillies."

Matlock always works with colts individually, never handling them as groups. The amount of riding that a young horse gets depends primarily on how that horse reacts to training. "If a colt's knees are closed up, I'll ride one pretty much until they get going fairly well, and then slack off," Matlock explained. He doesn't make it a usual practice to X-ray yearlings' knees, but adds, "If I think there is something wrong with a colt's knees, I certainly will X-ray one."

Matlock's conditioning programs for young horses are basically the same—whether the horse is a halter horse or a performance horse. In general he initially uses a round pen and a walker followed by a program of gradually increasing riding.

Since Matlock is such a highly respected trainer he was asked what he recommends that an owner do to get young prospects ready for the trainer. "Feed them right . . . and exercise, of course," he quickly replied. Sixty days is about how long he feels that he needs to work with a young horse before deciding whether that horse is going to perform above or below average.

"When an owner gets a horse back from the trainer," Matlock remarked, "the owner needs to follow a common sense program, including health care, to keep the horse in condition." He added that it is important to "keep somebody that's sensible and knows something about horses working with the horse."

As horses get older Matlock explained that they frequently have a tendency to get sluggish or "ill" when they are getting too much exercise. "The horse begins to dread whatever you are doing with it."

On the other hand, Matlock says that a horse not getting enough exercise will "play around" and just "won't have his mind on what he's doing." When not using a horse he believes in "leaving them to their own devices" to get self-exercise in a pasture. He quickly added that if the horse is kept in a stall it would certainly need some kind of a forced exercise program.

Matlock was asked if he ever uses swimming as a method of exercise for his horses. In answer, he smiled and said, "Only when I cross the river."

There aren't any big differences in the exercise programs for studs, mares and geldings. Studs are ridden regularly during the breeding season and the off season. "I believe in riding a stud. If you exercise him and keep him in working condition, he will be a better horse," Matlock stated.

Broodmares are kept on pasture so that they get plenty of sunlight and self-exercise. At the Rose ranch, dry mares, nursing mares and mares heavy with foal are kept in separate pastures.

As to cutting horses, in general Matlock usually starts them as late

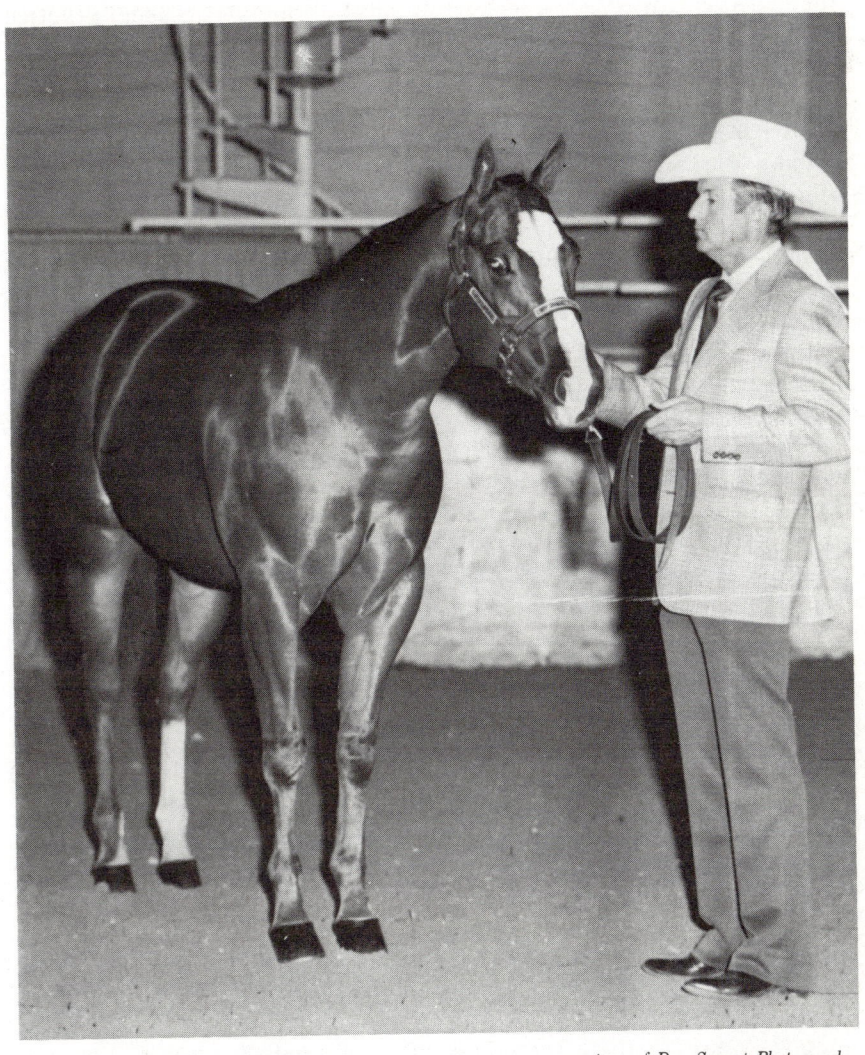

courtesy of Don Sugart Photography

All around horseman Matlock Rose at the 1974 State Fair of Texas with the outstanding two-year-old filly, Skipster's Lil.

two-year-olds. He has found that his young horses get all the exercise they need by riding, being put on a walker and being worked on cattle two to three times a week. To keep a young horse willing to work, he cautions, "Don't burn one out, keep a little desire in him."

Concerning the type of cattle he prefers to use with his young horses Matlock states, "You have got to have cattle they can hold so the horse won't be running all the time." He does use goats occasionally, commenting they are good for working young horses.

When asked how many calves, on the average, a beginning horse should work, Matlock said it depends entirely on how the young horse does. He then explained, "If the colt does good, I may only work one or two calves. If he doesn't, I will work with him slowly for 20 to 30 minutes—sometimes up to an hour if he doesn't get too hot."

With older horses he feels that it helps to work one in the pasture occasionally instead of in an arena at all times. Older, "finished" horses are often ponied as a method of forced exercise. In explanation Matlock added, "The horses we are hauling, the really top cutting horses, are worked or ridden on the days they aren't ponied. A finished horse is usually worked once a week, unless we are getting ready to go to a show, then the horse is worked two or three times during the week."

In answer to a question about when a cutting horse reaches his peak, Matlock replied, "Some horses will peak out as four-year-olds and others aren't at their best until they are eight—it depends on the individual horse." He believes that 12 to 14 is the maximum age for a cutting horse, if the horse stays sound. "I think cutting is harder on a horse than anything you can do with one," commented Matlock. In this area, navicular disease and pulled tendons are the most troublesome.

After a horse has been laid off for an injury Matlock brings it back into training slowly. "Walk the horse until he doesn't show any soreness, then start jogging some. Gradually work the horse back into whatever you ere doing—whether it's racing, cutting or whatever," he cautions.

Horses that get a little sore from work have their legs bandaged with liniment or DMSO as a precautionary measure. Blisters are used on horses under Matlock's care in situations such as splints and bumped knees. Also he feels that the practice of firing a horse is alright, with this stipulation, "If you've got somebody that really knows what they are doing!"

When a highly conditioned horse is to be turned out for a rest from training Matlock does it gradually. "Turn the horse out into a corral and let him play for three or four days," he recommends. "When the horse gets used to being outside, then it's time to turn him out."

To toughen up a performance horse he uses the following, "Riding—jogging and loping—just like you would any horse to get him in condition." Matlock doesn't believe you can set down any rules about a schedule to keep a performance horse at a constant, desired level of condition. "There's not a certain amount of exercise for every horse, it wouldn't work because of their individuality."

Matlock added that a reining horse is the hardest horse there is to keep going; in other words, keep fresh. "Most people wear them out at home working them 'dry' too much. Ride them, but don't overdo the spinning, turning and stopping once you have the horse going," he warns.

"A steady, consistent reining horse needs to be at least three years old, up to six," Matlock stated. When looking for a good reining horse he likes "a horse that has nerve and is athletic." He then explained, "The horse has to change leads easily and have a good way of going—the same things you would look for in any horse. If the horse is going to be an athlete, he's got to have maneuverability."

As for western pleasure horses he said, "I like a horse that has got some brains and travels well. If the horse doesn't move well, he won't make a good pleasure horse." Matlock smiled and added, "I like a horse that I could do something with besides pleasure."

"Any horse you show should be well groomed," he remarked when asked about specific grooming for show horses. He added that it takes a lot of preparation and daily work to groom a horse well. "You need to really clean a horse up before a class, but you can't wait until you show the horse to do it all."

Horses under Matlock's care are brushed daily for at least 30 minutes. He uses a rubber curry comb and a brush as the mainstay of his grooming program. To thin a mane or tail Matlock doesn't cut the hair, but pulls it. Also, he uses a hoof dressing regularly and blackens the hooves of horses before they enter a halter class.

Very seldom are horses clipped all over, but their ears, bridle paths, whiskers and fetlocks are trimmed periodically in the grooming program. Horses going to sales are groomed just like any others. They should be "fat and pretty," Matlock says.

In the summertime, horses are bathed—sometimes as a part of cooling after exercise. Warm water, always, is used on the horses. If the weather isn't warm, horses are walked until their coats are dry.

As for blanketing show horses to keep their coats really slick, Matlock begins using blankets when the nights start getting cool, around the end of August, and continues until spring. "The blankets usually come off in May," he said, "but it depends on what part of the country you are in."

On long trips extra care has to be taken to keep the horses from becoming over-tired. Horses should be tied loose enough in the trailer so they can hit the back bar inside of the trailer. Matlock usually unloads horses every 400 to 500 miles and lets them walk around. "After a long trip, such as 1,000 miles, the horses need a day or more to rest before being shown," he added.

Matlock's feeding program varies with the individual horse, but all of the show horses receive bran, oats and alfalfa twice a day. A few horses are fed three times each day. Broodmares are fed oats twice a day and alfalfa once a day. All of the horses have access to salt and mineral supplements, plus plenty of fresh, clean water. When asked about horses shown at halter Matlock said that he does keep them a little fatter than other horses.

Regarding health management, all horses are vaccinated against sleeping sickness (Eastern and Western), VEE, leptospirosis and tetanus. Frequently, horses that are shown quite a bit are vaccinated against flu also. Ninety days is the interval between wormings and all horses are wormed by the stomach tube method. To keep the parasite problem down, Matlock says, "The stalls are kept *clean*. We clean them daily and twice a day in the show barn. That's about all you can do," he added.

Matlock was asked about blood tests and replied that he uses blood analysis when a horse gets "pulled down" and isn't doing well. Blood testing isn't done on a regular basis.

Trimming and shoeing is done on the average of every six weeks. His young horses are usually shod when riding begins. "Occasionally we don't shoe colts when the riding starts," Matlock commented, then added, "the terrain that you are riding them over can make a difference." Broodmares in pastures are trimmed as often as they need it, generally every two or three months.

In answer to a question concerning stall sizes, Matlock said, "I don't think you can get a stall too big, but mine are 12 feet by 12 feet." He prefers shavings for bedding and has dirt floors in the stalls.

"You can't ever get enough help," Matlock said when asked how many horses per helper he likes. "I think six to seven head is the most one man can take care of," and added, smiling, "I like to have horsemen for help—not hippies." When he hires help, Matlock looks for "somebody that wants to *work!*"

Work is basic to Matlock Rose's conditioning program. He stresses that each horse is an individual—you have to really know every horse and fit exercise programs to the horse. No hard and fast rules apply. Each horse is slightly different regarding the type and amount of exercise it needs to build and maintain winning condition . . . but riding and forced exercise are fundamental.

Ginger Hyland
White Oaks Ranch

Ginger Hyland of White Oaks Ranch in Lake Hughes, California is widely recognized for her success in many phases of the Quarter racing industry. Consistently, White Oaks ranch yearlings demand top market prices at prestigious sales across the country.

For example, the filly, Luci Brown, sold for $31,000 in the 1971 All American Sale. That same year another White Oaks Ranch filly, Gay Wings, topped the Twin Classics sales at $20,500. A sound conditioning program is basic in preparing horses for sale Miss Hyland believes and wrote the following article presenting her practices.

The superior market-breeding establishment, White Oaks Ranch, utilizes a complex, computerized breeding program developed by Miss Hyland who graduated from the University of Kentucky with Departmental Honors, the first time ever given, in their Department of Animal Science. In addition to breeding many top-flight horses, Miss Hyland, whose father is Executive Vice-President for Hughes Aircraft and one of the inventors of radar, has also owned several successful running horses during their racing careers. She is on the Board of Directors of the Horseman's Quarter Horse Racing Association which runs the winter racing meet at Los Alamitos, California.

Conditioning Yearlings
For The Sales

by

Ginger Hyland

Proper conditioning of yearlings for sales is a process that actually begins when a foal is born. Proper nutrition, hoof trimming, exercise, handling, safe facilities, and medical attention all determine the quality of an individual. If the foundation is well laid, then the final 10 to 12 weeks of sale conditioning will yield a yearling of which to be proud.

Different ranches have different methods for preparing sale yearlings. The purpose of this article is to familiarize the reader with the program at White Oaks Ranch which has been quite successful, but not to imply that other programs do not work also.

Before actually getting into the final conditioning program, a brief discussion of the "Proper Foundation" is essential.

1) Nutrition—Foals at White Oaks Ranch are creep fed from the time they can eat grain. Feedings of ½ quart of mixed grain or a sweet feed are given morning, noon and night. At weaning time the ration is increased to 2 quarts daily until December 1 when the grain is again increased at 2 week intervals at ½ quart until a level of 4 to 8 quarts (depending on the individual) is reached. It always seems that, about January, the yearlings are growing so fast that they can get too thin without frequent increases both in hay and grain. "Eyeball" the yearlings and level off the grain when their ribs no longer show, but before they become fat.

2) Hoof Trimming—The time to correct crooked legs is while a horse is very young—4 to 12 months. After that the bones are too mature and correction will do more damage than good. Trim or rasp a foal every 30 days beginning at 4 months of age to correct problems, and every 45 to 60 days if he stands straight. Sound straight legs are a major factor when a buyer judges a yearling.

3) Exercise—The horse is an athlete—whether used for racing, show, or pleasure. And an athlete should be raised like an athlete—not in a tiny paddock, but in a pasture of at least 1/2 acre where a colt can run and develop.

4) Handling—Halter breaking, brushing, picking up feet—all are important in raising a foal. When done early, wrecks and injuries can be avoided later on. A well mannered yearling is an asset at a sale.

5) Safe Facilities—Rocks, holes, sharp corners on troughs or feeders, broken boards or broken wire can mean injuries with resulting scars and swellings. Few buyers will pay much money for such an individual. The best way to avoid blemishes is to keep pastures free from hazards and all fences in good repair.

6) Medical Attention—Neglecting wounds can result in unsightly scar tissue. Daily doctoring of cuts and wrapping of leg injuries where indicated will greatly reduce scarring. Of course, a good worming program is vital to keep a horse looking and feeling healthy.

With the proper foundation laid, it is time to begin the actual conditioning program. 10 to 12 weeks is required. At White Oaks Ranch the yearlings are put up in the barns about June 1. If the first sale is the end of August—that's just about 11 weeks.

All of the stalls at White Oaks have 30 foot paddocks outside them which makes the transition from pasture to barn easier.

After the yearlings have settled down, which may take a day or two,

Shown against the background of their well-known White Oaks Ranch are Ginger Hyland, her parents, Pat and Muriel, and Spot.

each is taken to the training ring (50 feet in diameter) for their first longe lesson. The purpose of longeing here is not so much exercise as it is education: getting a colt to respond to a pull of the longe line in stopping and going; learning to take his leads; going in both directions; paying attention to the trainer.

Young horses are mostly jogged in the training ring, occasionally loped—never allowed to gallop out because of the strain on growing legs.

When the yearlings are responding well in the ring, the pony horse is brought in. It is important for the trainer to work slowly with yearlings. They are capable of learning only a certain amount at a time, and each colt is different. Usually, walking the pony horse around the yearling, forcing the yearling to turn in a small circle and then gradually a larger circle is enough for the first day. The next day should be a repetition and if the colt goes well, the other direction can be attempted. However, should the yearling balk, turn him again in a circle. Don't ever rush him—give him a minute to rest now and then and a few reassuring words. Always quit on a colt after he does his lesson correctly and always try to avoid getting a colt mad—then he can't learn anything.

At the end of a week the yearlings should all be walking and jogging calmly alongside the pony horse. Now it's time to go out on the race track.

Again, these are young immature horses. The aim of a conditioning program for a sale is to exercise and tone their muscles so they look fit without stressing or straining their legs and joints. So the surface of the race track is plowed deep for a good cushion, harrowed regularly, and watered.

The track at White Oaks is $3/8$ mile. The yearlings are ponied at a walk around the track for a day or two. Beginning the third day, the colts are walked $1/2$ round of the track; jogged $1/2$ round; and then walked back $1/2$ round in the reverse direction. This program is continued for two weeks at which point the jogging is increased to a full round of the track, but always with walking before and after.

For many yearlings 1 round of jogging and loping is sufficient, but others, particularly with hay bellies, may require $1^1/2$ or even 2 rounds. Usually with an individual like this the program is Monday, Wednesday, and Friday—1 round; Tuesday and Thursday—$1^1/2$ or 2 rounds.

But always watch the colt's legs. If they begin to fill or show signs of strain—back off.

Here again, variation exists. Normally a sale yearling is exercised Monday through Friday, but for some individuals Monday, Wednesday, and Friday is enough with just walking in between. Always the yearl-

An example of a White Oaks Ranch yearling conditioned for sale—Pampered Lady.

ings have Saturday and Sunday to rest. Leave them alone—they need it. Turn them out individually in pastures for $1/2$ a day twice a week to play. Then they won't become bored and sour when asked to work. Sometimes, about 6 or 8 weeks into the conditioning program, some of the yearlings may be turned out and left alone for an entire week.

Along with the ponying, the yearlings have an education program which includes many things—the hot walker, clippers, trailering, grooming, bathing, and leg wraps. Each of these is important for a well mannered yearling. But remember, teach a young horse one thing at a time. Don't trailer a colt and give him a hose bath both for the first time the same day. Lesson one first and when the colt understands and performs that one well, go on to lesson two.

A yearling should always be properly cooled out after a workout. Since a lot of trainers use hot walkers, yearlings may as well learn to walk on them at home.

Some people just snap the horse on and let him fight it out until he quits, but at White Oaks we try to avoid battles like that. First the yearling is cooled out by hand around the walker with the machine off. After a couple of days, the walker is turned on, but the colt is still only hand walked around it, not tied on. Then the handler holds the ropes of the walker and the yearling together just like the colt was snapped on. The machine is then stopped and started several times to get the colt used to the pull. After several days of this, a yearling can be tied onto the walker with very little fuss, thus avoiding possible injury.

Grooming is, of course, extremely important in presenting a yearling for a sale. Daily vigorous brushing with a rubber curry comb and a brush is required to get the dead hair out of the coat and to put a shine in it. Manes and tails also need daily combing. An unruly mane should be braided to one side till it lays flat, which usually takes about 2 days. Then the mane should be pulled until it is about five inches long and is even. Tails should be just below the hock; forelocks about the center of the eye. The bright sun during the middle of the day can burn the hair coat of a horse, so it is best to keep the horses in their stalls during those hours.

Breaking a horse to the clippers merely takes patience. Let the colt smell and feel the clippers before turning them on. Then work slowly while the clippers are running, perhaps clipping just the nose one day—the bridle path the next. Some horses take to the clippers right away and some never do. On those individuals, a twitch is necessary. But most of the time, if the trainer is patient, a horse will accept the clippers.

For a sale, a yearling should have his nose and chin whiskers clipped, his bridle path back 4 to 6 inches, and the inside of his ears clipped.

Proper trailer breaking is vital for a young horse. Stuffing a colt in a trailer for the first time the day before the sale has caused countless injuries. Gaunted up yearlings with fresh cuts and capped hocks don't sell well.

So, one month before the sale, trailer breaking begins. At White Oaks Ranch a step up trailer (no ramp) is backed up to a loading chute with seven foot tall sides with a stationery built in ramp. On either side of the chute is a platform on which an assistant can stand. The yearling is led into the chute by the trainer and an assistant follows on the platform. Usually after a minute or two the colt will walk in. Sometimes a light tap of a buggy whip from the assistant encourages a balky yearling.

The colt is stood in the trailer for a few minutes every day for a week. The second week he goes for a short ride every day, unloading without the chute. The third week the chute is taken away and loading is done alongside a fence. By this time the colt should be well trailer broken.

A few words of caution—the first ride is always the most traumatic for a yearling. Starting off very slowly and stopping slowly helps considerably. Also make certain that there are no hazards in the trailer on which a colt might hurt himself.

Hose baths normally frighten a horse the first time. Put the colt in a small pen (15' by 30'), the trainer holding the horse, the assistant with the hose. Begin by hosing the yearling's front legs below the knees, then the hind legs. Ease the spray over his neck, shoulder, and back, but avoid his tail and head. Scrape the excess water off and put the colt on the walker. The next day include a light spray on top of the head, and also spray the tail. By the third day the colt will be ready for a complete shampoo.

About a week before the sale, put leg wraps or shipping boots on each yearling daily for about fifteen minutes. It takes a few days for a colt to accept boots, but they do help to prevent injuries on a long trailer ride.

The Sale

By sale time the yearlings should be in good firm flesh, their coats shining, manes pulled, bridle paths and noses clipped, feet trimmed, manners excellent. Always arrive at least two days before the sale to allow the yearlings time to rest and settle down in their new and strange environment. Having your own feed helps since a change in diet can throw a colt off his feed. Bathe and groom yearlings before you ship them. They should be prepared for viewing by prospective buyers the moment they step off the van. Put a new leather halter on each yearling—buckstitched or silver mounted halters are even better for nothing dresses up a colt more. Remember rub rags and coat conditioner, combs, brushes, feed and water tubs, a pitchfork, lead shanks, sponge, hoof pick, and hoof black. And, of course, be sure someone is there all the time to show the yearlings, to make them stand square, and walk them for a prospective buyer.

In conclusion, conditioning yearlings for a sale is a long, careful process that begins when a foal is born and peaks during the last ten to twelve weeks before the sale. It includes a proper fitness program along with nutrition, education, manners, and grooming.

Never has this program, in some ten years in the racing Quarter Horse business, failed to produce a yearling of which White Oaks Ranch was not proud. The moment that a well fitted yearling enters the sale ring and thus commands a good price—then you know—it's been well worth the effort.

Allen Jerkens

(Interview by Mary Jane Gallaher)

Allen Jerkens, a husky Thoroughbred trainer who looks as if he'd be equally at home on a pro-football field as at Belmont Park race course, is a frequent visitor in the winner's circles of New York's race tracks.

Jerkens' peers in the training set frankly scoff at the notion that he has a "magic touch" but do admit a trifle enviously that they'd like to know how he takes horses he's bought or claimed from them and drastically improves their racing ability. Trainers shake their heads in disbelief when they see a horse they had virtually given up on not only winning, but doing so in top company.

This talent has enabled Jack J. Dreyfus, Jr.'s Hobeau Stable, which Jerkens trains, to head the Leading Money Winning Owners' list in 1967, and hold fourth position on that roster for the years 1970, 1971, 1972 and 1973.

Born in New York in 1929, Jerkens is almost as good a polo player as he is race trainer. Shy and taciturn by nature, Jerkens nevertheless is willing to answer questions about his methods of training individual horses and how he copes with their problems.

Seated in his Belmont Park office, his first field of concentration was the racing of two-year-olds.

"When I get a young horse, it is helpful if an owner has a farm where he can break his yearlings and put a good foundation under them before sending them to me.

"Once they are in my barn I pretty much let them tell me when they will race. I believe racing two-year-olds, if you don't overdo it, is no more harmful than letting them fool around and get too fat. Some people think that not doing much with them at two is best; this hasn't been proven to me. The likelihood of leg troubles are the main reason you have to go slow with your young horses. There is no special time or age to start a horse; if he is training well and is up to a race, you may as well run him.

"Two-year-olds, however, will fool you. The real bad looking or highly impressive ones you can spot. But they are the exceptions. Some don't show much speed for months; they just get going late. Then there are the speedier ones that don't improve and turn out real cheap. It usually takes about four months to know what you have.

Lots of times you will have an idea of their value if you trained the sire or dam.

"You don't work the babies as far as you do the old horses, but in most groups of any age some can take more distance and more training than others.

"If the colt has been training good, has shown good speed with company, has broken well from the gate, eats well and looks good, he should show a good effort in his early races.

"Before they actually start, I usually take them to the paddock in the afternoon to get accustomed to the usual stable area noises; after that, crowd noise in the afternoons seldom bothers them.

"I hardly ever give a horse an excuse because of the race track. They all have to run over the same surface."

Jerkens, whose fame and fortune have risen with the likes of Onion, a known speed horse which unexpectedly and handily beat the mighty Secretariat in the $1^{1}/_{8}$ mile Whitney, and Prove Out who downed Secretariat in the Woodward and the powerful Riva Ridge in the Jockey Club Gold Cup, is regarded as the best around at getting a Thoroughbred to give his all. Jerkens' particular forte has been the returning to action, usually in stakes company, of older horses generally considered over the hill or too infirm to take on the best.

Jerkens says that buying and selling horses is not a one-way ticket to success.

"There's another side of the coin," he adds, "such as Never Bow. We sold him for a little more than $100,000 and Pancho Martin won a $100,000 stakes and a lot of other races with him before he was eventually sold as a stud prospect for $500,000. Unfortunately, Never Bow suffered a fatal accident when he was being loaded into a plane for Europe."

When asked for his formula for getting mature horses to travel in top company, he explains:

"I do the basic things such as jogging, galloping, breezing slow, then increasing distance and speed. If a horse lightens up too quickly, I slow up. Some real class horses want a lot of work and benefit from it. The horse will show you when he's getting too much work; he loses weight, gets nervous, backs off his feed. If he's not getting enough exercise, he'll slow up in his works and blow a lot afterwards. I try to fit the exercise to the horse; I know, for instance, that some fillies need a lot of work also.

"When I'm leading up to a race, I train them pretty hard if they haven't raced in a long time. Most of them don't need too much work if they run a lot.

Allen Jerkens, the highly regarded Thoroughbred trainer, keeps the owner of Hobeau Stables, Jack J. Dreyfus, Jr., among the top money winners year after year.

"If you get a horse that doesn't want to train, which you come across occasionally, 95% of the time there is something bothering him. Horses don't mind galloping and working if nothing hurts them. I believe that some horses get too edgy if you don't gallop them enough.

"If I get a horse that's obviously nervous, I try not to work him too fast—I give him a lot of slow works, graze him and hack him around the stable area. If a horse goes to race in a warm climate, it is probably best to have a good workout at least once or twice in the weather.

"It seems to me," he continued, "that a race horse reaches his peak at four to five years if he hasn't been overdone as a young one. I try to turn out at the farm before a horse is completely drained. I just bring them along, increasing the works as I go. If a horse is to be turned out, I gallop him every other day for a little while, then send him to the farm.

"When it comes to exercise on the track just before going in the gate for a race, I like to see my horses warm up, then stop for a few minutes before they go in the gate. When they get back after a race, we wash them if it's real hot, but with water that's lukewarm or cold. We walk ours by hand to cool them out."

In equine feeding, Jerkens is more particular than a mother with a first baby; in fact, he is known on the backstretch as "Dandelion Man" because he can be found in his spare moments gathering the yellow-topped plants to entice especially finicky eaters.

"Feeding horses boils down to getting the nutrition into the horse. Good quality hay and grain are about the best you can do. Supplements can be overdone. You do need them if the hay is bad. I have tried a lot of them but never stayed with 'em. I mainly rely on B_{12} powder and Vitamin E."

Then came the question of unsoundness and what to do about it. Jerkens obviously has advice to offer in that area as he's the first to admit he runs a geriatics stable. His success with taking older horses and improving their performance speaks for itself.

"If there is any particular key to success with older horses," Jerkens explained, "it is stopping on them before they are worn out. If you can stop them and turn them out one race before they are completely used up, I think you have a little edge. You're putting a little less pressure on them, and that makes it easier for them to come back."

Starting with basics, he was asked about trimming and shoeing. He recommends a once-a-month schedule for this. He worms his horses three times a year. As for swimming his charges, he says he would if it were handy. He thinks horses might enjoy it and that it might help bad legs but does think it can be overdone.

"It is a constant fight to keep your horses sound. I do anything that will help. We brace legs with liniment, tub with ice or hot water, use poultices, paints, sweats—anything that brings results. Blistering is alright when you lay a horse up for awhile. You have to see which blister works on each horse, as some can't stand some medications on their skin. We also use a whirlpool or other type therapy if we think legs will respond.

"I use all the standard equipment for racing when warranted, i.e., blinkers, speed patches, run-down bandages, shadow rolls, change of bits. I seldom use a breast harness; rubber pads usually will prevent a saddle slipping. I don't use racing bandages very often. I've always thought that with them, one slip, a sudden storm or even a wet track could prove disasterous.

"I like to cool horses out in water bandages. Bad-legged horses I put in ice after works, especially in warm weather.

"When I can't find a horse's trouble, naturally we get the veterinarian to take X-rays and whatever else is necessary. We run a blood analysis if a horse doesn't look good or isn't training to suit.

"As to clipping, if it's too warm, clip. When it's cold, clipping depends on the type of barn. In a barn that's snug, they don't need blankets except if you see one shivering or turning up his hair, then you have to use your own discretion as to whether to use a blanket. I don't use heat in the barns but a lot of successful trainers do. I've always heard that horses love cold weather but the longer I am around, the less I think so. I go to light weight sheets, light or heavy blankets as the weather changes.

"As to housing and help for our horses, I like a stall 14 feet by 12 feet, certainly not smaller than 12 feet by 10 feet. As for bedding, I like straw, but shavings will do if you have men that will keep it clean. We use solid walls. If a horse needs to see another horse, and occasionally he does much better when he can see a pal next door, he can see while looking out over the webbing.

"With my help, I don't use more than one man to three horses. If it's a 'big horse' (stakes horse), I use one man to two. In selecting my men, I want them to like horses and to want to see their horses do well, and I don't want any of them to be mean to a horse. We need people that like horses and like the racing game."

Jerkens thought a minute, then reflected, "Of course, you've got to have the horses in the first place . . . I'm fortunate in that I'm working for a man who, when his home-breds don't turn out the right way, is willing to buy horses. We make bad purchases too, but he doesn't get discouraged."

And owner Dreyfus pays Jerkens a like compliment: "Allen certainly isn't super-human and can't make a silk purse out of a sow's ear, but give him the silk ingredients and he will bring out the best in any racehorse he trains. I know of no one who cares so much or tries harder. He loves horses. To him, they are his friends ... not machines."

Jerry Wells

Jerry Wells is an outstanding breeder and trainer of Quarter Horses. Across the nation his fame and success are familiar to all horsemen. Mr. Wells has the distinctive honor of training and showing the first American Quarter Horse Association Supreme Champion.

The Supreme Champion, Kid Meyers, holds Certificate Number 1. The AQHA Supreme Champion Jetaway Reed, holder of Certificate Number 4, is another Wells-trained and shown horse. Adding to his esteem are several other AQHA Supreme Champions, including Magnolia Pay, Diamond Duro and Diamond Dividend. This is quite a feat since there are only 30 AQHA Supreme Champions.

The success of Mr. Wells' conditioning program is even further illustrated by the numerous AQHA Champions and Register of Merit horses that he has also trained and shown. His program is based on the idea that each horse is an individual and requires carefully considered care and conditioning to best fit its needs.

His 160 acre ranch near Purcell, Oklahoma is the site of one of the largest AQHA approved one day horse shows. The Jerry Wells Quarter Horse Show draws outstanding entries from all over the United States.

Mr. Wells himself makes quite a few shows, averaging about eight a month. He generally logs a total of over 50,000 miles a year traveling to and from shows.

The Wells ranch is the home of approximately fifty outstanding Quarter Horses including such superior horses as Cookies Gay Way (1969 Superior Halter Horse, AAA, AQHA Champion) and another Superior Halter Horse, Splash Bar Maid.

As a breeder, trainer and all around horseman, Mr. Wells' continuing success provides ample evidence of horses truly conditioned to win.

Jerry Wells' success as a trainer is fundamentally based on treating each horse as an individual. He pays special attention to every horse from the time it is very young and, therefore, is more accurately able to determine what a particular horse needs regarding exercise and feed to maintain winning condition.

Talking about young horses Jerry said, "I'd rather keep them turned out, it helps to make them really good horses." He firmly believes that when foals are allowed to run out and exercise on their own, they will be as sound as possible in the feet and legs.

He does, however, recommend halter breaking as early as possible. "I think if you can halter break one at two or three days old, you take a lot less chance of crippling a colt—there's no problem then." Jerry is a firm advocate of "the younger, the better" regarding halter breaking.

Under his management, all foals are creep fed. There is a definite advantage, Jerry feels, in having a colt already eating an adequate amount of grain before weaning. Weaning takes place when a colt is five months old.

Two months prior to weaning, Jerry prefers to keep the mare and colt stalled and turned into a big paddock at night. "This gets a colt used to the stall and easier to work with," he commented. The same routine of keeping the colt up during the day and turning it out at night is followed after weaning. As a rule, there is no forced exercise program until the horse is a yearling, preferably a long yearling.

"Of course all foals have a tendency to belly up when you take them off their mother and pour the feed to them," Jerry remarked, "so, you might have to use a forced exercise regime." In this case he uses a round pen or a longe line and the exercise rarely consists of over five minutes of long trotting in soft sand. He emphasizes that getting foals to buck and play on their own is most important.

Under Jerry's care, horses are prepared for breaking by work in a round pen. The young horses are trotted until they can slow down, stop and turn around. These exercise sessions usually last 10 to 12 minutes, never longer than 14 minutes. Also, the horses are driven four or five times before anyone actually rides them. "I don't like to ride a horse before he is a pretty long two-year-old," Jerry replied when asked at what age colts are broke to saddle.

"Don't overdo it," he cautions, "when a horse is willing and wants to try, 30 minutes of riding every other day is enough." Jerry feels that the size and temperment of a young horse determines the size person that should ride it, commenting that, "My wife is small and she rides quite a few of the colts—those that aren't too rank and rowdy." With young horses, Jerry believes that it is especially important to let them rest for a week or two after breaking begins.

By the time a horse is three, Jerry has worked with the individual enough to accurately judge how much exercise the horse needs and just how much he can stand. "Of course, the older a horse gets, the more you want him doing," Jerry remarked. "At this point, you can go faster with a horse and determine what he is capable of doing."

Regarding performance horses, Jerry is of the opinion that you can show a pleasure horse sooner than any other type. "By the end of their two-year-old year you can have them ready. With any young horse the most important thing is to break the horse right—go slowly and get him handling like you want to; then the horse should be ca-

Jerry Wells and one of the many champion Quarter Horses he has trained and shown—the outstanding halter horse, Sonny Go Lucky.

pable of doing whatever you want him to."

When asked about specific problems with young horses, he brought up the fact that frequently a young horse will be going extremely well in one event and then may go "blank," not doing anything well. "You've got to keep cool and really be patient with this type," Jerry cautioned, then added, "any young horse that was good in the first place will nearly always come back as good or better than he was." A 40 to 60 day rest period is the best remedy for this that Jerry has found. "In fact, I believe that this rest, after a horse has been started, is an important clue to successful work with young horses."

Jerry doesn't make it a practice to X-ray knees before the onset of intensive training since his horses are started at a relatively late age. "I'm around my horses from the time they are babies on up, so I pretty well know their problems. We just don't put that much work on a young horse." He does, however, recommend more caution with a valuable animal or extremely good prospect. "The better a horse is, the harder he'll try and the more apt he is to have trouble," Jerry explained, adding that, "when they really try, problems occur."

Young horses are accustomed to crowds and other horses by the practice of hauling them to shows in the general locale of Jerry's ranch. "Really, you just need to get them there, whether or not you show them, and eventually the young ones will overcome their fright," he stated. When hauling horses Jerry always wraps their legs for protection. "I think it's a precaution that a person ought to take."

In answer to a question concerning differences in Quarter Horses depending on the amount of Thoroughbred blood he has, Jerry replied that he has not found that it makes any difference while the horse is young. He added, though, "When a horse has some age on him, the Thoroughbred blood usually makes one develop more and have room left to do more."

As to the amount of exercise older, more seasoned horses need, Jerry feels that depends entirely on the individual horse. "When a horse is seasoned and doesn't need a lot of work, the main thing is to keep him tight enough so that the horse has adequate air and physical fitness for whatever you want him to do—don't overdo it. Young horses most commonly show signs of too much exercise in the form of leg problems. If this happens, let them exercise on their own."

In some cases, injuries may require that a horse be laid off, or one may be laid off simply for a rest. After being laid off, Jerry feels the most important thing is to start the horse back slowly and get him toned up again before he is subjected to any hard work. "Although it depends most on what you plan to do with the horse, be certain to start him back a little at a time, gradually increasing the exercise as you go along."

Regarding forced exercise without a rider, he overwhelmingly prefers the round pen and longe line. When asked about swimming horses Jerry answered that he has not had an opportunity to try it. He did say, "I think it's hard to beat that natural exercise—let Old Mother Nature do it her way!" He incorporates generally the same exercise regimes for studs, mares and geldings, finding no different overall techniques are needed.

Studs in service, however, are exercised most intensively beginning a month before and continuing daily through the breeding season. "Naturally, it depends on the horse, but I've found that studs breed better and handle better if they're exercised daily," Jerry reported. He also prefers to have mares foal outside, weather permitting. If the weather demands that mares must be brought in, he likes to have the mares and foals back out on pasture as soon as possible.

Since performance horses are Jerry's specialty, he was asked at what age the average performance horse reaches a physical peak. After explaining that it depends on the horse and when he was started, Jerry said, "To a certain extent, the older they get, the better they do." He feels that six to eight is the ideal age for a performance horse. "However, when a horse is this old and has been shown quite a bit, it is sometimes hard to keep the horse from anticipating the rider's signals."

"It is really important that you keep the horse guessing so he will do what you want him to," Jerry emphasized. "To keep a pleasure horse from souring in the arena, you must ride in different places and avoid doing the same thing over and over. That's tough to do, especially if the horse has been shown a lot, but you have to stay awake and use different routines."

As performance horses go, Jerry feels that reining horses are the hardest to keep fresh and ready to work. A horse needs to be $3^{1}/_{2}$ to $4^{1}/_{2}$ years old before beginning intensive training for reining, Jerry believes. To keep a reining horse from getting a tough mouth and anticipating your signals Jerry recommends, "After you get him going and see that he's capable—leave the horse alone. A reining horse is extremely difficult to keep eager to work. Leave off all unnecessary training after the horse is ready to show—just stay with enough exercise, such as longe line, round pen and easy riding, to keep the horse in peak condition."

Jerry is widely known for the excellence of his winning halter horses. Rubbing and brushing are the basic practices of his grooming program. "Each horse gets at least 30 to 40 minutes of rubbing each day," Jerry said, explaining that "this is broken into two sessions—before and after exercise." He uses a rubber curry as the mainstay of grooming, remarking that, "The whole point is to get as much hair off as possible every day."

Jerry also uses a rubber curry on the mane and tail feeling that frequent combing has a tendency to pull out too much hair. He does use a coat conditioner and hoof dressing at a show, but the coat is always smooth and lustrous from continual brushing—not the conditioner. When asked about blanketing, Jerry said he rarely uses blankets from May to September. "I don't like to see a horse sweat under a blanket. It's just too hot in the summer."

In the summer Jerry frequently bathes horses to rinse sweat and dirt from the hair coat and skin. "I do not use anything except warm, clear water. It's hard to brush that sweat and dirt off," he remarked. As for clipping, Jerry never clips a horse all over. "I believe that it is best to let nature take her course, aided by plenty of brushing and rubbing."

When asked about feeding methods, Jerry answered that he uses whole oats and high quality "rabbit" alfalfa. He is fortunate enough to live in an area where outstanding alfalfa is produced. Regarding supplements Jerry said, "I've tried a little bit of everything and haven't found any difference. I always go back to alfalfa—really good alfalfa takes the place of almost everything."

Usually hay is fed free choice, but it depends on the horse. Jerry takes care to not get a horse too fat, but just maintain condition. Mares and colts on pasture get free choice hay kept in racks in "loafing" sheds, and grain once a day.

Concerning general health management, stalled horses are stomach tube wormed every 90 to 120 days. Broodmares on pasture are wormed every six months. To keep the parasite problem down, pastures where horses are concentrated are harrowed periodically. Stalls are bedded with shavings and cleaned daily.

Under Jerry's management, physical exams, including blood analysis and dental work, are a regular part of health care. Horses are vaccinated annually for tetanus and encephalitis. "I've never had any problem with flu," Jerry remarked. Shoeing is done at regular intervals, depending on the horse; broodmares are trimmed every 70 to 80 days and colts are trimmed and watched carefully for problems requiring corrective trimming.

Lots of individual attention from the time a horse is foaled summarizes Jerry Wells' conditioning program. He makes it a point to know just how much exercise a horse needs and just how much a horse can stand by following a program of gradually increasing work. Another basic is protection of the physical and mental condition of every horse. Techniques such as starting colts relatively late, and minimal training of the "finished" horse are all aimed at preservation of the physical condition and mental attitude of a horse.

James Bartholomew Cummings

(Interview by Jack Greathead)

As Australia's foremost Thoroughbred trainer, James Bartholomew (Bart) Cummings has experienced unprecedented success. The excellence of Mr. Cummings' conditioning program has been proven time and time again by the superior ability of his horses.

Mr. Cummings is the first Australian to train winners of over a million dollars in stakes during a single season. As a great trainer of stayers Mr. Cummings has won Australia's premier race, The Melbourne Cup, three times. This feat is totally unique in the history of the Cup. Light Fingers in 1965, Galilee in 1966, and Red Handed in 1967 are Mr. Cummings' Melbourne Cup winners. To make the achievement even more meritorious, he also trained the runners up in 1965 and 1966. (Ziema and Light Fingers, respectively).

In fact, every prestigious staying race in Australia has been won at least once by Cummings-trained horses. He also has proven himself with sprinters. Tontonan, Century and Storm Queen are a few of his champion sprinters.

Mr. Cummings became a public trainer in 1954 after serving as foreman to his late father, Jim, for several years. Jim Cummings won the 1950 Melbourne Cup with Comic Court, whom Bart strapped. 1958 brought Bart Cummings' first major success as a trainer on his own, when Stormy Passage won the South Australian Derby.

At the time of this interview Mr. Cummings had 70 horses in training, including 50 at his headquarters in Adelaide and 20 in Melbourne. As another unparalleled achievement, Mr. Cummings has three times been the leading trainer in South Australia and Victoria in the same season. He races horses regularly in all States of Australia and travels more than 100,000 miles annually in supervising their preparation.

"The psychological well-being of a horse is as important as his physical well-being," states Bart Cummings. For this reason he firmly believes in taking a horse slowly and gradually building him up with steady work and a good nutritional program.

Bart comments that, "As a public trainer, I do not have any contact with young stock until they are purchased at yearling sales." Because of this his conditioning commences with getting a yearling ready for breaking. "Before breaking it is vitally important to have a yearling in a sound, healthy condition. For breaking to be successful, the yearling should have a foundation of good condition," Bart explained.

If a yearling is in poor condition, he will make certain that it gets up to 16 pounds of oats a day plus protein (amino acid concentrate), vitamin and mineral supplements. Along with this the horse gets $1/2$ gallon boiled grain and bran at night. This treatment is continued until Bart is satisfied with the yearling's condition. The nutritional building-up treatment for yearlings does not include a formal exercise regime.

Bart recommends that foals be halter broke soon after they reach one month in age. To help make a foal more obedient, it is led off a pony after halter breaking. Bart comments that colts are usually broke to saddle a little earlier than fillies, but the same practices are followed with both. The yearlings are broke to saddle individually, but ridden in groups of four. Bart explains, "Riding in groups speeds their education, and also makes them less shy of movement."

When yearlings are first ridden, the exercise amounts only to a steady trot and a slow canter. "Horses are under no pressure whatsoever," Bart added, stressing that the psychological state of a horse is just as important as the physical state. He prefers a boy less than ten stone (140 pounds) to first ride colts. When asked if he has ever used girls to break colts, Bart replied, "I've never known of a professional woman colt breaker in Australia."

He insists that the rider be an expert with much practical experience in horsemanship. "Breaking-in is the most important part in the making of a champion. I've never seen a champion in this country with a bad mouth," Bart said, then added, "The good breaker is the one who gives a young horse confidence."

Concerning exercise during this period, young horses are handled first by the breaker for 14 days. Then the horses are trotted gradually until after five weeks they are doing two miles a day. "This muscles them up and counters the effects of a high-grain diet," Bart said in explanation.

Bart was asked where he likes to keep young horses and commented, "Most Australian studs are in a climate that lends itself to grazing." He added that, "In Victoria some farms box (stall) yearlings in extreme cold, but not mares. Because of the temperate climate in Australia, it would be unique to find mares boxed. Foals are boxed for a week after weaning, then they go back to the paddock."

When asked how his conditioning program differs for specific types of horses, Bart replied that he trains sprinters and stayers. He then

Bart Cummings, Australia's most successful Thoroughbred trainer.

explained that, "A likely stayer, the horse with a late maturing pedigree, would be put aside in a two acre paddock during the early stages of training." In comparison, prospective sprinters, or those horses with precocious (early maturing) pedigrees, under Bart's care are put into work two months after having been broken. Work for these horses increases at a slow, steady rate.

Bart believes that a young horse needs to be in training for about 60 days to accurately determine the relative athletic ability of the horse. "I work on the basis that it takes a horse 100 days from the time it comes into the stable for training to be fit enough to win. There are exceptions, but 100 days is a good general rule. After about 60 days of training a horse is let run for the first time," he explained. The degrees of condition sets the age that a young horse enters his first race—there is no specific deadline for horses under Bart's care.

He does, however, pay special attention to a yearling's knees before the onset of intensive training. Although Bart does not necessarily insist that the knees be completely closed, he does advocate the use of discretion according to radiological findings as to the extent that pressure can be applied. "Use veterinary advice," he warns. With horses that are late maturing Bart recommends "slow, steady muscling work . . . but, extremely late maturers must be put back into the paddock for safety and economic reasons."

In answer to a question concerning getting young horses used to crowds before they are actually entered in a race Bart remarked, "Young horses learn quickly, but I make use of barrier trials under race conditions to accustom them to the race atmosphere. These trials in Australia often are attended by quite large crowds which simulate a race-day atmosphere." He has no trouble keeping people away from his horses because, "the security on courses in Australia is reasonably good and the horses are protected from the public by a barrier."

Bart was asked his opinion on racing two-year-olds and he commented, "Because they are born to race, the Thoroughbred industry is becoming increasingly geared to two-year-old racing." In addition he said, "In this country it is possible to win more than $100,000 in two individual races as a two-year-old." Bart believes that if the horse is well reared, of good bone and properly conditioned, he can win at two and still be winning top class races at five years old. In explanation he said, "Comic Court, trained by my late father, Jim, won the Fulham Plate, four furlongs, when not 24 months old and yet was still able to carry topweight of 131 pounds and run a record of 3 minutes, 19.5 seconds in winning the 1950 Melbourne Cup, two miles."

To emphasize individual care, Bart firmly feels that the secret of training two-year-olds is tender, loving care. "It's a matter of judgement, too," he adds. Bart also believes that the individual breeding of a horse makes a difference in the way a horse is going to respond to training and what the individual horse needs. "Some, because of their nervous make-up, require only trotting and cantering to bring them to their peak. Others need a strong gallop a couple of days before a race to clean their wind," he explains. Therefore, he does not believe that there is a specific age for the "performance peak" of a horse—the physical condition and psychological state of the individual horse are the true determining factors.

The individual animal's peak is determined by the way that animal has been reared, Bart feels. "Modern breeding and feeding techniques are producing animals of earlier maturity and it is not unusual to see a horse reach his peak in his mid three-year-old career. In earlier years, horses reached their peak at four or five," he stated.

Bart firmly believes that track work, as a part of a conditioning program, is to get a horse fit, *not* display his speed. "A good jockey, with a good judgement of pace is essential." With the ungenerous type of horse he often finds it necessary to force them hard on the track to produce their best. "These horses frequently respond well to a little track work, but plenty of exercise without a rider is also important," he added.

Bart's primary objective with a staying horse is to control their speed and conserve their energy. "Both sprinters and stayers are never subjected to undue strain before they are thoroughly seasoned and their system is conditioned to accept the work," —this is a fundamental of Bart's program.

Generally, he feels that the older a horse gets, the more exercise he requires—especially to reduce the build-up of fat inside. "The cardinal rule is never to subject a horse, no matter what his age, to an exercise he is not fit enough to cope with." For this reason, two-year-olds under Bart's care are never worked beyond six furlongs and his best results have been with restricted gallops of four furlongs. "In my opinion," Bart states, "most training troubles are the result of horses being underfed and overtrained."

Regarding exercise regimes, Bart remarked, "In Australia, with the warmer climate, dehydration is a problem." He has found that when a horse is getting too much exercise he will dehydrate and lose condition—often going off his feed, too. "In extreme cases of lack of exercise," Bart says, "there is a filling in of the hind legs, and even founder." He cautions that the amount of exercise is a matter of judgement by the trainer. "A gross stallion would naturally require more long, steady work to maintain peak condition than a light framed mare."

Swimming is one type of exercise Bart favors. He has found that swimming is an effective technique for developing wind in horses and also has therapeutic advantages. "On the average, we swim each horse three minutes about four times a week," he explained, then added, "In the summer we swim every day—weather permitting." Bart feels that walking horses in the Australian surf is excellent therapy.

Specific preparation, just prior to a race, involves walking a horse 30 to 45 minutes before saddling up. "Use your own discretion, it is simply a matter of judgment," Bart replied. He does not use mechanical walkers, reporting, "Walking machines are not accepted in Australia." On muddy tracks, he will tie up the horse's tail. After a race, horses are cooled by plenty of walking and minimal hosing. If a race is in a drastically different climate, a minimum of ten days with restricted training is allowed for physical adjustment.

Concerning horses that are particularly nervous Bart had several comments. "The best way to counteract this nervousness," he said, "is to take these horses to the races several times before they are raced, just to look around. This will improve the horse that sweats up before a race, too." He also believes that music helps in that it "keeps the staff happy and contented and, so, keeps the horses contented." Vitamin B-complex concentrate powder and rest, whenever needed, even if it means missing a race, are incorporated in management of highly strung horses.

Bart has had no particular trouble with bad habits. "Generally I take early action to prevent formation of bad habits. However, some bad habits are characteristic of specific bloodlines. In this case, you get in first and take early corrective action," he stated.

If horses must be laid off, due to injury, Bart emphasizes steady training to bring the horse back. His practices include giving the horse a few days off in the stable just trotting and cantering easily. He also said that two-year-olds may require antiphlogistine poultices for a couple of nights after a race to minimize the effects of shin soreness. "Although," Bart remarked, "with the turf tracks in Australia generally no specific leg treatment is needed for protection during racing."

Leg wraps are used on horses under Bart's care. The wraps are used at night *just* as support and to help circulation. Liniments are used very sparingly—he prefers to put a horse up in a paddock and use a blister. When asked about firing Bart answered, "External firing has given good results with bowed tendons and needle point firing has been successful with recurrent shin soreness."

As for general health programs, Bart requires that every horse be wormed at five week intervals via stomach tube. Also, blood analysis is run on a regular schedule of once a month. As part of the routine, each morning prior to work the feed left and droppings are checked. A veterinarian regularly looks for unusual paddock bruises, scars, etc. and performs needed dental work. A farrier examines every horse in the stable each day. Generally, horses are reshod about every three weeks.

Yearlings are the only horses that are bathed as a part of the program. Warm water and a preparation to prevent the spread of skin disease are used in every case. Older horses, after a race, are hosed only on the chest and legs—the back and loins are kept dry. Bart uses blankets from the time a horse is broken in. "Blankets keep horses warm and minimize the risk of infection resulting from a sudden drop in temperature," he explained.

Double blankets are used on horses after clipping. Once a year, Bart's horses are clipped all over. This is to remove long hair and facilitate drying to reduce the risk of colds.

Concerning facilities, the ideal stall is 16 feet by 14 feet bedded with oat or rye straw, Bart feels. The minimum size is 12 feet by 14 feet. "Horses are happier when they can see each other in adjoining stalls," Bart said. For this reason he favors concrete or brick walls, 4 feet 6 inches high, topped with bars or screen so that the horses can see others, but not fight. Stalls are cleaned daily.

Bart keeps three horses per man—he demands that his hands be patient and kind. "Hands must be experienced, with good references," he listed as requirements, and added, "abstainers are preferred and smoking is prohibited in the stable."

When asked about feeding Bart replied that his horses are fed three times daily, as follows:

Morning
    4 pounds oats
    1 pound cracked corn
    1 quart lucerne and oaten chaff, 3:1 ratio
    2 pounds lucerne hay in elevated bag

Midday
    4 pounds oats
    grated carrots
    vitaminized, electrolyte mixture

Night
    oats, minimum 6 pounds
    $1/2$ gallon boiled barley mash
    4 pounds lucerne hay and sheaf of oaten hay
    Vitamin and mineral supplements, morning and night.

As a trainer, Bart prefers that owners do nothing to get their horses ready for him. "Generally, the best results in my stable are gained by horses spelled (or kept) under my supervision." He likes to start them on good pasture and light exercise, working up to two and three miles a day of trotting and cantering and a high grain ration. He feels that he needs to have a horse at least five or six weeks.

In conclusion, Bart Cummings firmly believes in taking a horse slowly and building him up—paying special attention to the psychological well-being of a horse. His techniques involve taking advantage of the Australian climate—for example, the therapeutic quality of walking horses in the surf. Each horse is treated as a distinct individual and watched carefully at all times. This Australian trainer credits his success to excellent health care, steady exercise, plenty of patience and individual attention.

W. L. Anderson, D.V.M.

(Interview by Barbara Wright)

Dr. W. L. Anderson, past president of the Texas Veterinary Medical Association, has an extensive large animal practice in the Dallas-Fort Worth area specializing in equine medicine. Repeatedly he is faced with problems in all areas of equine conditioning and is often sought for counseling.

Widely recognized for his continued interest in horses, Dr. Anderson serves on the Advisory Committee to the House of Delegates Representing Large Animal Practice of the American Veterinary Medical Association and has been cited for outstanding service by the Texas Animal Commission and other veterinary organizations.

Through study at Texas A&M University and the wide scope of his practice, Dr. Anderson firmly concludes that proper conditioning is vital to the successful campaigning of any athlete. He feels that conscientious management programs "following the basics" in equine care make up the "backbone" of all successful conditioning regimes.

"Conditioning of horses is the same as it is with human athletes; it means being in excellent physical condition to be able to successfully cope with any physical competition expected of the animal. It is a vital necessity as far as any athlete is concerned, including horses."

When asked about conditioning programs for weanlings, Dr. Anderson replied, "I believe that it is best to keep them in pasture in groups of weanlings, segregated as to sex. Not more than eight to ten weanlings per pasture is preferable. After they are taken off their dam, weanlings should not be creep fed. Ideally, they should be fed individually, twice daily, if possible.

"If weanlings must be kept in a stall, an exercise program needs to be initiated. Assuming they are halter broken, it would be prefereable to pony them behind another horse at a trot. Other than riding, this is the best means of conditioning any horse. A mechanical walker would be the second choice and free exercise in an arena or small pasture would be third. Care should be taken to see that the animal's hooves are properly trimmed.

"For the yearling, I would continue with the same program," Dr. Anderson commented, adding, "ponying at a trot behind another horse is an ideal form of exercise. At a trot practically all the muscles of the animal's body are utilized. Of course, in many instances this is not economically feasible and other methods of exercise would have to be used. If free exercised in a pen, I would limit the number of horses to two, because they might get hurt."

In answer to a question concerning breaking performance horses to saddle, Dr. Anderson said, "I wouldn't break any horse before 18 months of age, and preferably later, to wait until the knees are closed. I think this is true for performance horses, race horses—any kind. It is better if the knees are closed but I don't think it hurts to break them out with a saddle and a little light riding, provided that the epiphyseal plate is not too open. Of course, the horse's feet should be cared for properly.

"Also, they should have high quality rations to assure that the bone is ossifying properly. The necessary minerals, such as calcium and phosphorus, are vital at this time. I believe it is very important to X-ray knees, because there is no way to determine that the knees are closed without X-raying. We see quite a few horses damaged permanently because they were ridden at too early an age, before the epiphyseal plates had closed. In essence, don't break any colt before 18 months and preferably 24 to 30 months."

Dr. Anderson was asked about the physical stress of various types of performance training and remarked, "Generally speaking, I think cutting is tougher on a performance horse than anything else, especially if the horse is subjected to an ambitious trainer."

He recommends "following the basics," such as proper shoeing, good nutrition and physical fitness to avoid injuries during training. "Get the animal in shape by not starting out too fast, leg him up properly and see that he is in excellent physical condition. I think many times we tend to push horses before they are capable of being pushed. That is, their muscles and bones are not developed, or possibly they don't have a blood count that is sufficiently high and consequently are receiving an insufficient oxygen supply. This is something that is often neglected."

When asked about different types of exercise for specific areas of performance, Dr. Anderson commented, "I think physical fitness is basically the same for every horse. He should be in good shape. This is also true for the halter horse. The halter horse should be in good condition and not overly fitted, or too fat. I believe being in good physical condition is vital for all horses in any type of performance.

"I think that we see more navicular disease and fractures of the phalanges than any other problems in cutting horses and roping horses," he replied when questioned about specific injuries in performance horses. "Problems of the third phalanx are certainly not unusual

Active in the service of many veterinary organizations, Dr. W. L. Anderson is an expert in the field of equine conditioning.

in performance horses, especially where they are asked to perform on hard ground. Arenas that are properly sanded or soft enough will keep concussion to a minimum and you will have fewer problems. Quite a few horses pop splints, but these are usually due to poor conformation, poor nutrition or training on hard ground.

"In clarification, fractures of the second and third phalanx are not extremely common, but are seen more often in cutting and roping horses. With most of these injuries, the horse cannot be expected to regain his former ability. Navicular disease is a problem that is very difficult to treat with any success; fractures are always difficult to handle and expect a horse to come back and perform normally."

When asked about wintering a horse, Dr. Anderson stated that he believes the horse is always better off in a pasture, if there is adequate room. "If there are too many horses per acre, a horse should be kept in a stall to avoid poor sanitation and inadequate grazing conditions." He also remarked that the horse should be kept at a reasonably constant temperature, not too warm. In addition he commented, "Personally, I think horses are much better off without any blankets, but it is impossible to keep a good hair coat on an animal without blankets." He also emphasized the importance of high quality nutrients and plenty of clean, fresh water.

After the winter, or a rest of any kind, Dr. Anderson strongly advises legging a horse up slowly, ideally by ponying behind another horse. "Start out at a walk for thirty minutes twice daily and gradually work up to a point where the horse is able to trot that much, or more, twice daily. I feel that it is impossible to beat ponying to get a horse in the shape where he can be ridden. Swimming is also an excellent method of exercise, but the animal needs regular exercise as well.

"After the horse has reached the point where he is physically fit for riding, he should be exercised with someone on his back. The rider, the individual horse and the duties to be performed are all factors to be considered in deciding how much riding should be done. However, after a horse is in good condition, I believe that too much exercise is highly unlikely, under normal circumstances, provided the horse has good nutrition, the feet are properly cared for and he is ridden over reasonable terrain."

"Good cooperation between stable management and the veterinarian is vitally important in establishing the routine procedures to assure the best health possible for horses", Dr. Anderson firmly states. Working with the veterinarian, management must make the decisions to implement routine health practices, enforced at specific intervals.

"There are various good feeding programs that can be followed, but these programs should be as natural as practical. If possible, proper nutrients should be gained from high quality grain and hay.

"Immunization programs are very important, especially for the young horse. The program should be started when the horse is very young utilizing strangles bacterin, influenza vaccine, tetanus toxoid, Eastern and Western Encephalomyelitis, rhinopneumonitis, and, in some areas, Venezuelan Encephalomyelitis. Generally, I prefer to start out when the foal is very young and repeat with boosters annually.

"Worming schedules vary with the way the horse is being kept. It is important that horses be wormed at regularly scheduled intervals, especially the young horse, to avoid later parasite problems. I recommend worming the foal at six to eight weeks of age, and every 30 to 60 days thereafter until the horse is two years of age. At this point, begin taking stool samples every 30 to 60 days to determine if infestation has occurred. (This schedule is for horses raised in concentration.)

"Horses stalled individually, in properly cared for stalls, probably won't have to be wormed more than three times a year, and only twice in some cases. Tube worming is by far the best method and the worming medication should be changed with each consecutive worming.

"Any animal in performance should have a blood analysis consisting of at least the hematocrit and hemoglobin determinations, every three to four weeks. If the findings are abnormal, complete blood chemistries should be run, including routine liver tests, muscle tests, calcium and phosphorus determinations, etc. Blood analysis should be utilized anytime that a horse appears to be abnormal—for example, not eating or responding to usual medication, antibiotics, supportive treatment, etc."

Concisely, to assure optimum health for any horse, Dr. Anderson stresses proper management, good nutrition, a sound immunization program, a regular worming procedure and regular blood analyses.

When hauling a horse to several shows, or from track to track, strict sanitation practices should be followed to avoid the spread of disease, he adds. "Never let a horse eat or drink from receptacles that could have been contaminated by other horses. Also, unless the horse rests at periodic intervals while he is being trailered, it is very important to see that the animal is eating and provided adequate water. Sometimes a horse will need to be given mineral oil on trips. Again, I emphasize the importance of proper immunization."

When asked what indicators the average horseman can use to determine the state of condition of his individual animal, Dr. Anderson stated, "The hair coat tells a lot, also the flesh that the animal carries—the amount of flab the horse has tells a lot about his condition.

It varies with the horseman and his experience, but I believe that most horsemen can tell when their animal is fatiguing prematurely. The experienced horseman should be able to tell when a horse is not in condition and doesn't have the vigor and vitality that he should. Actually, it is very difficult for the novice horseman to determine these things, especially when he sees his horse only once a week.

"Blood pressure and heart rate can give a fair indication of the physical condition of a horse, but I don't think they should be relied upon exclusively. Different horses have different chemistries and there are numerous other factors that can give a false impression if you place too much emphasis on pulse rate and blood pressure."

In answer to a question concerning the QRS complex or heart score, he said, "I think that this does have merit, but I don't believe that we can use this exclusively to determine a horse's capability of performance. It should be utilized along with the conformation, size and general physical condition of the horse."

Dr. Anderson feels that heritability is very important in influencing an animal's athletic success. "Excellent conditioning techniques and heritability are both essential for a horse's success.

"Personally I would like to see the same testing in performance as there is in racing," he commented when asked about drug testing. "It is very important to see that these animals have not been stimulated or depressed; drugs are used as 'crutches' too often in both racing and performance. They can be used therapeutically in many instances to keep a horse from soring too much, but we emphasize pre-race medication frequently and should use post-race medication.

"Vitamins and minerals can be used as conditioning aids, provided the animal is not receiving proper amounts in his feed. Supplementation is essential, but too much stress is placed on the use of vitamins immediately before a race—in a few instances you may see slight improvement, but it is usually negligible."

He doesn't feel that daily bathing is good for a horse's skin. "I think this should be done as infrequently as possible. The brush, the rub rag and the curry comb are much preferred to bathing. Granted, daily bathing is done by many successful trainers, but I don't like the practice."

Dr. Anderson states that exercise is vital for any breeding animal. Stallions should have adequate exercise, he feels, explaining that, "The most outstanding stallion, as far as settling mares, that I ever had the opportunity to work with, was ridden every day. Mares also need adequate exercise to function properly. Every breeding animal ideally should have access to adequate free exercise."

For mares coming out of training, he recommends about a six

months "let down" period before breeding the mare—depending upon the age of the mare. "Allow her to lose some weight, start gaining again, and be on the upswing nutritionally, when she is being bred." Emphasizing that the age of the mare can make a difference, Dr. Anderson commented that in some cases a maiden mare coming out of training can be successfully bred during her first heat period. If the mare fails to conceive during this first heat then it is generally advisable to wait for the "let down" period to have its full effects.

"To keep older animals in breeding condition, you should follow sound health, nutritional and exercise programs—this includes proper care of the teeth. Any lamenesses should be corrected, to keep the animal from experiencing pain." In explanation he added, "Many times we will nerve breeding animals that we wouldn't consider nerving as performance animals."

Dr. Anderson was asked about stall foaling versus pasture foaling and remarked, "Stall foaling is fine provided that the mare is watched around the clock. If not, I would prefer that one foal in the pasture. When a mare foals in a stall it is extremely important that she be watched constantly because if she starts to foal against the wall, it is very easy to kill the foal in the process of foaling."

If a mare does foal in a stall, Dr. Anderson stresses the importance of exercise to aid the mare in recovering from foaling. He advises turning the mare out for exercise within an hour or two of the time she passes the placenta. He also feels that a mare can be in acceptable condition to be bred back during her foal heat.

"Some very successful horse gynecologists skip the foal heat entirely, but in my opinion it is certainly alright to breed a mare at this time. The mare must be examined by an experienced veterinarian to make certain that she is in proper condition for foal heat breeding."

To assure a foal of becoming as good as he has the genetic capability of being, Dr. Anderson emphasizes excellent mare care, including proper nutrition and health programs. Also, the foal should be born in sanitary surroundings and properly treated immediately following foaling. "Beginning at one to two weeks of age, the foal should be offered creep feed. His immunization program should begin at three weeks of age and the worming schedule at six to eight weeks of age.

"A foal should be broke to lead while he is a suckling and adequate exercise is vitally important. Many people make the mistake of failing to allow the foal to have the natural exercise he needs to stretch and grow as he should. Also, we often tend to over fit the suckling by feeding the mare too much, forcing her to give too much milk. This can bring about problems, especially when the foal is too heavy for his bone structure. The middle of the road is very difficult to attain, but we can do as much damage by overfeeding as we can by underfeeding.

"The foal should be weaned when he is four to six months of age. Many times we wait too long and cause damage to the mare, especially old mares, by allowing her to act as a nurse animal for an extended period of time and thereby taking too much nutrition from her for the colt."

Dr. Anderson was then asked about facilities for the performance or race horse. "I feel that a stall should be at least 12 feet by 12 feet; saddlebred animals will need a larger stall to accommodate the tail board. As far as construction is concerned, I believe that wood is preferable, but have seen some acceptable stalls manufactured from concrete, steel, etc. It varies with the part of the country, but I prefer to bed on wood shavings. Of course, tanbark is the Cadillac of bedding, but it is very difficult to obtain.

"I would much rather have stall walls solid all the way up, as I have seen many injuries that could have been prevented had solid walls been utilized." He was then questioned about the insect problem with a stall-kept situation and commented that there is no ideal insecticide for use with horses. "Methoxychlor and pyrethrins are probably most commonly used, but both have their disadvantages. Although long lasting, methoxychlor leaves a white residue on the animal; while pyrethrins are effective, they are extremely short lasting. We certainly need an effective, long lasting insecticide safe for use with horses."

In summation, Dr. Anderson emphasizes a program of preventive health care and a more natural life-style for the horse. He stresses slow starts in all phases of training to assure proper development; frequent worming according to the way the horse is kept; and frequent blood tests for horses in competition. He feels close management-veterinary relations, strict sanitation, regular exercise and high quality nutritional standards are basic to all successful conditioning programs.

Newt Keck

As a trainer of running Quarter Horses, Newt Keck is widely known as one of the very best. In his approach to conditioning, Mr. Keck most strongly emphasizes the individuality of each and every horse. He believes in knowing the individual characteristics of a horse and devising a unique conditioning program to best fit each separate horse. Another of Mr. Keck's fundamental conditioning theories is to treat each horse as if he was the best runner in the stable.

The quality of Mr. Keck's conditioning techniques has been proven time and time again by his continuing high rank among Quarter Horse trainers throughout the country. Newt Keck has achieved one goal matched by no other trainer. He has trained three separate individuals who have won the World's richest horse race, the All-American Futurity at Ruidoso Downs, New Mexico. Three of the first five runnings of this elite event were won by Newt Keck-trained horses. Galobar in 1959, Pokey Bar in 1961, and Goetta in 1963 are his All-American winners.

Mr. Keck has trained many other great running Quarter Horses. His list includes Ruby Charge, winner of the 1965 Kansas Futurity, Nippy Bars, winner of the 1965 Rainbow Derby, Jet Too, winner of the 1966 Sunland Park Fall Futurity, and the superior runner, Mr. Jet Moore, the World Champion Quarter Running Horse in 1972 and winner of more than $340,000.

Mr. Keck was injured some time back and due to these injuries, forced into semi-retirement on his ranch in north central Texas. At the time of this interview, he and his wife, Flo, were preparing to resume training operations in California in the near future. If past performance is any indication of things to come—watch out California!

"Keep a horse contented," Newt Keck remarked, "and any horse that can run will run good for you." Every horse in the Keck barn receives a lot of Newt's personal attention. Newt prefers a small stable so he can give each horse as much care as he would his best runner. He feels that the looks of a horse are a valid indicator of the general condition of that horse.

Each morning, Newt feeds the horses himself and takes a close look at each one. "The most important thing for any one man to do as a trainer is to watch a horse's eye. A horse that is doing good and is sharp will have a real bright eye." Although Newt strongly stresses treating each horse as a unique individual, he does have some general recommendations.

Regarding weaning, Newt likes to leave a foal on the mare as long as possible, that is, as long as the mare gives plenty of milk. Seven months is the ideal weaning age he believes. Newt was quick to add that this isn't always possible. If a mare doesn't milk, he will take the foal off and feed it, making sure that the foal gets all the grain it will eat. Creep feeding foals is another practice Newt likes. "If they get plenty of exercise, I don't think you can feed a foal too much," he remarked.

Following weaning, Newt gives his foals plenty of room to exercise. He makes certain that the foals have a good place to run and aren't "bothered too much." "I like for them to just grow and rest," he commented. However, Newt does strongly recommend breaking a foal to lead while it is still nursing. "If a foal is taught to lead and stand tied while it is still small you decrease the chances of a colt hurting himself." At this time Newt also likes to get a foal used to having his feet picked up.

Newt breaks his yearlings to an exercise saddle in the fall, if possible. When asked about his methods Newt replied, "I've got a lot of confidence in driving a colt and I've done it every way." When you have the facilities, such as a safe, small corral, he feels that driving can be a very successful technique. "You have to have plenty of patience when working with yearlings," he warns. When starting to work with yearlings Newt stalls them at night but keeps them in a small corral during the day so they can look around and exercise on their own.

A hackamore isn't used on the yearlings under Newt's care. He begins with a light snaffle bit, always making sure to be easy on their mouths and protect them. When a youngster gets used to the bit, quits fighting and chewing it, a light gyp (longe) rope is snapped to the bridle and he is exercised in a small corral. Newt doesn't encounter any great differences between fillies and colts just starting. Naturally, some horses are more nervous than others and he takes it slower and easier with these.

Under ideal conditions Newt likes about a 100 pound boy to first ride young horses. "Usually you have to use a 120 to 140 pound boy," he comments, and doesn't feel that "the weight hurts a young horse being ridden around slowly." When running a young horse, he is always sure to have the weight down. "A yearling is worked a little every day until he starts going. After a young horse gets this far along, ponying and a boy are used twice a week each, just to lope the horse." Breaking foals early enough so they can be turned out for six weeks afterward is Newt's favorite method.

When asked about deep sand to leg up a young horse, Newt said he liked it. "But you definitely need a man riding him that knows when to

Newt Keck, pictured with an example of his training success, Pokey Bar, winner of the 1961 All American Futurity and winner of over $160,000.

get him out of the sand," he cautioned. "It's easy for horses, particularly young ones, to strain themselves in sand—they have to be handled right," Newt added. In general, he advocates breaking yearlings anywhere besides a track; "a colt learns that he goes there to run."

Once a week is the most Newt really works a young horse and never farther than 250 yards. "You have to build up courage in a young horse," he says. To do this, he'll work one at a "two minute clip," never letting anyone outwork him. "Don't let a horse get used to running behind another." Newt firmly feels that horses will really try when you take the time to build up their courage.

When asked about how much exercise a young horse needs Newt answered that he goes strictly by the individual. Watch them closely and you'll know how much exercise and training a young horse can stand. "A horse is just like a person," Newt replied, "if you get him hot and tired, and he gets mad—then he won't work for you." He is always careful to point out that when a Quarter Horse runs, the horse gives everything from the very start. Newt stresses that you can only train a Quarter Horse to run as far as he is bred to, a longer distance only takes that "early lick" away from one. Newt feels the horse just won't feel like giving his best at first if you try to add distance beyond the horse's capabilities.

When asked about signs of too much exercise, Newt replied that too much exercise or training doesn't show up in any one specific place. "Just like people," he explained, "each horse has his weak place and over-training will show up in this weak spot." He feels that there are far more horses overworked than underworked.

To prevent injuries, Newt advocates keeping a horse tight—"have the horse ready before you do too much," he says. A slow lope for half a mile with a boy on his back is a good way to build up wind in a horse, Newt believes. "Naturally," he says, "you have to get a horse toughened up before any really hard work." He feels that it is extremely important to get a horse legged up and ready before starting to really sharpen one up.

When asked about swimming Newt said he thought it was an excellent therapeutic measure for horses that were sore. He added, however, that quite a few trainers have a tendency to rely on swimming as a way to get a horse in shape. Newt believes swimming is good therapy, but you can't use it instead of regular exercise.

Newt was asked about racing two-year-olds and answered "Well, that is something that has been talked about ever since I hit the race track. We all know that a three-year-old has more of a chance of staying sound. Naturally, I'd rather go with a three-year-old, but the big money is as a two-year-old."

Newt Keck, trainer of three separate All American Futurity winners, is pictured here at the inaugural running in 1959 with his first winner, Galobar, owned by Hugh Huntley, Madera, California.

"Any horse will be nervous and spooky when you first get him out around crowds," replied Newt when asked how he gets a colt used to crowds. He really doesn't worry about it too much, but does like to ride a horse around the barns to get it used to people. Also, he will let a car meet him, if he is in a place where he can handle the horse, so that it will get used to cars, too. A small track is also good for this purpose, he feels. "You can lope along the outside rail, where people are standing and watching, and the horse will gradually get used to it," Newt explained.

When a horse is ready to run, Newt prefers to pony it for exercise. He says, "After I get a horse ready to run, I'm not much to put a saddle and a boy on his back." In the evenings, he likes to take a horse out on a long rope and let him look around, graze and relax. Newt believes this helps keep a horse psychologically ready to run.

Before a meet Newt likes to be at the track as early as possible. "The longer a horse is there, the better he'll do," he said, then explained, "the horse gets a chance to get used to the stall and relax—they're more content." During his experience there have been some exceptions to this. When there is a big change in altitude the horses are "really sharp" for the first week, Newt explained. For the next couple of weeks after that, they really slow down and it generally takes a horse about three weeks to "snap back" after the first week at higher altitudes, he has found.

Newt is a real believer in blood analysis and thinks a horse should have a high blood count before he runs. If a horse has a low count Newt will work with the vet, using B-complex and iron to get the blood count up. A horse's teeth are also thoroughly checked and any needed work done during the routine of getting ready for a race meet.

For the two weeks prior to a big race Newt's horses *never* run. He will pony the horse, maybe lope it and possibly do a little light work—that's all. "I let the horse work pretty much like he wants to," says Newt. A horse's legs are wrapped the night before a big race, but the bandages come off at least two hours before the horse runs. Also, any horse Newt puts in a trailer has its legs wrapped for protection.

An alcohol bath is part of Newt's routine for getting a horse ready to go to the gate. After that the horse is warmed up, at about a two minute clip, until there is a light sweat on its neck. "Really, it depends most on the individual," Newt explained, "whatever it takes for a horse to get loose and warm up a little—it just depends on how a particular horse acts and feels."

Newt doesn't believe in spurs and doesn't want his horses kicked either. He explains that both of these have a tendency to make a horse wring its tail and that anything a horse does with his tail has a bad effect on speed. For the same reason, Newt avoids wrapping tails whenever he can.

A horse is walked for about 45 minutes to an hour after a race, or until he is cooled out. Then comes a good rub down, brace and leg wraps to be left on overnight. Newt likes geldings best for running. "A mare has her ups and downs," he says. Stallions often will take, and need, more training than others, he believes. "Studs have a tendency to look around in the gate and loose time," Newt added for explanation. He just feels that geldings are by far the most consistent horses.

If a horse stays sound, he feels the horse reaches his peak at five years of age. "At this time a horse has a full mouth and no problems; he eats better and just generally does better." However, he states that most of today's Quarter Horses are "burned up" by five years of age. In answer to the question of when to take a horse off the track, Newt replied, "When a horse has run good for several years and starts tightening up and getting sore in the shoulders, it's time to take him off. A horse has got to have heart and fight—he gives everything he's got when he's out there." Newt lets a horse down slow and easy, never giving one a chance to cripple himself.

As for hay, that depends on how an individual horse fills up on it. Newt likes alfalfa because he has good luck with it—his horses like it, do good on it and alfalfa puts a good finish on his horses.

Newt gives alfalfa a big part of the credit for getting the horse ready that won a thirty mile endurance race for him. The race took place in Washington state about twenty years ago. An eight-year-old Thoroughbred was the horse Newt rode and he conditioned the horse for the race by ponying others at a Thoroughbred race track. "The endurance race was comical," Newt recalled. "We were going through mountains, up and down hills all the way." Of the two hundred horses that started, many didn't finish—they were pulled out at vet check stops along the way. Newt's strategy worked—he stayed behind for most of the race, pulling ahead at the last to finish first.

A lot of rubbing and brushing are included in the grooming program. "I really believe in the rub rag," Newt states. "Grooming is nothing but work." Then he added softly, "I do a lot of grooming and I'm bad with a rag. I was always taught that a man can rub speed into a horse—I believe it. Gradually you feel that skin thinning out and the veins beginning to stick out." He has a lot of pride in his horses' looks and is well known for it. Newt likes a silky mane, smooth laying tail and a slick coat on a horse. "I'm pretty much on blanketing every night," he says, remarking that it keeps a horse really looking good. He uses a hood only when a horse has a bad cold. A hoof dressing goes on every day, but Newt emphasizes using good judgment and leaving the dressing off if feet get too soft.

Three horses to a groom are the most that Newt feels one can really take care of. The one quality he looks for in help is dependability. When asked about having girls for help, Newt commented that he doesn't like the idea too well, feeling that they just can't be knocked around like a man can. "A woman just doesn't fit in there, that's my opinion," he stated. ("I'd feel guilty with a woman cleaning a stall," he added.)

As for general health management, horses under Newt's care are wormed three times a year, but not while they are at the track. He feels it knocks a horse down too much. Shoes are reset on the average of about once a month—"When their feet start growing out, it depends on the individual," Newt said in explanation. Also, he watches a colt's feet closely and trims them, if needed. Teeth of all the horses are checked regularly. Breeding animals, both broodmares and stallions, get plenty of exercise.

In general, knowing your horses and watching them closely is fundamental to Newt Keck. He continually stresses individual attention. Exercise and training are regulated by the way each individual horse looks and acts. If a horse is "down," a blood count is run. Whatever a particular horse needs, he gets. Newt likes to keep a horse legged up and tight. Good grooming is basic to the program. In conclusion, Newt Keck believes in treating *every* horse as if he were "real class."

Floyd C. Sager
D.V.M.

Dr. Floyd C. Sager is the resident veterinarian for the prestigious Claiborne Farm in Paris, Kentucky. In this capacity he is continually faced with problems in every phase of equine conditioning. The superior racing record of Claiborne Farm serves to illuminate Dr. Sager's success with programs for conditioning Thoroughbred horses. The experience and repute of Dr. Sager certainly qualify him as an expert in the field of equine conditioning; he is frequently called upon as an author and lecturer to aid in the dissemination of information to the horse industry.

QUESTION: What kind of conditioning and exercise program do you recommend for weanling colts?
ANSWER: The needs of the indiviual horse must govern the feeding—enough oats to keep the weanling growing, but not too fat. They should be in pasture 16 hours a day during summer heat and in the pasture for 8 hours during winter months. This will give the weanling a rest in the stall away from flies and heat during the summer months and keep it in the barn at night during the cold months. The young horse should be led to and from the pasture and brushed daily.

QUESTION: How do you step up this program prior to breaking and what precautions should be taken at the time of breaking?
ANSWER: No change in the program until breaking is started. All Thoroughbreds should be broken as yearlings. Go slowly, never force the young horse.

The speed of the education depends on the ability of the animal to learn. Always be gentle; discipline must be exercised with great care and caution.

QUESTION: Do you advise X-raying yearlings' knees before putting them in training?
ANSWER: I believe it is wise to X-ray the knees of all yearlings before they leave the farm.

QUESTION: How do you feel about racing two-year-olds?
ANSWER: Ordinarily two-year-olds are not ready to race, or at least not until late in their two-year-old year. Under our present racing set up there will always be racing of two-year-olds and the smart owner

will wait until his horse is physically ready to race. I do not think they should ever start before August of their two-year-old year.

QUESTION: What can you do to prevent injuries to the young horse during training?

ANSWER: Except for the race horse, most horses are usually mature before starting special training. In breaking yearlings, make sure they are gentle and accept equipment and rider in the stall. To prevent injury, keep excessive weight off their backs and make sure they are ridden on a soft (not too soft) surface. No speed trials during the breaking year.

QUESTION: Do you think heritability plays as big a role in a horse's success as does proper conditioning techniques?

ANSWER: I think heredity comes first, but must be coupled with the proper training and conditioning techniques. On very rare occasions a horse with very poor breeding will become a great race horse with the proper training and conditioning.

QUESTION: At what age should the young horse with normal feet and legs start being trimmed and shod?

ANSWER: You should start trimming foals' feet at 90 days of age, and younger if the hoof is abnormal. Shoeing should be put off until required by the use of the animal. Yearlings being readied for sale or show should be plated to prevent breaking of hooves.

QUESTION: What should be done routinely to assure the best health possible for a horse as an athlete?

ANSWER: The horse should be immunized against tetanus and influenza. Such other vaccinations and tests may be required at the receiving points when shipped to trainers. Blood tests should not be necessary as long as the condition of the animal is satisfactory.

QUESTION: When a horse is at a track, what measures should be taken to prevent the spread of disease?

ANSWER: Have the van cleaned and disinfected, and take the same precautions with the stall. Use your own clean feed pans and water buckets.

QUESTION: When do you feel leg wraps, liniments, cold water bandages, etc. should be applied by persons other than a veterinarian?

ANSWER: Any attendant who is qualified should be allowed to do the above, but always on the recommendation of the veterinarian.

QUESTION: Do you believe swimming a horse has any merits in a conditioning program?

ANSWER: Yes, it allows the animal to use all the muscles without

The success of the famous Claiborne Farm is partly attributable to the knowledge and skill of Dr. Floyd C. Sager, resident veterinarian.

the concussion resulting from moving on a hard surface.

QUESTION: How can the indiscriminate use of medication and supplements affect a horse's ability to perform at his peak?
ANSWER: Used indiscriminately, antibiotics could sterilize the gut of a horse and corticosteroids could interrupt the actions of the adrenal glands. In conjunction with the use of certain minerals, the indiscriminate use of vitamins could be harmful.

QUESTION: Do you feel some drugs could be used with race/performance horses without possible harmful effects to the animal or fraudulent outcomes of their performance?
ANSWER: Yes, Butazolidin.

QUESTION: How often should a horse be wormed to keep him as free from internal parasites as possible?
ANSWER: Horses should be wormed once a year (February) for the removal of bots. If feasible, have fecal egg counts made every thirty days and worm every animal which shows an egg count of forty strongyle eggs or more per gram, or an ascarid egg. If it is not practical to do this, the animals should be wormed every sixty days. Worming by stomach tube is far superior to the use of any wormers in the feed.

QUESTION: Concerning the use of vitamin and mineral supplements as conditioning aids, what guidelines should be used to guard against toxicity levels?
ANSWER: Ordinarily, if the directions for the use of the supplement are followed to the letter, there will be no harmful effects.

QUESTION: What are your feelings about firing a horse before any injury has occurred?
ANSWER: Never fire as a preventive measure. Medically, the greatest good from firing comes from the rest given the animal. The longer the rest, the better results from firing.

QUESTION: How long after shinbuck should a horse be rested, before he is put back into training?
ANSWER: With bucked shins the animal should be rested and cooled out until there is no heat, above body heat, in the injured area and no soreness on pressure. This should be followed by either firing or blistering, then the horse can go back into training thirty days after the treatment.

QUESTION: Approximately what percentage of horses with bowed tendons return to the track?
ANSWER: About fifty per cent of those horses with bowed tendons

return to the track, but a very, very small percentage of these horses ever retain their original form.

QUESTION: Do you feel bathing a horse frequently is a good practice, from a medical viewpoint?
ANSWER: Bathing with clear water apparently does no harm. An animal which is showered with a hose and dried with a scraper will be much cleaner than is possible by ordinary grooming.

QUESTION: Is exercise necessary to maintain peak fertility in stallions?
ANSWER: Yes, without proper exercise there cannot be a bloom of health and without the bloom of health you cannot have optimum fertility and libido.

QUESTION: What medically based practices can be used to keep old mares and stallions in good breeding condition?
ANSWER: I know of nothing specific, excellent health is the answer. This can be attained by proper feeding, care and exercise. An animal that is permanently disabled—crippled, for example—should be placed in a paddock daily and allowed to take as much exercise as it will.

QUESTION: How long does it take to "let down" a mare coming out of training before trying to breed her?
ANSWER: There is a wide difference of opinion on this. Some believe it best to breed the mare in her first heat period after she arrives at the farm from the track. I believe she should have at least three months on the farm before breeding and six months would be better.

QUESTION: Do you recommend stall or pasture foaling; and, if the foaling occurs in a stall, how soon after foaling should the mare and foal be turned out?
ANSWER: Stall foaling is preferable. It is the only way you can observe and control the mare. The mare and foal should be placed in a paddock, weather permitting, the morning after foaling, the amount of time out depends on the temperature. The foal should not be allowed to lay down on the cold ground. Repeat the turn out in the afternoon and increase the time out daily, until the foal stays out all day.

QUESTION: What should be done for the foal from the time he is born until he is weaned to insure him of having every chance of fulfilling his genetic potential?
ANSWER: Make sure his dam has an adequate milk supply. Allow the foal to have grain as soon as he desires it. Also provide excellent hay and keep him on excellent pasture. Protect him from all disease by insuring no contact with diseased animals. Allow the foal plenty of exercise and provide him with a clean, comfortable place to rest.

QUESTION: What special care should an orphan foal receive to assure him of being in acceptable condition upon going into training?
ANSWER: The orphan foal should be raised on a "nurse mare" and treated the same as all others after weaning.

QUESTION: Do you recommend "balling out" every foal, or only those that indicate the need?
ANSWER: I believe in routine balling out of all foals the morning after their birth.

QUESTION: How important is colostrum?
ANSWER: It is important that every foal receive the colostrum because all the antibodies present in the blood of the dam are transferred to the foal at this time, with the resulting immunity in the foal to those diseases to which the dam is immune. The length of the immunization varies with the individual, but is always long enough to protect the newborn foal.

QUESTION: Do you recommend blood typing horses at a breeding farm in the event a transfusion is needed by the foal?
ANSWER: No, type the blood of the foal and the prospective donor at the time it is needed, and always before the transfusion.

QUESTION: Do you think the average mare is in good enough health to breed during her foal heat?
ANSWER: Yes, but only when the speculum examination reveals a complete return to normal of the vagina and cervix, with no bruising or hemorrhagic areas; and the rectal exam shows the uterus to be completely returned to normal in size and consistency, and in normal position.

QUESTION: Do you recommend creep feeding foals?
ANSWER: I, personally, do not believe in creep feeding, but it is a routine practice at some of our leading farms.

QUESTION: Can mineral supplements in the rations of young horses cause abnormal bone developments?
ANSWER: Yes.

QUESTION: From a health and safety standpoint, what size and type stall do you prefer?
ANSWER: A stall 12 feet by 12 feet; the bedding choice is variable. Shavings are preferable for extremely hot weather, straw for cold weather and sand for van, express cars, etc.

QUESTION: Are there any insecticides allowed by the FDA, EPA, etc. that can control the problem insects in a stall?

ANSWER: I do not know of one. Keeping your barn spotlessly clean and free of odors is the best protection against insects. Darkened stalls also help to control the insects.

Common sense appears to be the by-word for Dr. Sager. His program of horse care to achieve and maintain peak condition involves no drastic measures, only treatment as needed after a solid program of preventive health care. Exercise, proper nutrition and extremely sanitary facilities are the rule. This, along with conditioning individualized to the horse's capabilities, has proved highly successful for Dr. Sager and Claiborne Farm.

W. C. (Woody) Stephens

(Interview by Mary Jane Gallaher)

The son of a land farmer in Woodford County, Kentucky, Woody Stephens began breaking yearlings at thirteen. He wanted to be a jockey, so he hired on with trainer John S. Ward and later won for Ward's son at Hialeah in 1931 at age sixteen.

Stephens outgrew jockeying and wound up as a groom. In this trade he learned about the care of horses. Eventually he began training on his own.

He saddled the first of his long string of winners (including over one-hundred stakes wins) in 1940. In 1974 he won the Kentucky Derby with Cannonade.

Stephens is often remembered as the trainer best able to handle the brilliant but tempermental Nasrullah line. Included in those he trained are Red God, One-Eyed King, Bold Eagle, Victory Morn and Never Bend.

Fortunately for younger horsemen who want to follow in his footsteps, Stephens is loquacious, harboring few trade secrets. Because of his Kentucky roots, he believes in observing horses on farms as yearlings for early guidelines as to how he should work with a colt or filly once serious training begins.

"I'm back in Kentucky a lot and I always look at the young stock my owners have coming on. Then I see them again, plus the additions from the sales, in the Carolinas and in Florida during the winter.

"After yearlings are broken, I think it's a good idea to keep them going during the winter months. Years ago, people used to turn them out during the winter, then they'd lose muscle tone and condition. Because of this, my horses go to South Carolina where they are under saddle until I get them in the spring.

"When I check yearlings, I especially check knees to make sure they're mature enough to stand the strain and pressure of training. I often take a look at the registration papers to make sure he's two-years old by the calendar—I like my horses to be at least two before I get serious with them.

"For example, I had Missile Belle—she won $213,968 and some top stakes in New York. As a two-year-old I didn't think she was mature enough early in the year, so I didn't start her until September—she made five starts at two then won the mile-and-a-half Coaching Club Oaks for me at three.

Mary Jane Gallaher, Inc.

Woody Stephens (right) and Seth Hancock, President of Claiborne Farm, Paris, Kentucky.

"It all depends, too, if you think you have a real quick colt, and he's sound, you could figure 'I'd better run him now while they're going short,' but if I get one I think has classic potential, I only want to run him three or four times in the fall at two.

"You really never know completely about a horse's potential. Sometimes a horse doesn't come to hand until he's four, but if he's well-bred, then he'll show you something somewhere along so you know you shouldn't get rid of him, that he has ability. Some horses come around later, some mature early. Likely you won't see that one might be a good horse until he's raced at least four or five times."

Stephens, when queried about his exercise program, says firmly he tunes that important part of a horse's routine to each individual animal.

"First," he explains, "I take size into account. If I've got a big heavy colt, you know you'll have to take more time to get him fit than you do with a lightbodied horse that doesn't weigh too much. With a lightbodied horse, you should be able to move him quickly.

"A gelding also is usually a finer horse, as are fillies—fillies likely won't stand as much training as a colt. It all usually depends on the nervous system, just what they will stand and how fast you can advance them; you have to consider also how they eat, and how strong they stand while you're training.

"A horse that has been in solid training for two or three years and has been fit most of his life needs less training as he gets older. A four-year-old is then at his peak in age. A three-year-old's teeth are changing and he's not as good a doer as he might be later. A horse has to mature properly from two to three and from three to four to go on and be a good horse. Four-year-olds usually lead the handicap division."

When asked if he uses a different exercise program for stallions, geldings and mares, Stephens, said, "Not necessarily. Sometimes I might send a group of eight to the track—that would include maybe two fillies, two geldings and four colts. I'll have them all gallop once around, but on work day, it might be a different story. I might put a slow mile under a big stud while I would keep the little filly at five furlongs.

"Once in a while you get a horse that's getting too much exercise. I judge that as much from his feed tub as anything—if you're overdoing it with him, he wouldn't be eating up well or he would begin to lose his conditioning and wouldn't look the way he should.

"I've had people ask me about taking bad-legged horses to swim. I've never been in a position to do that. However, I do tub, hose and ice my horses many times in the mornings after they train. I think swimming would be a good idea if a horse has been laid off by an injury and you want to keep him in condition."

Stephens says that, when approaching a race, a trainer ordinarily must step up his work program.

"How much you accelerate depends on your horse. With a horse like Cannonade, if he was going to run a mile and an eighth on Saturday, possibly on Monday I might give him a mile in 1:39 or 1:40; then I'd work him a day, gallop him a couple of days, and probably on Thursday or Friday, let him go $^3/_8$ in around :36 seconds.

"After a race, you again adjust to your horse. Some horses I might work one day after they run—some I wait three days. Others I may give five days after they get back on the track to start breezing. Some I may even give seven or eight.

"I learned early that horses can get too playful if you're not doing enough with them to keep them tired; you don't want them running over you in the barn. At the same time, too little work is no good either. You want them happy and feeling good."

What happens on race day that varies from the ordinary routine? Stephens says his pre-race procedure usually goes like this:

"Before a race, I really don't have many of my horses warmed up. If I have a horse that is a little arthritic, I tell the jockey to keep him moving right up to the starting gate. With others, if it's hot, I try to keep them as settled as possible on the way to the post.

"After a race, I treat most of my horses the same way. If it isn't too cool, I give them a bath and a brace, usually using a couple of bottles of alcohol on their legs, back and shoulders. Then I put a light wool blanket on them for about 20 minutes, then lighten up until we're down to a sheet. We finally put a net on when they're cool and water off."

Most successful New York-based trainers have had, as Stephens tells it, "the experience of having to race in a sudden change of climates and on different race surfaces, California being the main point in context.

"When I ship West, I don't do anything different. From my experience, I know there are a couple of ways you can do it. You can ship your horse out several days before the race or send him out there three or four weeks before.

"People tell me that horses tend to get a little relaxed after they've been out there a couple of weeks. I don't know whether it's the climate or trying to get used to the track, but after a horse has been on the Coast a couple of weeks, he seems to lose condition. It then takes a couple of more weeks to adjust."

Like most of his fellow conditioners, Stephens puts great emphasis on proper feeding for members of his stable. He is quick to admit:

"Everything you can get a horse to eat, I try to get. And as to portions, I try to feed them what they will eat within a reasonable time. There's nothing better than the best hay; and, of course, good oats and different vitamins.

"My horses are fed three times a day—breakfast at three in the morning, then their midday feed at 10:30, and again at four in the afternoon. If I have a nervous, colicky type horse, I'll put him on crushed oats and feed him every six hours, four times a day. I did that with Never Bend.

"I use a mixture of hay. I feed a little alfalfa each day and also medium mixed clover and timothy. I don't like it to be too light unless I have a real fat horse and am tryin' to get weight off, in which case I'll use timothy; but with a good mixture of clover and alfalfa, you won't be too far off with any horse. I have a rack at the back of the stall, another on the ground, and a rope rack at the door of the horse's stall. Anywhere he turns he'll find some hay if he wants it.

"I also believe in mashes—I use cooked mashed for very delicate horses. I feed carrots, watercress and various green vegetables. In addition, I use a liquid supplement and all of my horses get vitamins of some kind."

Like most of his clan, Stephens is a frustrated veterinarian. Trial and error during his lengthy career makes it possible for Stephens to know what is effective and what is a time-waster.

When asked what he does about regularly scheduled physical exams, the taking of blood samples for testing, and the testing for worms at spaced intervals, he notes:

"As to planned physicals, I don't. If a horse is racing good, looking good, then I think he's letting me know he's in good health and I don't bother him. But when a horse shows me there may be something wrong with him, I call the veterinarian.

"It's almost the same with blood samples. If a horse doesn't look right to me, I might take a sample. The only other time would be with a horse like Cannonade who had just won the Derby and was coming up to other big races. Then I might do it just to satisfy my own mind that he is in top condition.

"When it comes to worming, it's been my experience that if you get four veterinarians to run a fecal exam, you'll get four different answers. If I have a reason to believe a horse might have worms, then I just go ahead and worm him. Then maybe I take a blood sample."

When queried about such major and minor leg ailments as bowed tendons, shin bceks and wind puffs, he answered:

"I do the best I can. To me, bowed tendons are the worse things that

Woody Stephens with Cannonade, the horse he conditioned to win the 1974 Kentucky Derby.

can happen to a horse. He will never be a good horse again. Buck shins and wind puffs need only time and care.

"Before and after a race, I never change my routine too much. If I'm painting a horse's legs before a race, I tub him for two or three days after the race to let his legs get back to normal before reapplying heat.

"I'm a strong believer in Absorbine or alcohol or different mixtures of leg braces which tend to keep a horse a little tighter. I also try to protect a horse that is a little playful or rough while galloping with some kind of boot or nice light bandage. I also bandage my horses in their stalls just to protect them.

"When it comes to blistering, it all depends on what I'm trying to do with a horse. I like best to do this in the fall. I hate to use a blister or to fire in warm weather. Buck shins you need to take care of almost immediately so as to get a horse back to racing.

"I believe in firing ankles, but not knees. If a horse has an osselet or growth on his ankle where he's collecting calcium, then I think firing will break it up and stop the growth quicker than anything else. I don't see how it does any harm.

"I also use a whirlpool with some horses. Once they get used to it, they really seem to enjoy it. If they have problems, it surely won't hurt. If you have a bony growth or osselet, then I think if you keep icing, it will kill the growth or at least cool it down.

"As far as foot care goes, I have the blacksmith in regularly. My horses' feet are trimmed at least once a month—some horses' feet grow more quickly or they wear out their shoes faster so they must be trimmed and re-shod every two or three weeks. Perhaps because of the dampness in the ground, horses' feet tend to grow more quickly in Florida than they do in Kentucky or New York."

Stephens is well acquainted with the particular ailments which are more common to Thoroughbreds than to most other breeds. When asked about a horse that is "wind-broken," or having trouble breathing while racing, he admitted:

"There's not any way really to increase a horse's wind. If a horse is choking himself while running with his mouth open, you can use a figure eight on him or if he gets his tongue back in his throat, you can tie his tongue down during a race. About the only other thing you can do is keep him from filling up before a race or workout."

This brought up the question about the kinds of equipment a top trainer like Stephens uses on his horses. Stephens answered:

"You naturally use different equipment on different horses. I believe in using whatever the horse requires. I ran three horses in New York today. One wore a tongue strap, two had run-down bandages behind, one wore blinkers. All three wore D-bits."

When it comes to bathing his animals, he admits, "In the summer months, you almost have to bathe them often to keep them from getting gummy and sticky, but at other times of the year, I bathe them as infrequently as possible—of course, a washy horse is an exception—he needs a bath frequently. Also, when it comes to clipping, I like them to shed their coats if they will. If I fly South from New York, I'll clip them in New York because it's just so hot on the airplane."

Woody Stephens is said to have the ability to bring a particular horse up to a planned race and win it. Stephens does this with a watchful eye that takes meticulous notes on a horse's condition from his first year on through his racing career. The individual conditioning he stresses includes waiting patiently on a young horse to come to adequate maturity before racing. Proper feeding and conscientious veterinary care round out Stephens' successful conditioning program.

Bob Loomis

(Interview by Jane Pattie)

Bob Loomis is a specialist in reining horse training. His ability to put a rein on a horse and develop a light mouth is reflected by the long list of champions he has trained. Some of his outstanding horses are Okie Power Leo, Janice Jo Leo, Monika and Nancy Edwards. Most notable in his stable is Joe's Red Boy, an AQHA Register of Merit Arena horse, Honor Roll Reining Champion in 1972 and a Superior Reining Horse.

Although Bob's family had gaited and jumping horses, Bob was fascinated with teaching a horse to handle lightly and quietly. Consequently, Quarter performances horses became his field and reining events became his area of special interest.

Joyce Loomis, Bob's wife, is a barrel horse trainer. One of her top horses was War Leo Dude with whom, in 1970, she led GRA competition, won the National Finals Rodeo and set a record for money earned in one year.

Both Bob and Joyce are very successful professionals in the world of Quarter Horse competition. One major reason for this success is the importance they place on having horses really fit, i.e., not only well trained but in top condition, physically and mentally.

QUESTION: How soon do you recommend halter breaking colts?
ANSWER: We halter break our colts when we breed our mares back. They're easier to handle. I think the sooner you handle a horse, the nicer animal he's going to be the rest of his life. The younger one is, the faster he learns.

QUESTION: What kind of feeding program do you have for your colts?
ANSWER: I keep a lot of colts and, if they're performance prospects, I like to keep them up in the wintertime and on a high protein ration. I keep all of my colts on a 20% protein diet the year around. I like to get my performance colts out on grass in the summer. I do my halter colts the same way, only I keep them at the barn rather than out on grass. I like to mix all my supplements in my feed. I figure out a good mixture; the only difference is that my colts get a 20% protein feed, and my other horses get from 14% to 16%. The feed mill keeps all the

ingredients that this mixture requires, they just mix it and bring it to me in bulk. My horses all have free choice salt. Then I also put a little horse salt in their feed, and a good A, D and E vitamin and a good supplement protein.

QUESTION: Could you describe your initial conditioning programs?
ANSWER: I have a round pen where we work all of our halter colts that we're showing and keeping in stalls and, of course, our colts that are on pasture get free exercise. Our round pen is 50 feet in diameter, and we just stand in the middle and work them in there each day at a walk, trot and lope both ways. In fact, we condition all of our halter horses this way. Our conditioning program for yearlings before they are broke is a continuation of the same thing. Just before I break them, I put them in a head-set and walk, trot and canter them and exercise them in the head-set, preparing them for being ridden. They're between 20 and 22 months old when I'll start exercising them with their heads set and getting them used to a snaffle, because I start riding my colts when they're two. If I'm showing a colt at halter, and he doesn't have enough withers, I will exercise him in a round pen with a light saddle on him to sweat him some and bring his withers out. This is done as early yearlings, but ordinarily, they would be 20 to 22 months old.

QUESTION: How do you break your young horses?
ANSWER: I don't drive horses at all. I can accomplish more once I get on their backs. But don't get me wrong. I think driving is very good. I think it helps any horse, but I don't like to walk well enough to walk them around. I'd rather either work them free in a round pen or ride them. And I don't really like to longe a horse unless I have to. I think it's hard on his legs to longe him, because you're holding his head and he's pulling out on you, where free in a round pen, he keeps his own balance. Then if you ever did want to rope on a horse, longeing him is the worst thing in the world. He'll be prone to run around on the end of your rope. I do pony a lot of horses. I pony them as babies, and I pony all my halter horses. It's four miles through the park that adjoins my place, and I'll pony through this park. This not only gives them exercise, but lets them see the sights.

QUESTION: Do you find it hard to accustom your horses to crowds and noise?
ANSWER: I have no problem getting horses used to crowds and noise before I take them to a show. The park is always full of people picnicking and motorcycling and bicycling and hiking and playing games and flying kites. By the time I've ponied and then broken a horse to riding in that park and have ridden him in there as much as I do, there's not

anything in the world going to scare him. That park is one of the greatest training assets I have.

QUESTION: Do differences in individual colts result in differences in their upbringing?

ANSWER: There is definitely a difference in the way we'd bring up colts as far as exercising and conditioning, depending on what we are going to do with them. We're raising some colts with whom we don't plan to do anything but run barrels. I just turn these colts out in the pasture and make sure they're on a good protein diet with plenty of feed. I worm them every 60 days until they're long yearlings, and from that time, every 90 days. I just don't mess with them much. Then I bring them in when they're two and break them to ride. I get them to riding very nicely and very quietly at a walk, trot and canter. They'll take both leads, back up and give their heads. Then I turn them back out and forget them again, other than continuing their feeding program. Then I'll get each one up as a three-year-old, and my wife, Joyce, will start him on the barrels at a walk and a trot. As a three-year-old, he'll do nothing but walk and trot and once in a while, a very slow lope around the barrels. Then as a four-year-old, we'll bring him back in and "ask" him. These are horses we feel have the potential of being a champion, or honestly, we just wouldn't mess with them this long. We're talking about a lot of time and a lot of expense. When we're done with a horse like this, we're talking about one that's got to be worth $7500 and up.

QUESTION: How does your conditioning program differ for specific types of horses?

ANSWER: With my halter horses, I like to get a nice muscle tone on them. You've got to get their weight up on their backs. This is done through a very careful feeding program, a very careful exercising program, and a lot of elbow grease. There's just no short cut to getting a halter horse sure fit. I don't like to carry quite as much weight on my yearlings as some people do, because I think it's hard on their bone structure. It's very unhealthy to have a yearling just pudgy, soft fat. By giving this colt an adequate amount of exercise, he can carry the same amount of weight as he would if he were fat, but look a lot better by having toned muscling. And, by getting his muscles toned and hard, you're getting his legs conditioned, you're keeping his tendons right, and you're keeping everything that packs all his weight in shape.

QUESTION: Who breaks your horses?

ANSWER: I do my own breaking of colts and breaking horses to ride for customers. I wouldn't have anyone help me unless he was an exceptionally good man with a lot of experience. I wouldn't let just a mediocre man help me, because that first 30 to 60 days with a colt is like a foundation on a house. If it gets put in wrong, then you're in trouble from then on. All of my performance show horses I start myself. A man would have to be a good hand and absolutely have no temper with a horse before I could use him. A man who can't control his temper with a horse will never make a good horse trainer no matter what other attributes he has.

QUESTION: What kind of exercise and how much riding do horses get after breaking?

ANSWER: How much riding a colt gets once I start riding him depends very much on the individual. Until one is a good strong two-year-old, I won't ride him over 15 or 20 minutes at a time, five days a week. I don't ever ride any horse Saturdays or Sundays. I think two days off for them to rest and think about it is as important as the riding they get. As the horse gets stronger and as he starts legging up, the riding is increased. I ride my colts a little bit more all the time, maybe a couple of minutes longer each day as they leg up and get stronger. But even then, I never ask a two-year-old to do anything more than walk, trot and slow lope. I don't like to stop a two-year-old hard; I don't like to make him run back. I want one to back nicely, but slowly and easily. I don't want him to do anything rapidly. Everything is very quiet and done very slowly. I just don't want a two-year-old to strain himself in any form, mentally or physically.

Once I start riding a horse, most of his exercise is done from his back. Sometimes I'll set his head and put him in the round pen and lope him with his head set. But I do 90% of this head set with my hands from his back. My round pen has sand in it. I don't like deep sand. I don't like for my horses to labor. I want them to move free, so the sand is maybe three to four inches deep. It's just a nice, light coating, enough where they can have some cushion. I think you can strain a horse in deep sand and hurt him as bad as you can on hard ground.

QUESTION: How long do you usually work with a horse before making decisions about his potential?

ANSWER: I can tell a lot about a horse's mentality and ability in 30 days of riding. You can tell a lot by just handling one on the ground, and you're usually right, but every once in a while, you can make a mistake. I know pretty well what I want to do with a colt after 30 days of riding. I know just about what kind of horse he is, but then again, after one's riding real good and is pretty well broke and you've ridden him three or four months, things will pop up then and you can still be wrong. But nine times out of 10, you can tell pretty accurately. If I thought a lot of the horse I'd sure give him 90 days before I made any drastic decisions. Some great athletes just come slow.

QUESTION: What are the signs of too much or too little exercise?
ANSWER: You can give any horse too much or too little exercise. If you're using a horse too much, he'll come up sore, usually in the tendons. When he's not getting enough exercise, it's a lot the same thing. He'll be stocking up on you; he'll be getting a belly, and all his weight will just start dropping. You just have to use some common sense in your conditioning program. I've never had a horse shin buck. Windpuffs, yes, I've sure had them get windpuffs, although if a good brace is used and the legs are wrapped, windpuffs are very easily controlled. Shin buck and bowed tendons and such have never been problems for me. I definitely think that they primarily result from lack of condition or asking a horse for more than he's physically ready to give you. It's just rush training. I've never had any trouble with jacks, curbs or any such unsoundness of legs. But I used to splint horses, so we designed a splint boot that I think is one of the finest on the market. We use these splint boots religiously on everything we ride, and we have been for over two and a half years now. I use them from the first saddling. We have never splinted a horse since.

QUESTION: Exactly, how are these splint boots beneficial?
ANSWER: When you start riding a young horse, he doesn't know how to carry weight and how to cross his legs over in turning around. There's a test that we have done in clinics to prove a point . . . You take the straightest legged horse that you're using in a performance event and put a set of brand-new splint boots on him. Ride that horse or show him like you would in a normal day, and when you take those splint boots off, I'll bet there's not one horse in a 100 that won't have some skinned and scrape marks on those splint boots. If those boots aren't there, they're going to be hitting themselves in the shins. If a horse starts hitting himself in the shins, he gets sore, maybe not enough to limp, but enough so that he gets to dreading it. He'll slow down turning around, and he'll lose a little bit of his sparkle, maybe just enough that you think he's sluffing, but really he's not. He's sore. I just think that on all performance horses and colts you're just giving them more of an advantage by protecting their legs. We put splint boots on just as religiously as we do a saddle blanket.

QUESTION: What specialized care do you give to a horse's legs?
ANSWER: It's very important to give a horse's legs the very best of care. I'll never wrap a horse after rubbing his legs with Absorbine. It

will put a scurf or light blister on one. I'll make a mixture of two bottles of Bigelow, a bottle of Absorbine and a bottle of vinegar in a gallon jug, and that makes a real nice brace. You can rub a horse down with that and wrap him. Or if I've got a horse that's bumped a leg or if there's any swelling in his legs, I'll do his legs up with numotizine, put Saran Wrap around them and then bandage him up. This numotizine is great medicine. It will really pull any soreness out, and it isn't dangerous in any way. You just wash it off the next day. I think it is one of the best and simplest things to use, and I recommend it for anybody.

On the back of the Absorbine bottle is a good brace formula. It's a nice, simple one, but you want to be careful. You don't want to use too much of that Absorbine. If I do a horse up with just straight Absorbine, I don't bandage him. But then the rubbing will do more good than the brace. People think the brace does it all, but the more you rub, the more it's absorbed. DMSO also helps medicine to penetrate.

QUESTION: What precautions do you take when traveling with a horse?
ANSWER: In hauling horses, I either wrap them with just cotton and a wrap, or with a good quilted bandage and a wrap, and I'll either use a brace like I mentioned earlier or no brace. This wrapping is more to keep them from getting skinned up if they should bump the trailer or step on themselves. And there's no doubt that the worst place you can cut, bruise or injure a horse in any manner is from the knees or hocks down.

QUESTION: How do you determine the health of a horse?
ANSWER: I can tell pretty much the kind of general physical shape my horses are in by just looking at them. If they're in good shape, their hair will be good and their eyes will be bright and their gums will look healthy. And if they are not in such good shape, it's just as easy to tell that. The first thing I do to a horse when he comes in training, no matter what age he is, is to check his teeth, Of course, you want to feed all of your horses good and that's hard to do if they have dental problems. Dental and worming programs are probably your main things to watch, not only with old horses, but with all of them. If a horse has bridle teeth, I pull them immediately. I can't get a horse bitted with bridle teeth. I worm him and go to work on him. I like to worm my horses every 90 days.

QUESTION: What do you do for the appearance of your horse?
ANSWER: I think a large factor in getting a good coat is your feeding program and your balance of protein, calcium and phosphorus.

Yet, even when a horse is fed properly and is in great shape, the hair looks better when you rub and brush and curry a horse. You pull that oil out and put life in his hair. Definitely, a lot of brushing is necessary for a halter horse, where maybe you don't need to brush a performance horse other than to keep him clean. I use a good rubber curry comb and a soft bristled brush, and that's hard to beat. I don't like to bathe a horse over once a week. You wash too much of the natural oil out of his hair. I like to wash a horse with just warm water about three days before a show. I used to use different coat dressings, but many are oily so that on a dusty day in an outdoor show you just get dust collected. I now use only Show Sheen, and it's the finest. I used to have so much trouble using hoods on horses. They'd rub their manes out. But since I started using this Show Sheen, I can keep a mane on a horse and keep him hooded all winter. It just seems to coat each and every hair. It's great. I bathe them and squeegee them off, and then I just spray Show Sheen all over them and let them dry and brush them. This Show Sheen coats them so that if you have a white-legged horse, you can put it on him once a week, and if he gets his legs dirty, you can brush those white legs off and they're just as sparkling. It won't let the dirt stain the hair. You can put it on right after you wash one or you can put it on dry and it works well. I think it works better if the horse is clean. Put it on when he's damp and let him dry with it on.

QUESTION: What about trimming and shoeing?

ANSWER: I never trim one of my own horses. I like to have the best vet I can get and the best farriers I can get work on my horses. I believe everybody should specialize in their field, and I honor the person that is specialized. I have an awful lot of my own ideas on shoeing and doctoring, but yet I have a vet and a horseshoer, and I respect them for their abilities, and I always let them have the last word in their field.

QUESTION: What do you do to maintain condition in a seasoned horse?

ANSWER: Once my reining horses are made, I ride them more like they were pleasure horses. I lope them straightaway a lot and circle them a lot. I just keep them hard, fit and pliant. And maybe three days before a reining, I'll pick them up and kind of put some life in them and sharpen them and get everything working good. Then the day of the show I just like to keep them very quiet and relaxed.

QUESTION: How do you warm a horse up before an event?

ANSWER: To warm a horse up before a reining event, I like to walk him. I like to ease on a horse and just kind of wander around a while. I then pick him up and trot him and put him into a bridle and set his head. I then trot him a while and maybe lope him a little bit. I usually don't mess with his handle much the day of the show, because that's all working. I just get him loosened up and set his head and get him bending at the poll and get him where he's moving loose and free.

QUESTION: How do you cool a horse out after an event or exercise?
ANSWER: After he has worked, I never put a wet horse away. The old-fashioned way of just walking one until he's cool can't be beat. How I do it depends on the horse. Most of my horses are very relaxed. When I "throw a horse's head away," he usually just relaxes instantly. If I have the time, I just like to loosen the cinch and crawl back on him and just wander around until he's dry. If I'm short of time, I put one on the walker. But either way, I clean him up. We keep a bucket of disinfectant and a sponge by the crossties all the time, and every horse that we put away, all of the saddle area and the legs where the splint boots were and any other sweaty area on his body is washed with disinfectant. He feels better, and you'll never sore a horse up or gall him if his back is clean. Then you don't get fungus and all the things that you can get by saddling a sweaty horse up day after day and never washing him. Then after a show, I'll give a horse a couple of days off. I'll go right back to pleasuring him and just riding him off across the field quietly.

QUESTION: Are the diets different for your breeding stock?
ANSWER: I like to keep my broodmares, just like my performance horses, on a 14% to 16% protein diet. I keep my stallions on the same as my other horses. I think one of the main things with a stallion is exercise. Keep him on a lot of feed and condition him like you would a halter horse or a good performance horse. Stallions with a low fertility count are usually horses that are not getting the proper amount of exercise. They can get all of the good feed in the world, but if they are not properly exercised and in physically top condition, they are not going to be as fertile.

QUESTION: What kind of exercise program do you have for a breeding stallion?
ANSWER: I think a stud should be jogged. I like to trot a stud at least an hour a day, either on him or on the walker. Trotting is the best gait there is to condition and leg a horse up. I would condition him the same way all the time. I think he should be kept in shape the year around.

QUESTION: Does exercise differ according to the age or sex of a horse?

ANSWER: I don't really think that a horse's exercise should ever decrease at any age. I don't have different exercise programs for stallions, mares or geldings. It all depends on what the individual horse requires. A stallion, mare and gelding all have the same bodies. The stud requires a little more work discipline-wise. Studs are tougher than mares or geldings, there's no doubt about that, but most of it is mental. I think you have to get into a stud's mind, not necessarily with abuse, but you just need to have his attention. A stud sure needs correcting now and then, but the need for correction after he's been in training a good while should slack off to very little.

QUESTION: When do you start to show a horse and at what age is he at his best?

ANSWER: I'd rather wait until a reining horse is four before I start showing him but I can't. I have to have them ready as three-year-olds for the National Reining Futurity. That's what I work for every year. I try to train a few good three-year-olds for the Futurity, but if it weren't for that Futurity, I'd wait another year. I would go ahead and start riding them just as early. I'd have them broke. I'd have them handling where they could go win a reining, but I wouldn't put that extra snap, that extra fine polish on them that I have to for the Futurity. If I could give them another year, they'd be stronger and better horses. I think a horse is at his physical peak from five to seven, but his mental peak is up to the trainer. It depends on who is training him, and how his training is applied.

QUESTION: What causes bad habits?

ANSWER: Boredom is one of the worst things for a horse. Stall weaving, cribbing and a lot of other bad habits are caused from boredom. You can overcome much of it by just a lot of good, quiet miles. You can't beat quiet miles on any horse. You can go slow and put those quiet miles on them, and you just won't believe how much you're teaching them, and you won't figure out how you did it.

QUESTION: How do you prepare a horse for a sale?

ANSWER: When I get a horse ready for a sale, I want him carrying a lot of weight. I want him fat. I don't care if it's not a halter horse but just a performance horse. I'll condition him just like I'm getting him ready for halter, but I'll put a little extra weight on him and have his hair coat polished. Fat and polish bring you more money than anything. I definitely exercise them, but I wouldn't be exercising them for a horse race or for reining or for a barrel race, but just to get their muscles and their bodies in the best possible condition. Actually, if a horse is in that kind of a condition, he's really in pretty good working shape, too, other than packing some extra weight.

QUESTION: What do you recommend when transporting a horse?

ANSWER: In hauling horses, I like to tie them loose. I don't want to tie them too short. I want to give them plenty of room, but I do want them tied. When they're loose, any age horse can get his head down and get in all kinds of trouble. I think the main thing in hauling horses is how you drive. I don't use the brakes much. I usually slow my vehicle down with my transmission and also start out slow from a stopped position, and I make sure to turn the corners slow. Right there I think is the big secret to hauling horses, how you drive . . . Ease into your stops, ease into your going and ease around corners. Don't do anything that makes your horse have to brace real quick.

QUESTION: How long before an event do you like to arrive?

ANSWER: I hate to get to a show and just back a horse out of a trailer and go show him. I like to get to a one-day show or a week-end show within 150 or 200 miles of home three or four hours before the event in order to loosen the horses up. If it's 400 miles or farther, I like to have them there at least a day before to freshen them. If it's 1000 miles away, I like to be there two days before. You have no problem with your old seasoned horses eating and drinking. You do with young horses until they get a little seasoning on them. Getting there a day or two early kind of helps a young horse relax.

QUESTION: What do you do for a particularly nervous horse?

ANSWER: If I had a particularly nervous horse, I'd hang an old plastic milk jug on a rope in his stall and let him play with that. That will help. I think music helps, too. I've never used mascots for my horses. I've always had a goat around, but that's for me to look at.

QUESTION: What do you think is the ideal stall size?

ANSWER: I think the ideal stall size is 12'x12'. The minimum is 10'x10'. I keep my stud in a 12'x15'. If I'm foaling anything in bad weather, I have two 12'x12's with a removable center partition, so I'll have a 12'x24' foaling stall. In my opinion, stall walls should definitely be solid. I think horses being able to see each other is what causes them to kick and tear your stalls up, and they will hurt their legs more. I like the fronts open where a good breeze comes in, but I want solid walls between my horses.

QUESTION: What kind of bedding do you use and how often do you clean your stalls?

ANSWER: I use shavings as bedding in some of my barns and straw in some of them, but I prefer the shavings. It's easier to work with and is better for the horses. The stalls are cleaned every day and bedding is added as needed. I would say every four days there would be a complete new bedding, but it's done a little bit every day.

QUESTION: What can the horse owner do to help the trainer?

ANSWER: The main thing the average horse owner could do to help his trainer (before he sends his horse to him) is to never lose his temper with his horse. When they run across something they don't know how to cope with, instead of getting mad and knocking their horse around, go find out what the right thing to do is. Or take him right on to the trainer. From the average run-of-the-mill people, I'd rather get a horse not even halter broke. From owners that are better horsemen, I'd like for them to handle their young horses some—maybe even start them. But from the average, general public, I'd rather they'd not even be halter broke. I'd rather they'd just bring them to me.

QUESTION: Do you have any special recommendations for training?

ANSWER: In anything I do with a horse, I use good strong equipment. Don't ever let a horse get away from you, but don't handle him rough at any stage of training. Take your time. Do it slow without scaring him. If I bring a horse back after he has been laid off by an injury or just for a rest, I'd leg him up slowly just like a young horse. You can go a little faster with him than you can a baby, because his bone structure and everything is solid and his knees are closed, but still, you want to ease it on him a little bit at a time.

QUESTION: When do you use blankets and sheets?

ANSWER: We start blanketing our horses as soon as there is any chill in the air, and we add to it gradually. We use sheets in the summer to keep our halter horses from sun bleaching. I don't use sheets on my performance horses.

QUESTION: What do you do about a horse whose throatlatch is too thick?

ANSWER: If a horse's throatlatch is too thick, I use a good throatlatch band. I'll also use a little glycerin and alcohol and sweat him. How often that's necessary depends very much on the condition of the horse's neck and throat. You can exercise a horse with a sweat hood on for his neck, but I won't exercise a horse with a throatlatch band because I think it affects his breathing. But if you just religiously keep a throatlatch band on a horse, it will help tremendously. A lot of that thick neck is purely from lack of proper exercise. I've ridden lots of horses that have had heavy necks, but when I rode them and got their muscle tone right, that neck just kind of evaporated. You can ride an awful lot of it off.

QUESTION: What methods do you use in breaking colts?

ANSWER: When breaking colts, I like to concentrate on one colt at a time. When I'm done with him, I'll go get another one. I wouldn't handle fillies any different than stud colts, other than the ground work is a little different with a horse than it is with a mare. It all goes back to manners, mostly. But I wouldn't break colts any earlier than fillies. That all goes back to the size of the individual.

QUESTION: What do you normally look for in a good reining prospect?

ANSWER: The main problem I had with Okie Power Leo was that he just had so much gas. And that takes just a lot of riding. A lot of gas is not necessarily what you look for in a top reining horse. I've ridden some reining horses that were extremely quiet horses, but their minds were good. I look for a good, willing mind on a horse and a good, beautiful way of moving and for a horse that changes leads easily and naturally and for a horse that doesn't have a temper. A good-minded horse with a good mouth and a good way of moving doesn't necessarily have to be a "gallopy" horse. He can be a very quiet horse. Joe's Red Boy is one of the best pleasure horses I ever rode, and I can run a reining on him and use him hard and go right back five minutes later in a pleasure class. So the gas isn't all that important. It's the mental attitude and the athletic ability that you look for.

QUESTION: Could you give a specific example that demonstrates your goals?

ANSWER: I rode Okie Power Leo four to five hours a day for one year. This was quiet trotting and loping circles and straightaway through the park. It was a lot of quiet miles. He's a horse that, if I had gotten on and tried to do a lot of hard training at a young age, it would have blown his mind. You had to ease yourself on this horse. He was a very quiet, relaxed, beautifully moving horse. He had had some rough treatment before I got him, and he was a regular gazelle. He had so much ability but he was scared, so it just took me a long time to get his confidence and to get him to perform and do things hard but quiet. This is the art ... to get the horse to turn inside out and then just walk away like he hadn't done a thing. This takes time.

Spendthrift Training Center

(Interview by Mary Jane Gallaher)

Once there were fewer race tracks; these ovals raced seasonably and even when a meet was on there were always stalls available for yearlings and their big brothers, the 2-year-olds, all just learning the hows and whys of racing.

No more. With each racing state wanting an increasing share of the daily mutual take, young horses who cannot compete have become racing's step-children.

Hence the development of equine kindergardens, the most elegant and proficient being Lexington, Kentucky's Spendthrift Training Center.

Based deep in Kentucky's Blue Grass heart, the center operates under the direction of Brownell Combs II from July's end until late November, then packs its tack and moves into Florida's West Coast sun. There it has the advantages of Florida Downs' quiet backstretch and early in the year, actual competitive experience. Besides the educational opportunities offered at Tampa, for the more precocious colts and fillies, it is well within striking distance of Florida's Hialeah and New Orleans' Fair Grounds. Spendthrift remains at Tampa, testing and teaching, until just before Keeneland begins around April 1.

Major domo of the Kentucky division is John Cinnamon who has a thorough grounding in the ways of bringing out the best in any horse.

Cinnamon vividly remembers the beginning of Spendthrift's yearling breaking program, started as an adjunct to the stud's extensive breeding and marketing program.

"I came here in 1955—the second summer we decided to break four or five fillies that Mr. Combs wanted to keep to race. Well, that handful turned out to be 24. We now average about 60 at any given time. We begin on August 1 and ship, often in shifts, from mid-November to December 1 to Florida.

In the late '60's, Leslie Combs bought a sizable tract of Blue Grass land about 10 miles from Spendthrift proper. Well toward the rear of it, he designed and built a complex expressly for yearlings and horses-out-of-training.

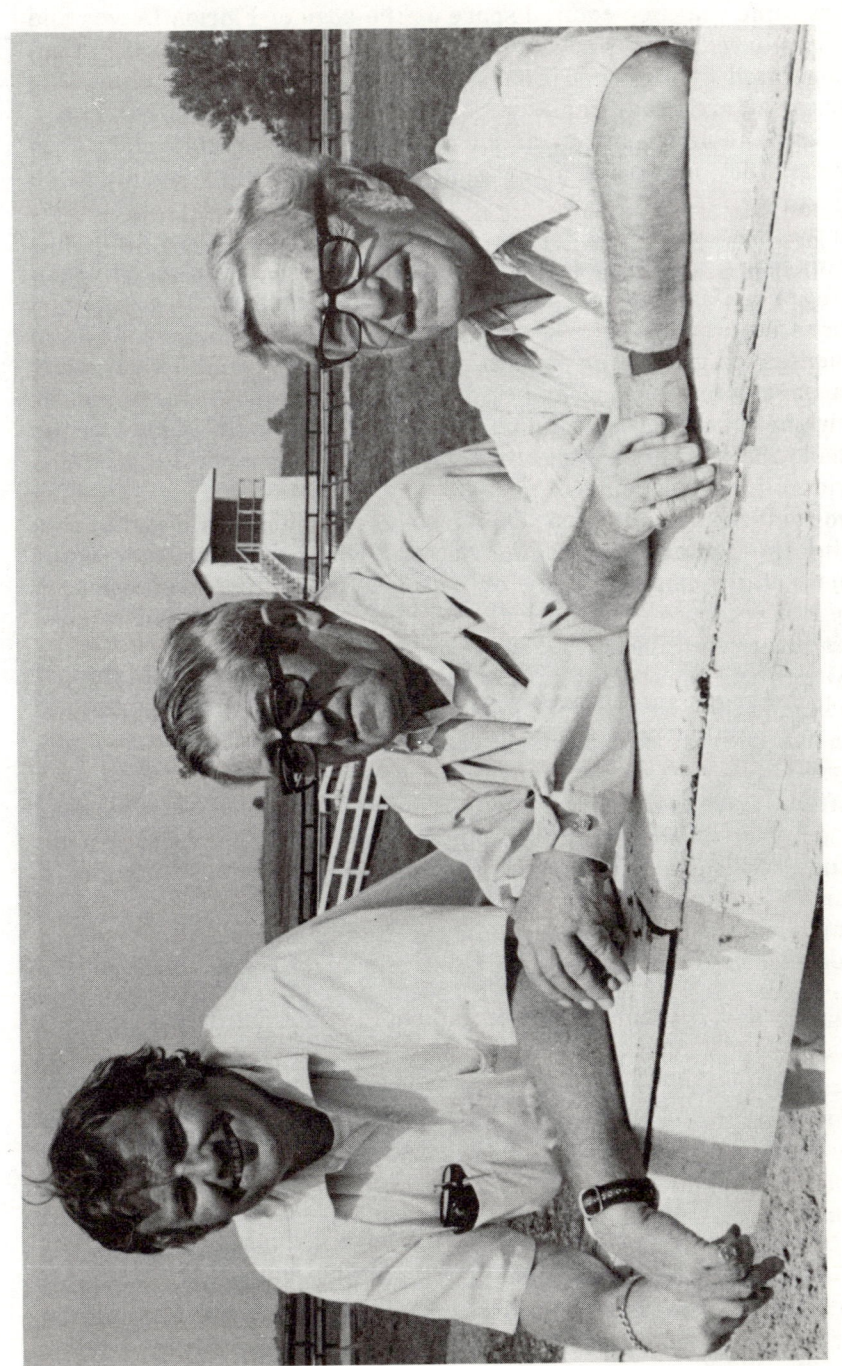

L. to r.: Brownell Combs II operator, John Cinnamon of the Kentucky division and Dick Fischer of the Florida division of Spendthrift Training Center.

That same year he acquired space at the edge of Florida Downs and built two barns. This is the winter headquarters of Spendthrift's Center, operated by Brownell Combs II and Trainer Dick Fischer. The horses that are ready for more intense training are shifted into a tougher schedule when they arrive from the North. If they show good progress, they may race a few times before returning home in the early spring.

On the Kentucky property, there are two mammoth barns each with its own jogging path outside the stalls but well underneath the roof. Nearby there is a half-mile dirt track, complete with starting gate and clocker's stand.

When asked the secret of turning out perfectly conditioned young horses, ready for a trainer to begin teaching them to use the speed for which they were bred, Cinnamon gives a seemingly simple reply: "Time is the answer to well-broke yearlings—but, particularly in this business, time is expensive."

Brownell Combs II then explained the Combs' philosophy concerning the Center: "Everything else at Spendthrift is as modern and efficient as we can make it. For instance, every time we replace a barn, it is with fire-proof fiber glass and poured concrete. But when it comes to breaking yearlings, we turn back the clock.

"With young horses, my father believes the best way, and I agree with him, is the way my great grandfather, Daniel Swigert, did—those horsemen knew much more than the present generation about giving a horse a good foundation from which he could do his best running."

"After we are satisfied a horse is completely schooled, then we send him to his owner's trainer, or to our own racing stable. At that point we know we've done the best we can for him; from then on, what he does is up to him."

Cinnamon then began to explain the highly workable methods he has developed over almost 20 years of preparing young colts and fillies.

"We like to take at least 90 days with each one; we break in the afternoon 'cause we can get better exercise boys then. They stand in line to work for us because they know we don't cut corners."

What does the yearling that goes the Spendthrift first-class route enjoy that is not readily available to his poorer equine relations?

"First," Cinnamon says, "any horse that comes on the place—mares, studs, anything—is quarantined for 21 days. Then when the yearlings come to us, we turn out at night as long as it's warm and take up first thing in the morning. We reverse that when the nights get cool. I give every summer-sales-yearling 30 days before we try to do anything with them. I cut back on their feed—they lose the sales fat mostly just by being turned out.

"They usually are in our barn three or more weeks before they see a race track. We start breaking in the stall. For a week we just put tack on. Then the boys get on and practice turning them so they'll understand that. When we bring them out under the shed, we just put tack on for several days. When we finally put a boy up, the men lead the yearlings for about three days.

"It's usually then that we find out if any are going to cause trouble. I know from experience that certain bloodlines have built-in troubles and I hate to see them come in the barn. With colts we only geld if the owner wants it, and then not until they are two years old."

To a practical horseman like Cinnamon, equipment is all important and in most cases he has simplified rather than over-complicated the riggings for his charges.

"For instance," he notes, "we have gone to a soft, felt saddle with a soft girth. The boys got to liking the felt saddles and they are easier on a horse's back. Also, they're a little lighter and are less expensive.

"We also use foam rubber pads with canvas duck covers under our saddles and girth covers; both are changed everytime a horse is saddled. We had a couple of horses with sore backs and I went down to the local Army Goods store and noticed the foam rubber. I had the man cut out a pad for me, and then I sold the idea to the harness shops. I paid about two dollars for it and now they sell for about ten. First we had them made with a zipper but that didn't work. Now it laps over on top. We put them in a washing machine and dryer because you can't depend on the men to wash them up every day. A couple of kids go around picking up after each set is unsaddled. These covers help preserve the saddles and the pads, and help keep down skin disease which, once it starts, goes through the whole barn.

"As to bits, we use a regular D unless a horse requires something different. And I don't give a boy a stick unless a horse is on the rough side, which yearlings usually are not.

"I also break all mine using a yoke with rings (martingale). A lot of boys don't have good hands for a horse and lay on their mouths. I learned to use those rings from a pretty good horseman, Duval Headley."

In answer to a question about the development of bad habits, Cinnamon sighed and said, "I think any bad habit a colt forms, he forms when you first begin to break him. If you let him get away with something like throwing a boy, it gets to be a habit. What he learns in those first 20 days sticks with him the rest of his life.

"Of course, we do get horses that are just nervous. These we try to handle with kid gloves and kindness. Use a boy who is kind and has good hands. We'll do almost anything to calm them down, to stop things like stall-walking. Mascots, like a goat, often are a help."

Cinnamon went on to tell of the unhurried routine his charges enjoy before going off to the racing wars. "We let our yearlings stay in the barn about three weeks or better—we have big aisles with three inches of sand so we can do almost anything with them. The first four or five days they are at the track, the men lead them back and forth. They learn to line up and to stand. You can't rush 'em—you'll ruin one if you do. You can only do as much as the horse himself can learn. Some you can tell about; others are like kids, and they don't get straightened out until they're two-year-olds.

"We start jogging gradually; then they learn to gallop and to stand in the starting gate. After about six weeks we have them go the wrong way of the track. They need to develop evenly and know how to shift themselves around going both ways.

"We just give them about two miles of slow gallops. We try to gallop them three abreast, four abreast, and let them get used to galloping beside one another. And we stand them in the starting gate with the gates open. After you watch for awhile, you can tell if a horse has a good stride, is not clumsy and handles himself like a cat on his feet. But you can't tell how they are going to run until they hit that starting gate in the afternoon.

"I also believe after a yearling is broken and well-mannered, it should be turned out for six or eight weeks. The lessons usually come back fast unless you've got a bad baby and his lessons don't come to him anyway."

Spendthrift has an interesting feeding program; and one man, Tommy Cooper, does *all* the feeding, a unique set-up on any Thoroughbred establishment. As Cinnamon tells it, "We have our own feed mill and mix our feed according to our own formula. It is delivered to the barns already prepared. We use a little salt, oats, barley, some prepared feeds (mostly Chevinal) then put blackstrap molasses over it all. We don't feed mashes because they are turned out at night, and with the green grass they don't need it.

"I'd say we average about 8 quarts a day, depending on the horse. You don't feed that much to a fat horse—to a skinny little filly you've got to give them all you can.

"Tommy does all our feeding because we found that it doesn't work for each man to feed his own horses. They are often careless about how much to give, then forget to tell us when a colt or filly didn't eat up. Now Tommy does it all—if a special feed is needed he knows it. If one is 'off his feed' he gets on me about giving him a tonic."

He continued: "We do another thing that only a big farm can do—we keep two blacksmiths, and one does all the yearlings, putting flat steel

Mary Jane Gallaher, Inc.

Young horses at Spendthrift Training Center displaying the calm, well mannered look that results from proper handling.

plates on them in front, nothing behind. They have their own shop right at the yearling barns. We reset and trim every 30 days."

Illnesses, surprisingly enough, are a minor problem at Spendthrift. It is likely that Brownell Combs' and Cinnamon's basic use of common sense is responsible for this. Cinnamon says yearlings' knees are X-rayed to see if they are closed only if an owner requests it. "Certainly," he says, "you can't start serious work with a horse until knees are closed. But here you need a vet's opinion. When we have a horse that looks like he's getting too much exercise, we have a vet check him. Also when we get a few shin splints I always do what the vet recommends. We use bandages only on horses we're treating—and we do ship in bandages. We use liniments and braces when the vet says we should.

"I don't believe in firing yearlings; after all, they are only babies. You want to develop them first, then see what's needed.

"We run blood tests on the yearlings on the farm about every 90 days and we definitely run them on the yearlings in training. There will be one period during breaking when we will run a blood count on them. We check for worms every 90 days. Some seem to have worms come back oftener than others; according to Dr. Bill McGee, you can run a fecal test on a horse today and then two or three days later the fecal count will be different."

Spendthrift is the farm that has turned out more stakes winners than any other in the world, so Cinnamon's advice can be well taken. In this case, the proof of the pudding is in the number of winner's circle appearances the Spendthrift graduates make.

Mary McPherson

(Interview by Jane Pattie)

Mary McPherson is an accomplished horsewoman, proficient in all areas of equine conditioning. As a professional she presents tough competition in western horse shows across the country. With Quarter Horses, Appaloosas and Palominos, Mary McPherson consistently places at the top—especially in the pleasure (western and English), reining, cutting and halter classes.

Cindy Dodger, Miss Bar Wa and Leo's Sunny (all AQHA Register of Merit Arena horses) are a few of the notables she has trained and shown. Honey Bar Mist, Bos'n Filaree and Miss San Skip represent Mary's success with Palominos, while her most successful Appaloosas include Kiowa Son, Torrington Sue, Son of Quanah's Little Deer, Miss Rusty Ann, Top Value and Top Dollar M.

This versatile horsewoman strongly emphasizes the importance of proper conditioning for every horse from early foalhood. The statement, "I am one of the few women, that I know of, who can break a horse from the very start," exemplifies the active interest she takes in her horses.

Mary has achieved recognition in all competitive areas of the horse world. As an example, she was widely acclaimed one of the top trick riders in the country before turning to training and exhibiting western performance horses. She now operates a large public training facility located near Haslet, north of Fort Worth, Texas, and is active in the breeding, showing and training phases of the horse industry.

QUESTION: Concerning performance horses, what is the importance of conditioning?

ANSWER: Just before a performance or halter class, you don't have to do an awful lot of grooming if you've had the horse on a proper diet and proper exercise. You can brush him and trim his ears and his fetlocks and go over him for that last minute touch-up, but the rest comes from conditioning, and you can't do that in a week or 30 days. That takes at least six months.

QUESTION: What type of conditioning program do you provide for foals?

ANSWER: My conditioning and exercise program for foals after they are weaned depends on whether I'm going to show them at halter or not. If I consider them not eligible to show, I just let them grow up naturally out in the pasture. If I'm going to show one, I'd start with the colt after I'd weaned it. I'd teach it to longe and I'd pony it horseback. I'm not too high on putting one on a mechanical walker until it's almost a year old. There's just something about a young horse being ponied and longed that's very beneficial. He's grasping certain things that will help him in later life. Longeing a colt teaches a certain amount of obedience, and when you are riding a broken horse and leading the colt, you are accomplishing a certain amount of good recordings in your animal's mind as it is being exercised. Also, if you are ponying or longeing, you will be less inclined to over-exercise, because you're right there. It's too easy to leave one on a walker too long, and if you over-exercise a young animal, he can begin to dread any form of connection with you.

QUESTION: How young do you halter break your horses?
ANSWER: I've halter broken colts all the way from four or five days up to three years of age. I really prefer to halter break them at two to three months old.

QUESTION: At this stage, what type and amount of exercise do they receive?
ANSWER: I alternate between longeing, walking and ponying. I have a filly of my own that was ponied while she was still on her mother in the halter breaking process. She was actually halter broken on foot the first day, and from then on the mare was tied up and the colt was ponied horseback right in the same area. I am now putting this yearling on the walker for conditioning purposes, being very careful not to let her go as long as I do the older horses. I put her in a trot 10 minutes and rest her 10 and trot her 10 and rest her 10. My walker will walk, trot and lope in either direction.

Every form of exercise such as ponying, longeing and free in a round pen properly done all achieve the same end. A calf roper frowns on a longe line, but saddlebred people, running horse people, halter people, jumping horse people, all use a longe line. I also like to pony a horse. There are a lot of people who prefer a round pen. I have facilities for all three. I have a round pen that I use, but I do not use real deep sand. I do use a medium cushion.

The kind of horse equipment to use depends on each individual trainer, as well as the horse. But no matter what you use, never use anything that will break. If the horse is heavy-headed, I use a heavy hackamore, and if it's light-headed, I use the light hackamore. I longe in a hackamore, because I want that horse to learn how to give to the

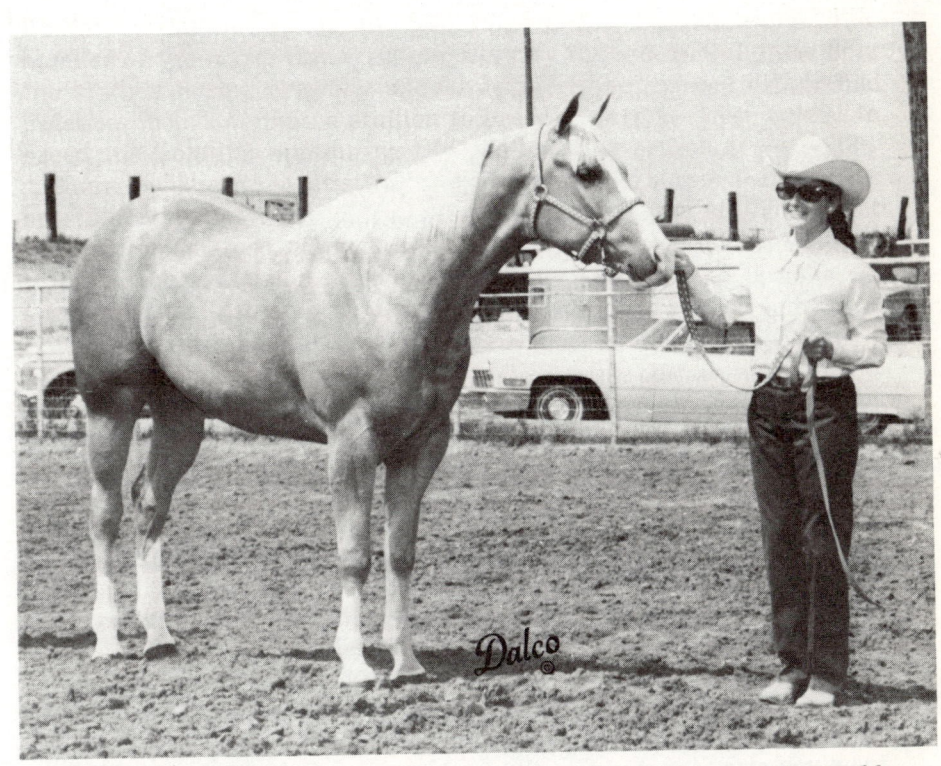

Noted trainer of Western horses, Mary McPherson is shown here with one of her outstanding Halter and Western Pleasure horses, Bos'n Filaree, owned by Dr. C. D. Fitzwilliam.

direction I want him to go. I want him to listen to me, which he might not do with just a halter on. The method I use accomplishes the same things as driving, but I don't drive, because I don't have the strength to control a horse. I have to use something on a horse so that the horse thinks I have control. I outsmart him by using the equipment that I do.

QUESTION: Is there a difference in the way you condition young horses, depending on what you're going to do with them?

ANSWER: You would definitely condition a halter colt a little bit differently than you would a horse that you were going to use in performance. You would want to put a little more weight and a little more glisten on the halter prospect. You could turn that performance horse out in a pen when you weren't riding him. Your halter horse is going to have to be kept out of the sun, and he's going to have to have a little more "bloomy" ration, where your performance horse is going to be allowed to grow normally, and you don't care whether he's sunburned or not; you can be a little bit more lax on appearance of performance horses. Even then, I always try to let my halter horses run out to a certain extent.

QUESTION: At what age do you plan on entering a young horse in an event?

ANSWER: The trend is to start showing performance horses at two years of age, and you have to have enough size on a horse to be able to have him ready to show when he's two years old. You have to start when he's about 18 months old to have enough training in the horse to get him in there as a two-year-old. It can't always be done. Some horses seem to grow overnight and are real good doers. Then others are very slow developers. So it has to be a fast developing horse to show it as a two. But I think you take a terrible chance in growing your colts too fast. It not only can upset their digestive system, but too much rich food can get colts too big too fast and they tend to break down more easily. So in breaking colts, I handle each one individually. I make no special allowance for the difference between colts and fillies. Eighteen months of age is about as early as you should start riding one, and that is determined by the size of the colt and the size of the rider.

QUESTION: Are colts started in performance as two-year-olds more likely to break down?

ANSWER: In the performance aspect, I don't think it hurts to work a two-year-old colt unless he has a terrific conformation problem. Any horse with a conformation problem is going to break down 10 times as fast as your good conformation horse. Of course, it depends on what performance class you're going to put him in and how you work him.

QUESTION: What methods do you use when breaking young horses?

ANSWER: If I have already taught the colt to longe, and if he's already used to being blanketed every night during his yearling year, then I saddle him with a lightweight pony saddle the first few times, and then I graduate to a larger saddle. I also longe the horse saddled. Then I cross-tie him in my barn to get on him in the beginning. I cross-tie him and get on and off until he is not afraid of having somebody up over his head. The alleyway of my barn is about 20 feet by 100 feet, and that's where I ride one the first time. I spend one or two days just getting on and off him and patting him, having him cross-tied where he can't move and where he can't fall over backwards with me. Then the third day, after I repeat the same process, I put the hackamore on the colt and close my doors at the ends of the hall. The colt is unafraid by this time of my getting on and off, so I don't cross-tie him while I get on him. Some horses will not untrack . . . that is, take their first step. I pull them around in a circle in that enclosure, or do anything to make them step out, because they're going to be fearful of their first step with weight on their backs. They have overcome the fear of something above their heads, so step number two is learning to move with that same weight on their backs. They're not sure what to do, and they're a little bit fearful of taking that first step. I usually circle them or turn them. There are all sorts of ways to get them to move, and I have had horses that I had to have somebody to lead forward, because they were so fearful. Then I get them to walk and stop and back up. The first day I ride them, they're backing up good. I don't require a lot of back-up, but they're backing four or five steps. They have already been backed from the ground, and they know what the word *back* means and that pressure on their nose means to back away from it, and it only takes a very few minutes to put a good back-up on a horse, if you have put your preliminary ground work on one.

I ride each colt in my enclosed alleyway according to the horse and how he reacts. You slowly and patiently remind him how to turn and go and stop and back, with someone on his back, because this sudden riding is a complete change from the earlier ground work. A horse has to have everything done real slow, one step at a time, and redone the next day. Each day you go back through steps one, two and three, then you teach him something new.

I usually spend three saddles in the hallway of the barn. The third saddle I open the door and ride to the arena. I generally like to have somebody open the gate for me, so I don't have to get off and on until after I have ridden him around in the arena. And I have no other horses to bother me the first few times in the arena. I want his whole attention. Then I may get on and off of him four or five times out in the arena after I've broken him into a pretty good sweat. I take the edge off him first.

QUESTION: How much arena riding do you like to do before you ride one outside?

ANSWER: I spend a good deal of time riding in the arena. I put lots of control on them and want to be sure they can pack weight real good. I usually take my first ride out with somebody, so if the horse balks at, say, crossing the road, the experienced horse calmly goes in front and helps alleviate the young horse's fear.

QUESTION: How do you determine how much to increase the riding at this early stage of conditioning?

ANSWER: The amount of riding a colt gets right after breaking depends on what he requires. Horses are like people. Some of them are of a lazy nature and some of them require miles of riding. It also depends on his bone structure and what he can stand. If a horse is a little crooked legged, even though he has a lot of energy, you're going to have to take that energy out without riding, and then ride him briefly.

On the average horse, I increase the riding gradually. You ride by feel, and you never want to overdo anything. That's the worst thing you can do.

Feel tells you how and when to increase his exercise. Then I think it is extremely important that after a two-year-old horse's back is hard and he is more or less conditioned, I'd say you've spent six months on him, then that horse knows what a hard day's work can be. He has to learn that you might ride him all day long. That will teach him how to travel better and how to do a lot of things better. A day's work takes a lot of that foolishness out of them, and all through one's life, he'll never forget that some days he's going to have to work hard.

I might also add that it depends on his eyesight. I am a fanatic on eyesight in horses, and I think it is something that a lot of people take for granted. Poor eyesight with some horses is a real problem. When I say poor, I mean horses that can't focus fast. They can see off at a distance, but when it comes to focusing up close quickly, there are a lot of horses that can't do it. You can ride by the same rock in the pasture 500 times, and they will jump higher every time. I've been bucked off more horses that couldn't focus their eyes quickly than I have any others.

QUESTION: What do you do for a particularly nervous horse?

ANSWER: There are some horses that are naturally more nervous than others. I don't use mascots or music or any of that to calm a nervous horse. I think routine helps a nervous horse more than anything. I definitely ride my real nervous horses more to burn up that nervous energy.

I've seen horses become very attached to each other, too. They have certain friends that they seem to like better than others. If you'll just study your horses, it's sometimes better to keep them stalled by each other. You'll have less kicking and less breakage of your stalls. I think it helps a nervous horse if he is congenial with the horse stalled next to him.

QUESTION: What do you look for as signs of over-exercise and under-exercise in horses?

ANSWER: You can overdo or underdo any horse's exercise. A horse that is getting too much exercise will naturally have a fatigued look. He will often put his ears back and be ill-tempered. A horse that is not getting enough exercise will have more spirit, but he also will be just as "ill" because he, too, is unhappy. I don't believe horses realize what being happy or unhappy is, but I have found out that if my horses are exercised every day, I have less kicking and less goofy habits such as weaving or cribbing. A certain amount of exercise every day takes away boredom and tends to make a horse better adjusted. If I see a horse that is starting to pick up a bad habit, immediately that horse is given priority to exercise and more prolonged changing of his environment, say, turning him loose more and filling his life with more variety and excitement.

QUESTION: Is free exercise important for young horses?

ANSWER: Every colt should have the opportunity to run out in pasture and learn balance and how to handle himself. Even my colts that I'm going to show at halter, prior to breaking, I turn out from two to six hours a day in quite a large enclosed area and let them run. I take their blankets and halters off. They need to run and play like a little child needs to play and have relaxation and change of environment.

QUESTION: What type of stall do you prefer?

ANSWER: If a horse is stalled, I prefer that he can see the other horses in the next stalls. I definitely think it keeps them from getting bored, and if they don't like each other, I change them around. Now I don't want them to be where they can get to each other. I'd want something very sturdy between the stalls. We have very thick boards mixed with four inch pipe between stalls.

If I had my choice, I think that 14' x 14' is a good sized stall, and, of course, if you had the space and the money and the bedding available, an even larger stall would be marvelous. We have some stalls that are 20' x 12', and they're twice as easy to clean. The larger a stall, the easier it is to clean. I think the minimum size for a stall is 10' x 12'. Wood shavings are my preference for bedding, but straw is nice, also.

QUESTION: What special practices do you follow for older breeding animals?

ANSWER: If you have a very old mare that is a good producer, I think that she should definitely be kept separate from other horses, or at least with other friendly old mares, due to the fact that she is an asset to you and like having money in the bank. She's like a dividend check, and you should take extra precautions with her. Her teeth should be checked more regularly, because more malnutrition is caused by bad teeth than worms. Of course, she needs to be parasite-free, also. I would watch that mare daily for any kind of reaction or any problem. I might feed her ground alfafa and all the hay she would eat, plus a good grain ration.

We are now living in an era of pelleted feeds. Some of these are too hard for an old horse with poor teeth. But there are several brands of soft pellets, and they have the correct ratio of hay and grain. This can be a life saver for the real old horse.

QUESTION: What type of supplements do you use?

ANSWER: I've used several vitamin and mineral and protein supplements. I use a protein supplement to give a little bit of extra push, especially when I wean a colt. They need something to keep them growing as fast as they were while they were on their mother, providing the mother was well-fed and producing the right amount of milk. If she wasn't, and they came off a poor mare from poor conditions, it is to stimulate their growth and to make them look as good as possible. But you don't want to push them too fast.

QUESTION: What kind of hay do you prefer?

ANSWER: I think a person has to feed hay according to the best he can get in his own locality. Even though we're close to Oklahoma, it is very difficult to get what I consider A-1 alfalfa hay consistently. If I had my choice, I wouldn't feed any hay to my show horses but alfalfa. We raise our own coastal, which is nearly 20% protein, and it's not overly fertilized. I've never had any trouble with coastal hay.

QUESTION: How often do you worm your horses and which method do you prefer?

ANSWER: For a horse to properly utilize his feed, he must be parasite-free. I believe in first worming colts when they are two to three months old. If a colt is very wormy, I worm him every 30 days to every six weeks. If he doesn't appear to be very wormy, I think it's still necessary every 90 days. I worm my grown horses three to four times a year, especially for bots.

I start all of my baby colts while they're still on the mares by tubing them, and I'm liable to have them tubed two to three times. As soon as they're off the mares, I hand worm them if they're eating well. If I can't get a horse to eat like I want him to, then I have to tube worm him.

QUESTION: What about dental problems?
ANSWER: Many people think that young horses don't suffer from bad teeth. They think they have to be old, but in fact, it's usually quite the contrary, I've found. When they have sharp points they can't chew their food. When they can't chew their food correctly, then they lose the nutrition they're supposed to get out of the feed. I've had horses that, within a few days after having the sharp points removed, started getting glossy hair and by the end of the month they looked great. I don't think that shedding teeth gives them nearly the trouble that sharp points do. If they're not grinding their food, it is not digested correctly. Also, when a horse has a bad tooth condition, he will often carry his head sort of sideways when you are riding him.

QUESTION: Do you blanket your show horses?
ANSWER: Yes, blanketing is necessary. I think that you could blanket a halter horse all year if you live in a climate that will allow you to do it. Any form of cover on that hair is going to help. But if you live in a hot climate where that horse is going to sweat profusely, even a sheet is a hindrance. You're going to have to use your judgment on what your conditions are. But you can always help a horse's hair by putting a blanket on him. No matter if his hair is two inches long, that horse will look better with a blanket on him and long hair than he will by clipping him.

If the nights start getting cool in the latter part of August, I start blanketing with a sheet, and I add to that as the weather changes. I'm liable to have a sheet and two blankets on a horse if it gets real bad, or say a wool blanket and two other blankets and two hoods if we drop down around zero weather.

When I turn horses out during the day in the wintertime, those blankets stay on them until the temperature gets around 60 degrees. At 60 degrees I take all the blankets off. The blankets stay off until just prior to feeding time at night, and then they are put back on for protection as the night becomes colder again.

I don't think a hood is too detrimental to a horse's mane if you'll put it on during the night and take it off for a period during the day. I've noticed that when I'm lax and leave a hood on a horse for from 36 to 48 hours without removing it, satin-lined or not, it rubs the mane out.

In the summertime, to keep a horse's hair good, I keep him from being out in the sun a lot. Sunshine will sunburn a horse's hair coat. There are some horses that don't show a sunburn on their hair as much as another color of horse will. Chestnuts, sorrels and blacks are more prone to sun bleach than any of the other colors. A gray horse can stay in the bright sun all summer and look just the same as if he were never allowed to get out in the sunshine, but a Palomino will sun bleach.

QUESTION: What kind of trimming and shoeing program do you follow?

ANSWER: Foot care is another important aspect of conditioning. As a rule, we don't trim colts until they are at least six months of age. This definitely depends on their conformation and what is required. I have one yearling that has never had to be trimmed. She is so straight legged that her feet wear evenly. Then I have some other colts that we trim regularly, because they're not quite so straight and they wear one side more than they do the other. You can't correct poor conformation by trimming, but you can help to keep a colt straight.

I've had horses that you had to shoe in order to finish breaking because they were more tender-footed than other horses. I let a horse go barefooted just as long as I possibly can. I live where it's quite rocky, so I shoe maybe earlier than people who live in less rocky terrain. You just nearly have to have shoes on a performance horse if you intend to show him. You cannot afford to bruise that horse's foot.

QUESTION: What special precautions do you take when hauling horses?

ANSWER: We generally always carry feed so that there won't be a drastic change in feed.

On a long haul, in the middle of the day we stop and unload, and then at night, we try to find water and a big pen where the horses can walk around and lie down and roll. I never encounter any trouble in hauling horses. A green horse might not drink water until he becomes adjusted to it, but after you've hauled a horse, say, for a year, he'll drink water anywhere.

If I'm hauling a long way to a show, I'd prefer to be there the day before to give a horse time enough to lie down and rest and to adjust. That will also possibly give you time to take the horse into the arena. The more you can work a horse in strange surroundings, the more it helps him.

If you're going to haul a horse, haul him in a good trailer, one that is well made and has all the features that reputable trailer makers have engineered for a safe horse trailer. Buying a cheap horse trailer is a waste of money.

Say I'm going to haul a mare and colt for the first time, I naturally will tie the mare, but I don't tie the colt until a colt has become halter broken and knows what it is to be tied up. I like to have an enclosed back end either with canvas at the top or a solid door, when I'm hauling a mare and colt. A baby colt can jump out the back through fear.

I prefer the first couple of times to haul a weanling with another horse that's older and more established, if at all possible. I definitely use a trailer tie for a weanling. I tie any green horse, no matter whether it's a weanling or a five-year-old, considering that this horse has already been broken to lead and knows what it is to stand tied. I always tie a horse until he becomes adjusted to riding in a trailer, so that he won't get his head down. I do not tie my older horses that have been hauled. If I do tie a horse, he's tied with a trailer tie, so that in an emergency, I could release him quickly.

Wrapping a horse's legs when hauling is important. I always wrap a horse's legs to haul him, for safety.

QUESTION: Do you have much trouble with horses that have bad hauling habits?

ANSWER: I've cured many bad hauling horses, and most of them can be cured if you'll just drive with common sense. It's not how fast you drive on a straight road, but it's how you turn the corners. You can drive fast, but slow that turn down. That's where the horse is apt to lose his balance.

Another thing . . . Get away from that solid partition in a two-horse trailer. Give that horse room to spread his legs out. I've learned the hard way that every horse that has ever been put in a trailer with a solid partition so that he can't spread his legs to catch his balance when a corner is turned too fast, turns into a trailer fighter. There isn't anything any worse to haul than a trailer fighting horse.

QUESTION: How do you exercise your horses prior to a show?

ANSWER: I try to exercise my horses very hard the day before a show, about double to three times what I generally ride them per day, so they will be a little tired. Then when I get to the show I don't have to wear myself out getting the edge off them. Although he is a little fatigued, he has had a night's rest. Any time he's done a hard day's work one day, he's not going to be dancing and prancing the second day, but he will be groomed and clean and look nice and behave nice at the show. I try to be very calm with a horse prior to going into the ring.

QUESTION: How do you exercise your reining horses?

ANSWER: I've actually had few horses that I considered exceptionally good reining prospects, and those horses required a lot of just plain, straight riding. On those horses, I have worked a pattern, but as I rode them down the road, I might give them a signal to turn back, or riding in the pasture, I would stop and pivot. A good reining horse is a fast thinking horse; he's a fast responding horse, and usually a highly energetic horse.

My reining horses have all had to be ridden quite a bit, but I always just pleasured them out in the pasture or down the road or I've worked cattle on them. Working cattle helped them a whole lot, too. You can goof a horse up by figure-eighting him too much. I want him to know how to do it, and every so often, I practice a couple of figure-eights or make six or seven circles and then a figure eight, but never just one figure-eight right after the other.

QUESTION: Do you ever recommend the use of spurs?

ANSWER: If and when I use spurs depends on the horse. The best reining horse I have ever ridden never needed spurs. A horse that's born that way is willing and mentally alert. You teach and cue a horse by different pressures of your body. Using spurs depends primarily on the nature of your horse. In breaking a horse, I never use spurs until the horse understands all the signals and knows how to pack weight. Not all horses need spurs used on them. If I need spurs, I always start the horse with a blunt cavalry spur, and I find that that's about the only spur I need 75% of the time, depending on the nature of the horse. Then I have another spur that's a little bit rougher, and then I have a set of spurs that will "jar the building." It depends on what event I'm in and the nature of the horse as to what spur I wear. I never start any horse with a rough pair of spurs unless it's just absolutely required and this is extremely rare.

QUESTION: How do you warm a pleasure horse up just before an event?

ANSWER: In warming a horse up before I show him, I would definitely take a little more edge off of a pleasure horse, even though his disposition would be quieter than a reining horse's. Of course, you can get one too dead, covering no ground, and then he is definitely no pleasure to ride.

QUESTION: What do you mean "covering no ground"?

ANSWER: This is caused from being too short strided, and there isn't much you can do about it. Some horses are just born that way. You can long trot one and lengthen his stride some, and you can help a horse's carriage by riding him distances. You can take a short-strided horse and ride him 10 to 15 miles, and he will learn to lengthen his stride when he gets tired and an overly long-strided horse will often learn to shorten his stride. They learn to take care of themselves. A horse learns a lot from a hard day's work.

QUESTION: Does the way you warm a horse up before an event depend on the type of event it is?

ANSWER: When I get to a show, I warm my horse up simply by riding him around. Every horse is a little weak in some areas. Maybe this particular horse is weaker, say, in turning to the right. Then I'd rehearse that horse to the right just a couple of times, and if he did correctly, I'd pat him on the neck and leave him alone. It doesn't hurt to turn one around a few times and kind of gin him up if you feel that's needed. I show him that I want a little more spirit. Say I'm riding one in pleasure and then in reining . . . I go into pleasure with no spurs at all. Then when I get ready for the reining, I put on my spurs and I gently let that horse know that I've got them on and that I expect him to turn around. I signal him on the neck, softly, and if he doesn't turn, I make the next signal pretty clear, and that generally wakes him up.

QUESTION: How do you feed before you show?

ANSWER: I don't like to feed too heavy before I show. I've found out that if you will withhold some of that feed, a horse is not quite as nervous. It's just like you and I doing something on a full stomach. I like to have plenty of time before I ride one for that food to be digested. At home I feed around daylight every morning, and I give my horses an hour-and-a-half before I even move them out to the arena where they can run around.

QUESTION: How do you "cool a horse out," after an event?

ANSWER: Most reining classes and pleasure classes don't last long enough to require a lot of cooling down. Speed event classes such as barrel racing or pole bending would require more cooling out. It also depends on the temperature and on the disposition of your horse. If he settles down and you can ride him around quietly for a little bit, I think that's sufficient. So many of our shows are outside, and I think it is very important to have a blanket to put on one if it's a chilly day. A horse has nerves, and if he seems nervous and hot, you just want to ride him around slowly to let him down quietly. You may want to uncinch your saddle a notch or two, too. I seldom hand walk a horse when I can ride him.

QUESTION: What grooming procedures do you follow?

ANSWER: Since I have a barn full of horses, I don't brush like I used to. I brush for two purposes ... to gentle a horse and to make him look better. I love to brush a horse, and I grew up with the old saying, "A good brushing is like a gallon of oats." There's no way that brushing can do anything but help a horse, disposition-wise and hair-wise. I use a rubber curry comb and a very stiff bristled brush. Then I go over them with a very fine brush to make them shine, and I use a plastic mane and tail comb. If I'm washing one, I'll use my metal mane and tail comb, but when it's dry, I use the plastic comb. Under very cold conditions, when I can't wash the halter horses to get them ready, I use an automatic brush that fits on my electric clippers and rotates. You have to be very careful, though, that you do not tangle the mane or the tail in it. Then I vacuum them after I brush them real good. A vacuum doesn't take the place of brushing, but it does take the dust out. You can sure put on that extra show polish with one.

I keep alcohol in my trailer all the time, because it's a fast cleaner. Say a horse gets a little dirt or manure on a white leg ... You can very quickly clean it off with alcohol. I put alcohol on a rag and use it for a cleaner and then take another clean rag and go over it like you'd shine a shoe almost, and alcohol dries in just a few seconds.

I roach a bridle path on most of my horses and I use a small clipper, an Oster A-2 with a No. 15 blade. I use that clipper for their fetlocks and everything. I have a little tooth knife that I use on their tails that I buy at a local western store. It's a little blade with notches in it, that is made especially to trim manes and tails. Then I also pull some of my manes. I shorten it and then pull it. I shorten it with just plain everyday scissors by working my scissors up and down, just like a beautician would do in a beauty shop. That keeps it from looking blunt.

I use this little knife on the tail and then occasionally, on heavy, heavy tails, I use the thinning scissors. I use the thinning scissors especially if I'm going to shorten the tail. First I thin it and then I shorten it. Every horse's tail is a little bit different, and some are quite bushy at the top, and you have to do a lot of thinning at the top. You work from the underneath up, so that you have the top hair to lay over where you have to remove any.

QUESTION: What can you do for a horse with a thick throatlatch?

ANSWER: There are any number of devices to help if a horse's throatlatch is too thick. I think you need to tighten up those muscles. Of course, some horses are just born with a thick neck. You can tighten those muscles, but you'll never get him a long neck and a small throatlatch. Sometimes a big neck is caused from lack of exercise. I use a sweat hood an awful lot. You often have this problem of a thick neck with a short necked horse. If you have a horse that's inclined to get a little "cresty", it helps him tremendously to put a sweat hood on him when you're riding him. Just lather that neck, and perhaps tie him up for a while after you've ridden him. Keep the sweat hood on him and you can take a tremendous amount of neck off a horse.

QUESTION: How often do you bathe horses?
ANSWER: If you own a horse with a lot of white on him, it's best to bathe him before a show. I use a little plastic scrubber that works on the end of a hose. I have a concrete wash rack with hot and cold water which I can adjust to lukewarm. I use almost the same washing method on a white horse that I use on a dark colored horse. I usually shampoo their mane and tail, and then I use this plastic attachment which has little teeth in it, like a little curry comb, on the end of my hose. I really don't use much shampoo on the horse's body, because I think the soap kills the oil, which will take several days to build back up in that hair. If that horse with white on him has bad stains on him, then I am almost forced to use shampoo on those stains. But if at all possible, I use no shampoo whatsoever except on his mane and tail, and possibly on the blaze on his face and on his stockings if he has any. I will rinse the mane and tail and use the little scrubber and lukewarm water on the rest of his body and try to get the dirt out that way. I am very careful around his face and foretop, to remove the scrubber and cut the water down to extremely low pressure. I work with my hand and low water pressure on the face, so as not frighten the horse.

QUESTION: Do you use hoof dressing?
ANSWER: I don't use any hoof dressing. In certain climates it is necessary. If he is not receiving the proper nutrients, you'll discover that it shows in his hooves. Also, you'll discover that horses' hooves grow better when there's a lot of dampness in the air rather than when it's dry. In other words a combination of good nutrition and sufficient moisture seems to do away with the need for hoof dressing.

QUESTION: Do you condition a horse differently for a sale?
ANSWER: Good grooming and conditioning are always important. If you think that you're going to put a horse in a sale, you should decide seven or eight months ahead of the sale. You should condition that horse through proper feeding, proper exercise, and blanketing at least six months ahead of a wintertime sale. Don't just take your horse out of the pasture, because nobody likes a long-haired, skinny, poor, un-

kept horse; I don't care if it's the greatest breeding in the world. That slick shine and fat will sell anything.

At the sale grounds people study the sale catalog prior to a sale and check on a horse's pedigree. You need to be available to answer any questions correctly and lead your horse out if they want to look at it. I think it is very wise to place a sign with the catalog number you have been given on your stall so that people can locate it easily.

QUESTION: What do you consider the most important advice you give owners of young horses before they give them to a trainer?

ANSWER: The most important thing an owner can do to save a trainer time and himself money is to halter break his colt and teach it to tie up. That is the fundamental of all discipline, and an owner should know how to tie a horse up and what to tie a horse up with. He's not going to accomplish one thing if he ties that colt up with a little, weak rope and it breaks away. If he doesn't have the proper halter and lead rope to tie him with and know the proper distance and proper height to tie that horse, then it would be smarter to take it on to the trainer who does know.

Always tie any horse to something that is very stout. In other words, don't tie one to the board that's nailed to a crosstie; tie it around the crosstie. The board can come loose. Another thing, don't tie a green horse to a tree that he can wrap around and choke himself. You want to have a halter lead rope, and definitely a snap that won't break. Tie him in a safe place to something that will not pull out or break. Always tie a horse fairly high and never lower than his head. Always be sure than you don't tie too long so that he can rear up or set back and get a foot over the rope.

If you have a young colt you're teaching to stand tied, it's a good idea to let him stand an hour the first day and then turn him loose. The next day, let him stand for an hour and a half. Periodically work up to where you can tie him four or five hours out of the day. Usually, in about two days he has learned how to take care of himself.

QUESTION: What techniques do you use to bring a horse back after an injury or rest?

ANSWER: To bring a horse back after he has been laid off from an injury or from a rest period, you just have to start right back like you were starting from scratch. You can bring him along faster than you could a green horse, but you've got to start him right back on a routine again to build up those muscles. It actually takes several months to get a horse in top shape for performance or running.

It's a similar thing when you quit showing a horse and turn him out. I think it's very hard on a horse that's been used to eating grain and being on a schedule and kept blanketed in a barn to suddenly be turned out in a pasture. I think it would be very wise to let him down slowly. If you're going to turn him out with no grain at all, you need to start reducing your grain and giving him more roughage to get his stomach to where it can hold enough roughage to keep him going. If he's been a race horse on high vitamins, minerals, protein and "pep-up" food, you need to change his grain diet to one not so high and increase his hay. Also, say you've had that horse in a stall and then he's injured so that you have to turn him out for six months and it's cold weather. I think you're very foolish to pull a blanket off that horse and turn him out, because he's going to shake just like you and I are. It would be much wiser to keep him under some sort of protection until the time of the year does allow him to go out without blankets.

QUESTION: How long does it usually take to evaluate a horse's potential?

ANSWER: I have to ride a colt 30 to 90 days before I make an intelligent decision as to whether he's going to make a good horse, a sorry horse, or an excellent horse. I've had horses that turned into fantastic horses, but it took nearly 90 days to find out they had that kind of potential. Generally, within 30 days, you can tell a lot about their temperament. I give myself at least that much leeway. I would say that if one hasn't done something halfway intelligent in 90 days, it would be wiser to change horses. I make my decision on how quick one learns and on his ability to handle himself. At this time, I can decide in what event the horse will do best by his nature and disposition. Of course, man can change the disposition of a good horse a lot of times, but my decision is made on the horse's natural disposition and ability.

BIBLIOGRAPHY

Adams, O.R., D.V.M., M.S., **Lameness in Horses**, Philadelphia, Pennsylvania, Lea and Febiger, 1972.

Allen, Thomas B., Editor, **The Marvels of Animal Behavior**, Washington, D.C., The National Geographic Society, 1972.

Asheim, A., V.D.M., Ph.D.; Knudsen, O., V.D.M., Ph.D.; Lindholm, V.D.M.; Rulcker, V.D.M., Ph.D.; and Saltin, V., Ph.D., "Heart Rates and Blood Lactate Concentrates of Standardbred Horses During Training and Racing," Journal of the American Veterinary Medical Association, Volume 157: 3, 1970, pp. 304-312.

Baker, H.J., D.V.M., and Lindsey, J.R., D.V.M., "Equine Goiter Due to Excess Dietary Iodide," Journal of the American Veterinary Medical Association, Volume 153: 12, 1968, pp. 1618-1630.

Bauer, W.W., M.D., Editor, **Today's Health Guide**, Chicago, Illinois, Department of Health Education of the American Medical Association, 1970.

Beeman, Marvin, D.V.M., "Conformation...The Relationship of Form to Function," Quarter Horse Journal, Volume 25:3, 1972, p. 82.

Burch, Preston M., **Training Thoroughbred Horses**, Lexington, Kentucky, The Blood-Horse, 1967.

Catcott, E.J., D.V.M., Ph.D. and Smithcors, J.F., D.V.M., Ph.D., Editors, **Equine Medicine and Surgery**, Wheaton, Illinois, American Veterinary Publications, Inc., 1972.

Catcott, E.J., D.V.M., Ph.D., and Smithcors, J.F., D.V.M., Ph.D., Editors, **Progress in Equine Practice**, Volumes One and Two, Wheaton, Illinois, American Veterinary Publications, Inc., 1969.

Coggins, Jack, **The Horseman's Bible**, Garden City, New York, Doubleday & Company, Inc., 1966.

Collins, Robert W., **Race Horse Training**, Lexington, Kentucky, The Thoroughbred Record Company, Inc., 1972.

Edwards, E.H., and Geddes, C., Editors, **The Complete Book of the Horse**, New York, New York, Arco Publishing Company, Inc., 1973.

Ensminger, M.E., B.S., M.A., Ph.D., **Horses and Horsemanship**, Danville, Illinois, The Interstate Printers and Publishers, Inc., 1969.

Frandson, R.D., D.V.M., M.S., **Anatomy and Physiology of Farm Animals**, Philadelphia, Pennsylvania, Lea and Febiger, 1965.

Harrison, James C., **The Care and Training of the Trotter and Pacer**, Columbus, Ohio, The United States Trotting Association, 1968.

Hughes, J.P., D.V.M.; Stabenfeldt, G.H., D.V.M., Ph.D.; and Evans, J.W., Ph.D., "Estrous Cycle and Ovulation in the Mare," Journal of the American Veterinary Medical Association, Volume 161: 11, 1972, pp. 1367-1374.

Jones, William E., D.V.M., Ph.D. and Bogart, Ralph, Ph.D., **Genetics of the Horse**, East Lansing, Michigan, Caballus Publishers, 1971.

Lamkin, William G., D.V.M., "Control of Orthopedic Inflammation," Quarter Racing World, Volume 5: 5, 1972, pp. 64-67.

Lindholm, Arne, D.V.M., Ph.D., **Muscle Morphology and Metabolism in Standardbred Horses at Rest and During Exercise**, Stockholm, Sweden, 1974. (From the Department of Biochemistry, Royal Veterinary College and the Department of Physiology, Gymnastik—och idrottshögskolan.)

McGee, W.R., D.V.M., **Veterinary Notes for the Standardbred Breeder**, Columbus, Ohio, The United States Trotting Association.

McKibben, Lloyd D., D.V.M., "A Review of Splints," The Backstretch, Volume 12: 1, 1973, p. 16.

Miller, W.C., F.R.C.V.S., F.R.S.E., **Practical Essentials in the Care and Management of Horses on Thoroughbred Studs**, London, England, The Thoroughbred Breeders Association, 1965.

Moore, Ruth, **Evolution**, New York, New York, Time-Life Books, Inc., 1968.

Official Handbook of the American Quarter Horse Association, Twenty-Second Edition/January 1, 1974, Amarillo, Texas, The American Quarter Horse Association, 1973.

Ommert, William, D.V.M., "Help Mother Nature Increase Your Live Foal Rate," Horseman, Volume 17: 7, 1973, pp. 14-23.

Pickett, B.W. and Voss, J.L., "Reproductive Management of the Stallion," Proceedings of the Eighteenth Annual Convention of the American Association of Equine Practitioners, 1972, pp. 510-531.

Purvis, Alan D., D.V.M., "Inducing Labor in Mares," The Blood-Horse, Volume XCIX: 12, 1973, p. 1024.

Putnam, Harold D., D.V.M., "Lamenesses," Quarter Racing Record, Volume 13: 4, 1973, p. 16.

Reed, W.O., "Bowed Tendons Heal Slowly in Horses," Journal of the American Veterinary Medical Association, Volume 148: 4, 1966, p. 390.

Rossdale, Peter D., M.A., F.R.C.V.S., **The Horse**, Arcadia, California, The California Thoroughbred Breeders Association, 1972.

Rule, Fred, D.V.M., "Breeding Soundness in Stallions," Quarter Horse Journal, Volume 24: 3, 1971, p. 53.

Sager, F.C., D.V.M., "Care of the Reproductive Tract of the Mare," Journal of the American Veterinary Medical Association, Volume 149: 12, 1966, pp. 1542-1545.

Schalm, Oscar W., D.V.M., Ph.D., **Veterinary Hematology**, Philadelphia, Pennsylvania, Lea and Febiger, 1965.

Siegmund, O.H., Editor, **The Merck Veterinary Manual**, Rahway, New Jersey, Merck and Company, Inc., 1967.

Simpson, George G., **Horses**, New York, New York, Oxford University Press, 1970.

Smythe, R.H., **The Mind of the Horse**, Brattleboro, Vermont, The Stephen Greene Press, 1965.

Stein, M.R.; Vidich, A.J.; and White, D.M., **Identity and Anxiety**, The Free Press of Glencoe, 1963.

Stowe, H.D., "Reproductive Performance of Barren Mares Following Vitamin A and E Supplementation," Proceedings of the 1967 Convention of the American Association of Equine Practitioners.

Straiton, E.C., **The Horse Owner's Vet Book**, Philadelphia, Pennsylvania, Farming Press Ltd., 1973.

Strong, Charles L., M.V.O., M.S.C.P.,**Horses' Injuries**, London, England, Faber and Faber , Limited, 1967.

Swenson, Melvin J., D.V.M., M.S., Ph.D., Editor, **Dukes' Physiology of Domestic Animals**, Ithaca, New York, Cornell University Press, 1970.

Van Pelt, R.W., D.V.M., Ph.D., "Intra-Articular Injection of 6 a-Methyl, 17 a-Hydroxyprogesterone Acetate in Tarsal Hydrarthrosis (Bog Spavin) in the Horse," Journal of the American Veterinary Medical Association, Volume 151: 9, 1967, pp. 1159-1171.

Walls, Katharine F., Ph.D., **Kinesiology: The Scientific Basis of Human Motion**, Philadelphia, Pennsylvania, W.B. Saunders Company, 1966.

Williams, Dorian, **The Book of Horses**, Philadelphia, Pennsylvania, J.B. Lippincott and Company, 1971.

Williams, Moyra, **Horse Psychology**, South Brunswick, New York, A.S. Barnes and Company, 1969.

Williams, Waynon, "Walk Your Horse," Quarter Horse Journal, Volume 24: 4, 1971, pp. 76-77.

Worthington, William E., D.V.M., "Management of Stallions, Considerations of Feeding, Health and Fertility," Lectures given at the Stud Managers Course, Lexington, Kentucky, Stud Managers Course, 1973, p. 86-96.